August 20-22, 2014
Kyoto, Japan

I0044240

Association for
Computing Machinery

Advancing Computing as a Science & Profession

CABS'14

Proceedings of the 5th ACM International Conference on
Collaboration Across Boundaries

Sponsored by:
ACM SIGCHI

Contributors:
NSF and KANSAI OSAKA 21st Century Association

Association for Computing Machinery

Advancing Computing as a Science & Profession

The Association for Computing Machinery
2 Penn Plaza, Suite 701
New York, New York 10121-0701

Notice to Past Authors of ACM-Published Articles
ACM intends to create a complete electronic archive of all articles and/or other material previously published by ACM. If you have written a work that has been previously published by ACM in any journal or conference proceedings prior to 1978, or any SIG Newsletter at any time, and you do NOT want this work to appear in the ACM Digital Library, please inform permissions@acm.org, stating the title of the work, the author(s), and where and when published.

ISBN: 978-1-4503-2557-8 (Digital)

ISBN: 978-1-4503-3263-7 (Print)

Additional copies may be ordered prepaid from:

ACM Order Department
PO Box 30777
New York, NY 10087-0777, USA

Phone: 1-800-342-6626 (USA and Canada)
+1-212-626-0500 (Global)
Fax: +1-212-944-1318
E-mail: acmhelp@acm.org
Hours of Operation: 8:30 am – 4:30 pm ET

Printed in the USA

Welcome from the Conference Chairs

Welcome to Kyoto and the 5th ACM International Conference on Collaboration Across Boundaries: Culture, Distance and Technology (CABS '14). CABS '14 showcases the very best research exploring the nature of, and ways to facilitate, intercultural collaboration. CABS is a multidisciplinary forum that includes behavioral, socio-cultural and technical perspectives, with the objective of exchanging the latest knowledge about intercultural collaboration. This diversity of perspectives is mirrored by geographic diversity among contributors. CABS '14 is the 5th conference in the series formerly called the International Conference on Intercultural Collaboration (ICIC).

The CABS '14 program presents an exciting set of workshops, full papers, panels, and late breaking papers. For the papers program, submissions were solicited under three broad topics: Communication and Management, Computer-Mediated Collaboration, and Cross-linguistic Communication. We received 24 submissions and after careful peer review by an interdisciplinary team of experts, we accepted 13 (54%), The program also includes 8 Late Breaking Papers that report on work in progress or newly completed. These will be presented during a special interactive poster session.

Special highlights include our opening plenary talk, **"Language, Culture and Boundary-Spanning: Pushing the Frontiers of Research on Global Learning and Innovation,"** by Mary Yoko Brannen of Victoria University, our second day opening plenary, **"Cross Cultural Research, Innovation and Design in 2050,"** by Apala Lahiri Chavan of the Institute of Customer Experience, and our closing plenary, **"Evolution of Human Mind and Culture Viewed From the Study of Chimpanzees,"** by Tetsuro Matsuzawa of Kyoto University.

The conference also includes many exciting cultural events to help attendees get the most out of their stay in Kyoto. These include a "Meeting the Zen Spirit" at Kenninji temple - the oldest zen temple - on Thursday morning, a conference reception and calligraphy exercise.

Putting together CABS '14 was a team effort. We thank the authors for providing the content that is the core of our dynamic program, the program committee for their hard work in reviewing papers, and our entire hard-working conference committee, from the papers chairs to the treasurer to the webmasters. We also thank Lisa Tolles at Sheridan Communications and Ashley Cozzi from ACM for all of their assistance with arrangements and publications. Finally, we thank our sponsor SIGCHI and our contributors, The National Science Foundation and the Japan World Exposition 1970 Commemorative Fund.

CABS is a upcoming, mixed and vibrant community. We hope you will be inspired by this high quality conference program.

Naomi Yamashita
CABS'14 General Co-Chair
NTT, Japan

Vanessa Evers
CABS'14 General Co-Chair
University of Twente, The Netherlands

Table of Contents

Poster Session (Late Breaking Paper Session)

Session 4: Cultural Contexts for Interaction
Session Chair: Ari Hautasaari *(NTT Communication Science Labs)*

Keynote 3 (Closing Keynote)
Session Chair: Naomi Yamashita *(NTT Communication Science Labs)*

CABS 2014 Conference Organization

General Chairs: Naomi Yamashita *(NTT Communication Science Laboratories, Japan)*
Vanessa Evers *(University of Twente, The Netherlands)*

Program Chairs: Susan R. Fussell *(Cornell University, USA / Computer Mediated Collaboration)*
Carolyn Rosé *(Carnegie Mellon University, USA / Cross-Linguistic Communication)*
Mary Beth Watson-Manheim *(University of Illinois at Chicago, USA / Management and Communication)*

Late Breaking Papers Chairs: Astrid Weiss *(Vienna University of Technology, Austria)*
Marianna Obrist *(University of Sussex, UK)*

Panel Chair: Anne-Marie Søderberg *(Copenhagen Business School, Denmark)*

Doctoral Consortium Chairs: Scott Robertson *(University of Hawaii, USA)*
Ravi Vatrapu *(Copenhagen Business School, Denmark & Norwegian School of Information Technology, Norway)*

Proceedings Chairs: Duyen T. Nguyen Mary *(Carnegie Mellon University, USA)*
Heeryon Cho *(Yonsei University, Korea)*

Local Chair: Takashi Yoshino *(Wakayama University, Japan)*

Publicity Chair: Nanyi Bi *(Cornell University, USA)*

Treasurer: Ari Hautasaari *(NTT Communication Science Laboratories, Japan)*

Registration Chair: Yohei Murakami *(Kyoto University, Japan)*

Student Volunteers Chair: Saeko Nomura Baird *(USA)*

Cultural Experience Chair: Naoe Imura *(Kyoto Sangyo University, Japan)*

Steering Committee: Pamela Hinds *(Stanford University, USA)*
Vanessa Evers *(University of Twente, The Netherlands)*
Martha Maznevski *(International Institute for Management Development, Switzerland)*
Gary Olson *(University of California Irvine, USA)*
Anne-Marie Søderberg *(Copenhagen Business School, Denmark)*
Ravi Vatrapu *(Copenhagen Business School, Denmark & Norwegian School of Information Technology, Norway)*
Naomi Yamashita *(NTT Communication Science Laboratories, Japan)*

CABS 2014 Sponsor & Supporters

Sponsor: SIGCHI

Contributors: NSF

SUPPORT
The Japan World Exposition 1970 Commemorative Fund
KANSAI OSAKA 21st Century Association

Language, Culture and Boundary-Spanning: Pushing the Frontiers of Research on Global Learning and Innovation

Mary Yoko Brannen
Jarislowsky CAPI East Asia (Japan) Chair,
Professor of International Business,
University of Victoria

ABSTRACT

Building an integrated global strategy for ongoing growth and renewal across markets which are geographically remote and have differing native languages and cultures is undoubtedly harder than classical scholars of business strategy have cared to understand or admit. While our cumulative knowledge of the role of organizational learning in internationalization is considerable, it has generally been seen as knowledge transmitted from the home-organizational base to subsidiaries abroad. As such, current theories take little account of the capacity of the organizations to reverse the one-way vector of learning emanating from headquarters in order to learn endogenously, as it were, from knowledge resources available at the periphery and throughout its global reach. A major reason why theory has not advanced further in documenting and thus realizing the mechanisms by which firms can learn from their global footprint is that the methodologies used have been ineffective as they tend to take a "bird's eye" view of phenomena when what is needed is an "up-close" and contextually-grounded approach. In this keynote speech, Professor Mary-Yoko Brannen will discuss new avenues for research methods that facilitate the understanding of complex, micro level contextually embedded phenomena where research settings are rife with multilevel cultural interactions. Integrating current research on the multifaceted nature of language used in global organizations and the boundary-spanning skillsets that bi- and multi-cultural individuals bring to today's workforce, Professor Brannen will discuss new methods for researchers as well as practitioners to positively influence global learning and innovation outcomes.

Author Keywords

Language; Culture; Boundary-Spanning; Innovation

1998 ACM Classification Keywords

K.4.3 Organizational Impacts; J.4 Social and Behavioral Sciences

CABS '14, August 21-22, 2014, Kyoto, Japan.
ACM 978-1-4503-2557-8/14/08.
http://dx.doi.org/10.1145/2631488.2637430

BIO

Mary Yoko Brannen is the Jarislowsky East Asia (Japan) Chair at the Centre for Asia-Pacific Initiatives (CAPI) and Professor of International Business at the Peter B. Gustavson School of Business at the University of Victoria in British Columbia and serves as Deputy Editor of the Journal of International Business. She received her M.B.A. with emphasis in International Business and Ph.D. in Organizational Behavior with a minor in Cultural Anthropology from the University of Massachusetts at Amherst, and a B.A. from the University of California at Berkeley. She has taught at the Ross School of Business at the University of Michigan, the Lucas Graduate School of Business at San Jose State University, the Haas Business School at the University of California at Berkeley, Smith College, and Stanford University in the United States; Keio Business School in Tokyo, Japan, and Fudan University in Shanghai, China. Professor Brannen's expertise in cross-cultural management is evident in her research, consulting, teaching, and personal background. Born and raised in Japan, having studied in France and Spain, and having worked as a cross-cultural consultant for over 25 years to various Fortune 100 companies, she brings a multi-faceted, deep knowledge of today's complex cultural business environment. Her consulting specialty is in helping multinational firms realize their global strategic initiatives by aligning, integrating and deploying critical organizational resources. Professor Brannen's current research projects include research on knowledge sharing across distance and differentiated contexts, directing a global think tank focusing on biculturals and people of mixed cultural origins as the new workplace demographic, and developing strategic ethnography as a method by which global companies can realize sustainable competitive advantage.

Accelerating Cultural Capital:
Reproducing Silicon Valley Culture in Global Ecosystems

Julia Katherine Haines
Department of Informatics
University of California, Irvine,
USA
hainesj@uci.edu

ABSTRACT
A combination of infrastructure developments, accessible platforms and easy to use tools have dramatically lowered the barriers to entry for technology startups in recent years. Alongside this, seed accelerators, which provide the soft infrastructure and training to foster high-tech startups have spread rapidly worldwide. But little is known about how accelerators are impacting the global tech startup landscape. Through fieldwork at an accelerator in Singapore, we investigate the expansion of this Silicon Valley model of innovation, the cultural values inherent in its practices, and how it is transformed and implemented in other contexts. Drawing on Bourdieu's theory of cultural capital, we frame accelerators as sites of complex cultural interaction, reproduction, and tension. Accelerators both explicitly and implicitly propagate cultural values from Silicon Valley. We highlight the complexities this presents for founders of different backgrounds as well as the value and recognition it gives them in the startup community.

Author Keywords
Entrepreneurship; innovation; startups; cultural capital.

ACM Classification Keywords
K.4 COMPUTERS AND SOCIETY; K.4.3 Organizational Impacts

CABS '14, August 21-22, 2014, Kyoto, Japan.
ACM 978-1-4503-2557-8/14/08.
http://dx.doi.org/10.1145/2631488.2631489

Trust in Client-Vendor Relations:
An Empirical Study of Collaboration Across National and Organizational Boundaries

Thomas Tøth
Copenhagen Business School
Porcelænshaven 18A
2000 Frederiksberg, Denmark
tto.ikl@cbs.dk

ABSTRACT
In an ever more globalized world we are faced with the challenges of collaborating across geographical distance. This article examines how trust is established in an offshore outsourcing engagement of IT operations between a leading Danish media company and an Indian IT-service provider.

The findings presented in this paper are a subset of a larger ethnographic research project including more than four hundred hours of participant observation and twenty-nine semi-structured interviews. Thus, the article contributes with a empirical investigation of collaboration across national and organizational boundaries within the field of IT offshore outsourcing.

The article concludes that trust is primarily established when the teams are meeting face-to-face and in order to establish trust at a distance they are dependent on technology being readily available and on engaging in active trust building, by imitating the way they communicate face-to-face, when collaborating virtually.

Author Keywords
Trust; Virtual Team; Offshore Outsourcing; Global Collaboration

INTRODUCTION
One of the many manifestations of globalization is the increasing tendency for western firms to strategically outsource activities to Asia [30] and throughout the last two decades it has become increasingly popular to engage in offshore outsourcing [25] of IT activities. Success in such endeavors dependent significantly on the participants' abilities to work in distributed teams; and a large body of research within several academic fields has been devoted to understanding the inherent complexities of distributed

teamwork [16; 24]; and the role of culture in global collaboration [22]. Much of this research mentions the importance of trust in virtual teamwork, but without making much of it.

On the other hand, there exists a large body of research on trust [29], but within trust research only limited attention has been devoted to virtual collaboration.

In this paper I take upon me the challenge of investigating what the perceived challenges of distributed work is seen from the perspectives of the actors in the client organization as well as the supplier organization. Subsequently, I will enquire into how trust is established and maintained in the relationship between the actors from the two organizational entities, characterized, for the most part, by physical distance. Thus, in this chapter I seek to answer the two questions below:

• What are the perceived challenges of distributed collaboration?

• How is trust established in the collaboration between actors from the two organizational entities?

Additionally, I will – based on the empirical findings and the theoretical framework – discuss whether there are unexploited opportunities for advancing trustful relations between the actors from the two different organizational entities.

LITERATURE REVIEW
Trust is "a psychological state comprising the intention to accept vulnerability based upon positive expectations of the intentions or behavior of another" [27: p. 395]. This definition is widely accepted among trust scholars. It signifies that we can only speak about trust in cases where "some uncertainty and vulnerability that actors have to deal with by means other than pay-off calculations" [23: p. 32] is present.

Furthermore, there is a wide agreement among trust scholars that "trust in everyday life is a mix of feeling and rational thinking" [23: p. 44]. Thus, trust has a cognitive and an affective dimension and trust is based on assessments of the trustee's ability, integrity and benevolence [23], where and integrity relates to the cognitive dimension of trust, and benevolence relates to the affective dimension of trust. Thus, if one perceives another to be able and have integrity we say that that person has cognitive trust in the other and if one perceives another as benevolent we say that that person has affective trust in the other.

In order to cope with uncertainty actors need to take a 'leap of faith', which Bachmann [1] explains as a process in which "a trustor transforms fuzzy uncertainty (…) into a certain risk which a trustor is prepared to accept" [1: p. 207]. Möllering designates this as suspension, which he finds to be "the essence of trust, because trust as a state of positive expectation of others can only be reached when reason, routine and reflexivity are combined with suspension" [23: p. 110].

Trust is not a trivial research concept, despite (or I speculate, because) often unconsciously taken for granted highly unproblematic in everyday-life. Saunders et al. [29] have recently compiled a volume that highlights some of the complexities of trust across cultural contexts. The spatial dimension of such collaborations adds further complexity to the matter. Chung & Jackson [9] point out that "relationships cannot always be controlled by formal organisational procedures or policies and tasks inherently entail risk-taking" [9: p. 67] and Greenberg et al. [15] stress that "trust is critical to the cooperative behavior that leads to the success of all teams, but it is especially important in virtual teams" [15: p. 327].

Research has traditionally considered "the trustor as a rather passive figure who reaches (or fails to reach) the state of trust on the basis of "given" factors such as her/his own predisposition, the perceived trustworthiness of the trustee, and/or relevant institutional safeguards" [7: p. 70]. This passive path to trust is what Child & Möllering [7] calls *contextual confidence*. Child & Möllering criticizes this notion of the trustor as a passive figure as they are dissatisfied "with the notion that the trustor can only draw on "given" contextual variables" [7: p. 71] as the trustor "can play a more (pro)active role in trust production, perhaps especially where the contextual foundations for trust are weak". [7: p. 71]. They claim that active trust development can be used as a strategy in cross-border collaboration in order to strengthen the basis for trust by for instance working actively on establishing personal rapport.

Hinds & Bailey [18] conclude: "When trust is missing, team members are more likely to question others' intentions and make attributions that do not adequately account for situational factors" [18: p. 618] as lack of close proximity is a hindrance to establishment of shared context, familiarity, friendship and homogeneity among the actors. Hinds & Bailey [18] argue that when teams are dispersed casual encounters and the amount of passive information about the distant colleagues is significantly less than with collocated ditto which results in actors being out of sync with their remote colleagues: They do not understand their concerns, work processes and personalities, which lead to task-related

and process conflicts; and furthermore to affective conflicts due to the reduced possibility of friendship formation. Rosen et. al. [26] sums up the trust challenges in distributed teams by rhetorically asking: "Does a failure to make a promised entry in the team's web archive mean that a teammate is struggling with a complex issue, under pressure from on-site management to make other issues a priority, or just slacking off?" [26: p. 259]

From quite a different branch of academic literature Kimberly Elsbach and her colleagues [11] conclude that by "just being around" we tend to spontaneously and unconsciously draw positive conclusions about the character of our colleagues: We assign personal traits such as reliability, dedication, accountability merely based on co-presence. Elsbach et al. [11] furthermore demonstrate that employees that are not physically present miss out on promotions and salary increases, due to the lack of these spontaneous, positive conclusions. Being the virtual colleague can be quite challenging with regards to establishing a positive impression of one self and the work one performs and additionally a hindrance to one's career.

Thus, it seems that distance indeed matters as Olson & Olson [24] concluded in their widely cited article from 2000. However, much has happened since Olson & Olson did their empirical studies some fifteen years ago. Communication technology has developed and matured drastically and Olson & Olson were definitely right when assessing the future of collaboration technologies: "Good design and more horsepower in the infrastructure will solve a number of the limitations of current distance technologies. Greater bandwidth will solve the disruptive influence of today's delays in audio and video transmission. Greater bandwidth will allow for larger, smoother, more life-size displays of remote workers, making their interaction more similar to the flow of proximal interaction" [24: p. 143].

Today, high-quality video meetings with unnoticeable lack, cutting clear and undisrupted audio where groups of people can interact from different location are widely available. So are video-enabled chat services such as Skype, Microsoft Lync and IBM Sametime and a broad variety of web-conferencing software available. Thus, it is safe to say that Olson & Olson's projection that "advances in technology suggest that with careful human factors in design, there may be technical ways to come closer to some aspects of the face-to-face work" [24: p. 143] have come true.

But even though the technical achievements over the past fifteen years are impressive does that mean that it has become *easy* to collaborate across distance? A vast body of literature [2] suggests that technological advancement in it self does not guarantee smooth, frictionless collaboration. Rather, we should – as Ceci & Prencipe [6] suggests – focus on *how* we collaborate. That is, we need to pay attention to how do we organize virtual teamwork. Ceci & Prencipe [6] identify two generic approaches, namely to "(a) decompose activities through the definition of standard and stable interfaces among its components to reduce interdependencies; (b) create opportunity for ongoing communication for actors involved in the pursuit of interdependent activities" [6: p. 326]. However, as Brusoni et al. [4] point out, perfect decomposability requires perfect understanding of all interdependencies, which is a rare case. Consequently, actors have to communicate when collaborating in virtual teams in order to succeed in performing the tasks they are set out to do, which, as emphasized by Hinds & Bailey [18] is a challenge in distributed teams.

RESEARCH DESIGN AND METHODOLOGY
The findings presented in this paper are a subset of a larger ethnographic research project investigating trust.

When conducting empirical research on a delicate and complex matter such as trust it is of utmost importance to gain insights into how trust is established, maintained, confirmed, repaired and broken, in situ, as opposed to a "bird's eye view" [17: p. 16] where we are not only likely to "miss the more intimate sounds of people speaking, singing, or crying out to one another" (ibid.); but also confined to develop our understanding on the basis of retrospective interview data. Thus, in order to understand trust as it unfolds in reality I employ an ethnographic approach, defined as "participant observation plus any other appropriate methods" [13: p. 566].

The empirical foundation for this paper consists of participant observation to gain a deeper understanding of the phenomenon by investigating it within a real life context [5]. Additionally, semi-structured interviews have been conducted to gain in-depth understanding of the context of practices observed; and to grasp the "complex pattern of organizational, work-group, professional and interpersonal loyalties" [5: p. 21]. Finally, document analysis of company-internal documents as well as publicly available information has established a basic understanding of the organizational environment.

The ethnographic study was conducted over a twelve-month period starting in February 2013. Approximately five hundred hours of participant observation has been conducted. I have observed "office-life" at the client-side IT-department in Copenhagen, Denmark as well as in the Operations Management Center (OMC) at the suppliers premises in Chennai, India, including numerous virtual meetings mediated through phone or Skype between representatives of the organizations; physical meetings related to the outsourcing collaboration; local staff meetings; and substantial number of informal conversations with the staff.

Additionally, I have conducted twenty-nine formal semi-structured interviews, each approximately lasting one hour, with employees and managers from the client organization as well as the supplier organization. All interviews have subsequently been transcribed and coded into various themes and sub-themes. This paper presents one of these themes,

namely 'Establishing Trust in Virtual Teams'. Additionally three major themes have been identified: 'Intercultural and Interorganizational Trust', 'Trust and Control' and 'Boundary Spanning'.

The semi-structured form allowed the interviewees to elaborate and steer the discussion into areas they perceived as relevant [14]. Though my primary interest is to study trust I have made a point of not directly asking about trust during interviews, in order not to force an agenda of trust onto the interviewees. The actors themselves have started to talk about trust when asked about collaboration and relationships, and I have merely used the opportunity to explore the topic deeper.

All interviewed people were informed that their contribution and identity would remain anonymous to ensure a high level of confidentiality and pave the way for open and honest accounts. This was furthermore sought via my at-length ethnographic engagement, where I initially presented my overall research agenda and personal as well as professional background to all staff-members in the IT-department.

THE CASE
The case is an offshore outsourcing engagement between the IT-organization in a leading media company in Denmark (from here: 'the client') and an Indian-owned IT-service provider with more than 80.000 employees worldwide (from here: 'the vendor') embarked on in the second half of 2011.

The client's internal IT-organization is comprised of sixteen people of which four are dedicated to IT operations and the remainders are focused at development, project management and higher-level management, for example the CIO. The client has engaged with an outsourcing partner in Ukraine for web and mobile development and with the vendor in India for IT operations. The latter cooperation is the sole focus of this paper.

At the vendor's premises in India the client has an Operations Management Center (OMC) comprised of approximately 80 consultants dedicated to servicing the client. The OMC provides a broad range of services including application management; technical infrastructure; and data center management and is exclusively responsible for all of the client's IT-operations.

The OMC is essentially interfacing with employees from The client in two different ways: In cases where changes to applications managed by the OMC need to be introduced to cater for new web or mobile development or changed requirements within the client organization, they are interfacing with the client's project managers; and on operational aspects they are connected to the four employees in the IT-operations department. These four people have, like the project managers, managerial responsibilities; thus, all "hands-on" work is done at the OMC.

ANALYSIS

The Value of Face-to-Face Interaction and Collocation
Throughout my fieldwork it has been clear that the actors from both organizations value face-to-face interaction with their counterparts immensely. The value of collocation has repeatedly been brought up during interviews and furthermore substantiated by the means of my observation studies, where I have had ample opportunity to observe how the actors repeatedly turn to collocated counterparts – to the familiar faces conveniently present.

Actors from both organizational entities explain that collocation makes communication and collaboration easier. One vendor employee claims that being "somewhere near to them [the Danes], it is always easy for me to go and interact" while another elaborates that it may also be "more effective in a way. That is the reason we have a guy over here [in Denmark] all the time". The notion of collocated work being easier and more convenient is supported by the client's employees, who find it more convenient to interact "directly with them instead of writing short messages on instant messenger and [sending] emails" as one puts it.

"What is it that is easier when being collocated?" I ask them. Predominantly the answers are: 'being available' and 'understanding'. The first, 'being available' is perceived as a value in itself as eases communication, while the latter, 'understanding', is twofold: On one hand it is about the ease of communicating and learning about technical and domain specific issues. One the other hand collocation and face-to-face interaction are seen as means to gaining understanding of the people who constitute their client-side counterpart.

Communicating at a Distance: Three Challenges
While collocation of the actors from the two organizations results in the actors being available and understanding each other this is not the case when the actors have not had a chance to work in close physical proximity. Lack of collocation leads to three challenges that will be elaborated below by comparing the characteristics of collocated and non-collocated work as it unfolds in practice.

Challenge I: Going Directly
During my interviews several people have used the term "putting a face" to the other's, when asked to elaborate on why it is more cumbersome to collaborate with people they have met face-to-face as opposed to people they have only interacted with via mediated communication. For instance, one of the client employees explain that "it is important to put face on" as she feels "closer to them – and they feel closer too" One of the vendor employees, and one who performs a role that requires a lot of client interaction, recollects the how the collaboration changed after meeting her Danish counterparts: "I started feeling free to call in for any issues. Before I met them I used to have a fear [...] so after meeting there is a change". Another vendor employee, also with substantial interaction with some of the Danish employees explains that she used to think "what are they

going to think about me, why is this girl so much pestering", But after she met with her client-side counterpart, she realized that "he was a really cool guy" and that meeting in person was "definitely really important. And after he left from here I really did not hesitate to call him for any issues".

Thus, the actors perceived a challenge related to 'going directly', which is caused by lack of adequate social interaction. First, as elaborated above, there seems to be a mental barrier, where the actors maintain a depersonalized mode of communication as long as they have not met. Consequently, *physical distance becomes mental distance.*

Secondly, the actors also refer to another hindrance related to their ability to be 'going directly': The availability of technology. In order to conduct video-based meetings or to have phone conferences, meeting rooms "have to be book[ed] and it's very cumbersome" as the rooms need to booked well in advance. Thus, impromptu video meetings are not an option – unless there is an operational crisis, in which case other bookings will be overruled.

This is in stark contrast to the interaction with collocated actors. A vendor employee explains that: "if it is in our team anytime we can talk to them and we can make them understand what actually we are going to convey. So that thing is very easy here, but whereas with the client we have to schedule a meeting". Therefore, as he continues: "First we'll initiate with the mail trails and if this getting continuous mail trails then we'll go for a meeting". Thus, emails are the default way of collaborating. At least up to the point where the actors realize that the complexity of the matter inhibits successful collaboration via emails.

To sum up, the actors find it difficult to approach their counterparts from the other organizational entity, when they have not met face-to-face, as encounters in physical proximity facilitates communication that allow the actors to get to know each other. Furthermore, going directly is a challenge due to scarce technological resources in the form of meeting rooms with video equipment and phone conferencing systems.

Challenge II: Knowledge Gaps
In line with other studies [e.g. 10; 20] asymmetric knowledge across the geographical and organizational boundaries poses a significant challenge to the collaboration between the client and vendor employees in the context of the offshore outsourcing collaboration that constitutes the empirical foundation for this paper.

During my observation studies as well as in interviews it has repeatedly been brought to my attention that the client employees believe that the vendor employees working from offshore lack important knowledge about the client's business and the impact that technological changes and failures have on the business. One of the client employees explain that: "Even though we have executed a giant knowledge transfer [...] there is still a lack of overview of what they [the IT-systems] do and how they are interconnected. I don't think anyone has that now, except for myself and a few other people in our department [in Denmark]. It is not easy to communicate via these channels. I think here is a big difference". Consequently, he has "given up on getting them [the vendor employees] to understand how things are connected" and he furthermore states that he is repeatedly consulted on things that he had expected that the vendor employees would be able to figure out themselves, which he attributes to the distance, as "one has another kind of dialogue when one is sitting next to people and talking directly to them compared to writing short messages on instant messenger or email".

This point of view is widely shared among the client employees, though some express it in a softer tone. On the other hand, several of the vendor employees are exclaiming that they see themselves as what Markus [21] labels *expertise-seeking novices* – as someone who are who are in need of knowledge possessed by others to be able to perform their work – when asked to reflect on the collaboration with the client employees. One vendor employee explains: "I do learn from them. So my mistakes will be spoken to me so that I also improve" and furthermore he assumes that learning is not bi-directional, as the client employees do not seem to learn from her or her colleagues.

Interestingly, the notion of lack of knowledge among the vendor employees only applies to the one's who have not been stationed *onsite*, in Denmark: The vendor employees who have been working in close physical proximity with the client employees are repeatedly acknowledged for the abilities to understand the core business of the client company – during interviews and informal conversations where I was told that "these two guys [onsite vendor employees] are among the best […] They are really easy to work with and highly intelligent"; but also during a client visit to India, where the two aforementioned as well as other vendor employees working onsite were praised in front of their Indian colleagues for their business knowledge.

This difference in understanding of the business of the client is also recognized by the onsite vendor staff. One explains that: "If anyone sends a mail from the client they [the offshore team in India] will not be understanding the exact criticality of that issue, how the client is facing over there. […] So the website is down; […] so they [the offshore team in India] will consider this is as low criticality. So we [the onsite vendor employees] need to tell them that the entire Europe is using this. If this website is not working, then it's the credibility of [the client] and their name is going to lose in the market"

Challenge III: Lack of Transparency
The vendor employees who are deployed onsite and thus working in close physical proximity with the client employees are repeatedly praised for their commitment to adding value by following through on the issues that are

raised by the client employees by "making sure that it actually works" as one client employee phrases it. In contrast his experience is that when collaborating with the offshore vendor staff "things are just hidden or 'forgotten' if they [the vendor staff] don't know how to solve them" and sometimes he feels that he cannot be sure if the offshore vendor employees take responsibility.

The collaboration between the client employees and the onsite vendor employees is characterized by ongoing interaction, where the vendor employees are very conscious about 'proving themselves' both in terms of the quality of work they are doing but also, to a large extent about making sure that all enquiries from the client employees are responded to as fast as possible – as one of the vendor employees emphasizes: "your service should be effective and your response time should be very quick".

On the other hand, the interaction between the client employees and the offshore vendor staff is based on a so-called service management system, Remedy, where status and progress on tasks is communicated. In contrast to collaborating in close physical proximity, where there is an ongoing dialogue about tasks between employees from the two organizational entities, the client employees perceive the virtual collaboration as difficult, because "it is sometimes hard to understand why things take so long time – even simple tasks".

In order to cope with this lack of transparency the client employees have changed the way they specify assignments. One of the client employees explains that he used to assign tasks that were abstract, but as that did not work out he now has to "be more specific and split the tasks so they matches the siloes [functional areas]" in order to make sure that they are completed satisfactory, which he has realized after he has visited the OMC and "seen how they work […] which makes it easier to understand why things are happening the way they are"

Thus, one consequence of virtual collaboration mediated by a service management system is that the client employees perceive that they lack transparency. That is, until they have had the chance to visit the OMC and gain understanding of how the vendor staff works, which they can use to change the way they specify tasks. Another dimension of lack of transparency has to do with the faceless communication, where some of the client employees are unsure who are working on the tasks they have submitted in the service management system, which is further complicated because they – as one puts it – "can't separate one name from the other" when it comes to working with the offshore vendor employees, whose Indian names are difficult to remember for the client employees of Danish origin.

Establishing Trust in Offshore Outsourcing
In this section I will address the second research question, namely: *How is trust established in the collaboration between actors from the two organizational entities?* In order

to investigate how trust is established we need to understand how the three pillars of trust; ability, integrity and benevolence (see literature review) are perceived by the actors from the two organizational entities.

Assessments of Benevolence

Actors from both organizational entities find 'going directly' challenging, when they have not had the opportunity to meet their counterparts face-to-face. However, even short face-to-face encounters – such as the client employees' week-long visits to India, where the face-to-face interaction with individual Indian consultants is limited to one or two meeting, not lasting more than 45 minutes each, increases the actor's comfort-level with regards to making direct contact via e.g. phone. This is repeatedly attributed to getting to know each other on a more personal level or, as one Indian consultant puts it to "understand their characters well".

In each their way, the actors from both organizational entities all emphasize that meeting their counterparts cater for a more humanized image. As one Indian recollect about her image of one particular Danish employee – who has a very direct approach and usually talks rather hard, as I have observed repeatedly myself – before meeting him: "I thought he will be somewhat huge. Tall. Intimidating", whereas he is in fact quite small. Thus, she projects an image of him based on his hard, direct and somewhat confrontational virtual communication style, as being huge and intimidating. After meeting him she "feel[s] free to dial him and dial him anytime if there is an issue. I don't have second thought".

Even though no one specifically mentions the word 'benevolence' when referring to the change in perception, that happens when meeting face-to-face with their other-organizational counterparts, I argue that this word, benevolence, very well describes the change in perception that physical proximity leads to.

While the collaboration among actors who have met in person is characterized by positive assessments benevolence the same is not the case for actors who have not met face-to-face. In this scenario the collaboration is characterized primarily by the absence of assessments of the counterpart's benevolence.

It is important to stress the distinction between negative assessments of benevolence and the absence of such assessments: I have not observed a single incident where an actor has expressed that virtual communication has led to negative assessments. Rather, it seems that in cases where the actors have not met physically they refrain from assessing their counterpart's benevolence; and as a consequence they refrain from engaging in 'direct' communication, such as talking on the phone. Thus, is seems that *when positive assessments of benevolence is missing, the actors act as if they had assessed benevolence negatively.*

Assessments of Ability

With regards to *ability*, we have seen how vendor employees with onsite experience are praised for their ability to understand the client's business and use this to provide high quality in their work. Seen from the client employee's perspective the vendor employees with onsite experience are considered both technically savvy and knowledgeable about the client's business environment.

Thus, on one hand, the Danish employees assess the abilities of the Indian consultants they have been collaborating with in close physical proximity for period of time on the grounds of their perceived business understanding and in a more "holistic" manner. That is, their abilities are subjectively assessed as the perceived quality of their individual contributions. This stands in contrast to the assessment of the abilities of the Indian consultant with whom the Danish employees have not collaborated with in physical proximity: These actors are not individually assessed, but rather assessed as a part of the functional group they belong to and based on performance measurements derived from the monthly reporting as well as reports from the service management system. In some cases, systems have been running smoothly for a long period of time. This is reflected in the reporting and during the client's visit to the OMC such teams are praised for doing a good and competent job. Other teams, that cannot display equally good results, are questioned in terms of their abilities. These are the teams that are referred to when a client employee says that "there is still a lack of overview" despite a huge effort in transferring knowledge throughout the transition period.

On the other hand, the abilities of the Danish employees are assessed quite similar by the Indian employees who have had a chance to work in Denmark and the ones who have solely been working from India: Actors from both sub-groups acknowledge the Danish employees' business knowledge and in a similar vein they position themselves as *expertise-seeking novices* [21], who early in the collaboration are dependent on the Danish employees to understand the business. Though, the Danish employees' business knowledge is never challenged by the Indian consultants it is worth noticing that the Indian consultants with onsite experience express a level of reservation when it comes to readily accepting the needs and requirements expressed by their Danish counterparts. Whereas the Indian consultants that have not been exposed to collaboration in physical proximity with their Danish counterparts seems to accept the business knowledge of the Danish employees without any hesitation, the group of Indian consultants who are – or has been – working in Denmark are more reluctant and are deliberately challenging their Danish counterparts. As one Indian consultant says: "when you get requirements you have to be sure that he is absolutely sure about the requirement". This suggests that that the Indian consultants with onsite experience are comfortable questioning their Danish counterparts, which corresponds very well to the positive assessment of benevolence.

Assessments of Integrity
Finally, with regards to *integrity,* we have seen how client employees are counting on the vendor employees who are deployed onsite to "making sure that it actually works" and how the vendor employees working from onsite manage to prove themselves and as a consequence are given the freedom to plan their work without having to justify how they spend their time in detail. On the other hand, the lack of transparency, seen from the perspective of the client employees, lead the client employees to question the integrity of the offshore vendor staff. However, this only applies to offshore vendor employees who have not had exposure to working onsite – vendor employees returning to India after an onsite allocation continue to enjoy positive assessments of their integrity. From the client employees perspective they experience that the offshore vendor employees without onsite experience do not take responsibility. Thus, the client employees assess the onsite vendor employees' integrity positively and the offshore vendor employees negatively.

On the other side the Indian consultants draw positive conclusions about the integrity of their Danish counterparts, regardless of having onsite experience or not. This difference, I speculate, may relate to the nature of the collaboration, where the Danish employees are dependent on the Indian consultants to provide solutions that are critical to their business, i.e. the nature of the client-supplier relationship.

Collocation Facilitates Trust – Distance Inhibits Trust
As elaborated above the actors perceive collocation as beneficial as it makes 'being available' and 'understanding' easier. However, beyond these immediate values of collocation another benefit of collocation – one that is indeed subtler, more long-term oriented – surfaces: Collocation and face-to-face interaction are catalysts for building *trust* among the actors.

When the actors are collocated they engage in what Bjørn & Christensen [3] have labeled *relation work*. That is, the interaction necessary to establish "technical and social connections that are critical for the everyday interaction within organizations" [8: p. 2]. Through collocated relation work the actor's build interpersonal trust via positive assessments of the other's *abilities, integrity and benevolence* – the cornerstones of trust. Interestingly, this relation work has a positive impact on the collaboration that goes beyond

the period of time where the actors are collocated; its effect lasts when the actors are no longer working in close physical proximity, when they are engaging in distributed collaboration. Thus, vendor employees who return to India after onsite deployment still enjoy positive assessments of their ability, integrity and benevolence by their client-side counterparts; collocation facilitates trust.

On the other hand it seems that distance inhibits trust. However, while the conclusion about the exposure to collocation is clear cut as it facilitates positive assessments of both ability, integrity and benevolence for the actors from both organizational entities and thus creates both affective and cognitive trust, this is not the case when the actors have not met face-to-face. In such cases the client employees refrain from assessing the vendor employees' abilities on an individual level, they assess integrity negatively when the expected performance criteria are not met and they refrain from assessing the benevolence which leads to negative conclusions insofar they are reluctant to approach the employees directly. Thus, the client employees do not display any form of trust in the vendor employees they have not met in person.

The vendor employees' also refrain from assessing the client employees' benevolence when they have not met face-to-face, which also result in reluctance to approach their face-less counterparts directly. However, even though the actors have not met in person, the vendor employees assess both the ability and the integrity of the client employees positively. Thus, they display cognitive trust in their other-organizational counterparts.

The second research question reads: *How is trust established in the collaboration between actors from the two organizational entities?* In this section I have answered this question by investigating first the three challenges that the actors' face when collaborating virtually and afterwards by relating these challenges to the cornerstones of trust, namely ability, integrity and benevolence. The findings are summarized in Table 1.

DISCUSSION
What defines a virtual team? On one hand there are teams that are always working in close physical proximity. On the other side there are teams that never meet, where all communication is mediated by technology. Thus, we have a

	Exposure to Collocation		No Exposure to Collocation	
	Vendor's assessment of client counterparts	Client's assessment of vendor counterparts	Vendor's assessment of client counterparts	Client's assessment of vendor counterparts
Ability	Positive assessment	Positive assessment	Positive assessment	No individual assessment
Integrity	Positive assessment	Positive assessment	Positive assessment	Negative assessment
Benevolence	Positive assessment	Positive assessment	No assessment, negative conclusion	No assessment, negative conclusion

Table 1

continuum where it is difficult to clearly define when a team is indeed a virtual team.

In the specific empirical settings we are dealing with here we have team members that hardly ever meet. Over the course of the collaboration that has lasted more than one and a half year, they have met once or twice and seldom more than a few hours. It is safe to say that the collaboration between these actors can be characterized as a virtual team structure.

On the other hand we have team members who have been working in close physical proximity for a longer period of time. During the course of time where they are actually collocated, when the Indian consultants are working at the client-side office in Denmark, the team structure cannot be characterized as virtual. However, we have seen how collocation has a positive effect on the assessments of ability, integrity and benevolence, which lasts even after the actors are not working together in a collocated environment. That is, when the collaboration structure is changed to a virtual one, the positive assessments stemming from collocation are preserved. Thus, we can conclude that while trust is created when the actors are collocated it can be maintained at a distance.

Noteworthy Difference in the Creation of Cognitive Trust

With regards to cognitive trust we see that the vendor employees are assessing the ability and integrity of the client employees positively despite not working with them in a collocated manner. This is not the case for the client employees who only assess the vendor employees' ability and integrity positively when they have been working with them in close physical proximity for a period of time. What causes this difference? From the body of literature on trust we know that assessments of ability, integrity and benevolence are dependent on the trustor's propensity to trust; that is, a predisposition [15] that can be caused by a number of things such as culture [31] or macro factors, such as national wealth, income equality and education [12]. I speculate that two such factors may influence this difference in trust development between the client employees and the vendor employees: First, the vendor employees are working in an IT industry in India, where more than ninety percent of the employees are delivering outsourcing services to non-Indian companies. This means that the vendor employees are highly accustomed to working in virtual teams with people from the other side of the globe, which gives them an advantage: They are simply used to work with and build rapport and trust with counterparts they have not met.

Secondly, the difference in team sizes may have an influence. That is, on the vendor side approximately eighty people are servicing the client, who are represented by less that ten people that engage with the vendor staff – and in practice the vast majority of communication with the vendor staff is done by a group of four client employees. As mentioned in the literature review trust is a psychological state where one is prepared to accept vulnerability and in order to do so one has

to take a 'leap of faith', where fuzzy uncertainty, as Bachmann [1] calls it is transformed into an accepted risk. Given the organizational setup and the team sizes I speculate that taking such a leap of faith is easier for the vendor employees as they can make use of *referral trust* [19]: By the means of a colleague's trust in a client employee, the vendor employee can more easily establish trust in the specific client employee – the basis for trust is so to say transferred from one vendor employee to another. As the client employees have are significantly fewer and all vendor employees presumably know their names finding a colleague among the vendor employees who is able to vouch for the client employee in question is undoubtedly easier than finding a colleague among the client employees who can vouch for a specific vendor employee, knowing that the client employees are challenged by the Indian names and "can't separate one name from the other" as one of the client employees told me.

This furthermore corresponds well with Tsai & Ghoshal's findings that "individuals who enjoy more central positions within a network are likely to be perceived as more trustworthy" [28: p. 283].

Opportunities for advancing trustful relations

In the analysis above I have answered the two research questions. For the remainder of this article I will discuss if there are *unexploited opportunities for advancing trustful relations between the actors from the two organizational entities?* As we have seen throughout this paper building trust when the actors from the two organizational entities are collocated happens simply by the means of collocation itself. However, establishing trust in virtual teams is by no means a trivial matter. Berry [2] concludes that "Creating trust between coworkers and between employees and managers may be the greatest challenge in building successful virtual teams" [2: p. 10] But does this mean that trust cannot be created in such scenarios?

In the case that constitutes the empirical foundation for this paper we see that developing rapport, in the sense of a close and harmonious relationship where people understand each other's feelings or ideas and communicate well, is in fact achievable, when the actors are collocated. The question is whether this can be done *without* physical co-presence as well. Arguably, there are two barriers to this. One has to do with availability of (Information and Communication Technology) ICT and the other has to do with technology utilization.

First, with regards to availability of ICT the challenge is not the quality of the technologies, but rather the fact that video conferencing facilities are not instantly available (as elaborated in 'Challenge I: Going directly') Thus, impromptu video meetings are not an option, which is in stark contrast to the interaction with collocated actors, where one can easily move to another person's desk or office to talk. One can, of course, claim that there are other means of 'going directly' and thus paving the way for positive assessments of benevolence, such as instant messengers or phones. However, this leads us to the second barrier: *technology utilization.*

In quite a few interviews – sixteen to be specific – I have asked what the difference between meeting one another in person and communicating via video, phone or chat. The actors all agree that there is a difference as "virtual meetings are more straight to the point" as one puts it. The actors report that there is no small talk before or after meetings. Thus, the way the actors interact when using technology is substantially different from interacting face-to-face. Additionally, some are reluctant to use the technologies available. For instance one of the client employees exclaim that "I don't do stuff like that" when I ask him if he is communicating via instant messengers.

In order to advance trustful relations in the specific context of this virtual collaboration the actors cannot depend on what Child & Möllering [7] calls contextual confidence, as this is weak. Thus, in order to build trust in the virtual team they must actively engage in trust building by – as Child & Möllering [7] would put it – applying *active trust.* However, active trust development in virtual teams requires that technology is readily available and used; and that they actively seek to imitate the form of dialogue that occurs when they are collocated.

How can this be done? I believe there is ample opportunity. One technique is to raise awareness of each other's presence by imitating how the collocated team members greet each other when they arrive at the office, when they break for lunch and when they leave again at night. In the collocated environment they walk through the open office and with a few words or gestures they signal their presence to their colleagues.

This can be imitated by actively engaging with remote actors in the same situations, by a simple 'hi', 'good morning' or 'goodbye' conveyed through instant messenger. I speculate, that this would eventually lead to a situation where a short greeting on the way in or out of office would remind the actors of something that needs to be discussed, just as it happens between collocated actors when one see's another on the move in or out of the office. In other words, it would improve the ability to be going directly in virtual teams. Furthermore, such greetings would improve transparency as to the availability of remote counterparts.

There are several other techniques, such as leaving webcams and sound on for a longer period of time without necessarily having to speak to each other all the time or booking calendar time, where it is agreed that remote colleagues have first priority and can make contact at any point in time. Such techniques also aid help the actors to be going directly and increases transparency by the means of active trust building.

Undoubtedly, such techniques will feel odd in the beginning. Some will work and some will not. However, in order to advance trustful relations in virtual teams we need to,

somehow, engage in active trust building that may challenge our habitual way of collaborating.

CONCLUSION

The aim of this paper has been to answer two research questions, namely (a) What are the perceived challenges of distributed collaboration? and (b) How is trust established in the collaboration between actors from the two organizational entities?

We have seen that the actors perceive difficulties in going directly, knowledge gaps and lack of transparency; and I have argued how this leads to a situation where mutual trust is created only when the actors are collocated. However, I have also argued that the vendor employees are able to build cognitive trust in their counterparts even when not being collocated and I have argued that this may be explained by them being more used to work in virtual teams due to the characteristics of the IT industry in India; and furthermore that referral trust may contribute positively to trust building.

Finally, I have, in the discussion, argued that in order to advance trustful relations in virtual collaboration the actors are dependent on technology being readily available but also on engaging in active trust building, by actively imitating the way they communicate face-to-face, when they are collaborating virtually.

ACKNOWLEDGMENTS
This contribution is funded by the Danish Agency for Science, Technology and Innovation under the project "Next Generation Technologies and Processes for Global Software Development".

REFERENCES
1. Bachmann, R. At the crossroads: Future directions in trust research, *Journal of Trust Research 1,* 2 (2011) 203-213.

2. Berry, G. R. A Cross-Disciplinary Literature Review: Examining Trust on Virtual Teams, *Performance Improvement Quarterly 24,* 3 (2013), 9–28.

3. Bjørn, P. and Christensen, L. R. Relation work: Creating socio-technical connections in global engineering, *European Conference on Computer supported cooperative work (ECSCW), Kluwer Academic,* (2011) 133-152.

4. Brusoni, S., Prencipe, A., Pavitt, K.L.R. Knowledge specialization and the boundaries of the firm: why do firms know more than they make?, *Administrative Science Quarterly 46,* (2001) 597–621.

5. Cassell, C., & Symon, G. Essential Guide to Qualitative Methods in Organizational Research, (2004) *Sage.*

6. Ceci, F., & Prencipe, A. Does distance hinder coordination? Identifying and bridging boundaries of offshored work. *Journal of International Management 19,* 4, (2013), 324-332.

7. Child, J., & Möllering, G. Contextual confidence and active trust development in the Chinese business environment. *Organization Science 14*, 1 (2003), 69-80.

8. Christensen, L. R., Jensen, R. E. & Bjørn, P. Relation Work in Collocated and Distributed Collaboration, *Proceedings of COOP*, (2014) 1-16.

9. Chung, Y. & Jackson, S.E. Co-worker trust and knowledge creation: A multilevel analysis, *Journal of Trust Research 1*,1 (2011) 65-83.

10. Dibbern, J., Goles, T., Hirschheim, R., and Jayatilaka, B. Information systems outsourcing: A survey and analysis of the literature, *Database for Advances in Information Systems 35*, 4, (2004) 6-102.

11. Elsbach, K. D., Cable D. M. & Sherman, J. W. How passive 'face time' affects perceptions of employees: Evidence of spontaneous trait inference, *Human Relations 63*, 6 (2010), 735-760.

12. Ferrin, D., & Gillespie, N. Trust Differences across National-Societal cultures: Much to Do or Much ado about Nothing?, in *Saunders, M., (edt): Organizational Trust: A Cultural Perspective,* (2010), Cambridge Companions to Management.

13. Forsey, M. G. Ethnography as Participant Listening, *Ethnography, December 2010 vol. 11* 4 (2010) 558-572.

14. Gertsen, M.C., & Søderberg, A-M. Intercultural Collaboration Stories: On Narrative Inquiry and Analysis as Tools for Research, *International Business. Journal of International Business Studies 42, 6* (2011)*, 765–786.*

15. Greenberg, P., Greenberg, R.H., & Antonucci, Y.L. Creating and sustaining trust in virtual teams, *Business Horizons 50*, (2007) 325–333.

16. Hambley, L. A., O'Neill, T. A., & Kline, T. J. B. Virtual team leadership: The effects of leadership style and communication medium on team interaction styles and outcomes, *Organizational Behavior & Human Decision Processes 103*, (2007) 1-20

17. Hazen, M. A. Towards Polyphonic Organization, *Journal of Organizational Change Management 6*, 5 (1993), 15-26.

18. Hinds, P. J., & Bailey, D. E. Out of sight, out of sync: Understanding conflict in distributed teams, *Organization Science 14*, (2003) 615-632.

19. Jøsang, A. Trust management in online communities. *New Forms of Collaborative Innovation and Production on the Internet 75,* (2011), 75-89.

20. Madsen, S., Bødker, K. & Tøth, T. From Research to Practical Application: Knowledge Transfer Planning and Execution in Outsourcing, *Grand Successes and Failures in IT, public and private sectors,* (2013), 510-524.

21. Markus, M.L. Toward a theory of knowledge reuse: Types of knowledge reuse situations and factors in reuse success", *Journal of Management Information Systems 18*, 1, (2001) 57-93.

22. Maznevski, M. L. State of the Art: Global teams, in Gertsen, M.C., Søderberg, A-M. & Zølner, M. (Eds), Global Collaboration: Intercultural Experiences and Learning, *PalgraveMacmillan* (2012) 187-206.

23. Möllering, G. Trust: Reason, routine, reflexivity, *Emerald Group Publishing,* (2006).

24. Olson, G. and Olson, J.S. Distance Matters, *Human Computer Interaction 15*, (2000), 139-178.

25. Contractor, F. J., Kumar, V., Kundu, S., & Pedersen, T., Global Outsourcing and Offshoring: In Search of the Optimal Configuration for a Company. In F. J. Contractor, V. Kumar, S. K. Kundu, & T. Pedersen (Eds.), *Global outsourcing and offshoring.* (2010), Cambridge University Press.

26. Rosen, B., Furst, S., Blackburn, R. Overcoming Barriers to Knowledge Sharing in Virtual Teams, *Organizational Dynamics 36,* 3 (2005), 259–273.

27. Rousseau, D.M., Sitkin, S.B., Burt, R.S., Camerer, C. Not so different after all: a cross-discipline view of trust, *Academy of Management Review 23*, 3 (1998) 393–404.

28. Sarker, S., Ahuja, M., Sarker, S. & Kirkeby, S. The Role of Communication and Trust in Global Virtual Teams: A Social Network Perspective, *Journal of Management Information Systems 28*, 1, (2011), 273-309

29. Saunders, M. (eds). Organizational Trust: A Cultural Perspective, *Cambridge University Press* (2010).

30. Windrum, P., Reinstaller, A., & Bull, C. The outsourcing productivity paradox: total outsourcing, organisational innovation, and long run productivity growth, *Journal of Evolutionary Economics*, 19, (2009) 197–229.

31. Zaheer, S. & Zaheer, A. Trust across borders, *Journal of International Business Studies 37*, (2006), 21-29.

Avocados Crossing Borders: The Missing Common Information Infrastructure for International Trade

Thomas Jensen[1], Niels Bjørn-Andersen[1], and Ravi Vatrapu[1, 2]

Computational Social Science Laboratory (CSSL)

[1]Department of IT Management, Copenhagen Business School, Denmark

[2]Norwegian School of Information Technology (NITH), Norway

tje.itm@cbs.dk, nba.itm@cbs.dk, vatrapu@cbs.dk

ABSTRACT

This paper addresses indirect global interactions that involve collaboration across continents involving different cultures, languages, technologies and nations. Specifically, we are concerned with analyzing international trade of avocados from trees in Africa to grocery store shelves in the European Union. The methodology of the paper is a revelatory case study of a particular trade lane from Kenya to The Netherlands. Drawing on Activity Theory Framework and theories on Information Infrastructures, we provide an analysis of the complex inter-organizational systems and infrastructures involved in the selected case of international trade, identify critical issues in information flows, and propose ideas for design principles for a new information infrastructure for international trade. Our analysis shows that the existing infrastructure can be described as very fragmented and grossly ineffective. Our findings indicate that the implementation of a common integrated information infrastructure could significantly contribute to reducing costs especially by speeding up processes, by providing transparency in the flow and reducing the lead time for international trade of fruit and vegetables. Further, the description format developed for this case can be useful for visualizing and analyzing other supply chains involving collaborations across borders.

Author Keywords

International trade, information infrastructure, activity theory

ACM Classification Keywords

H.5.3 Group and Organization Interfaces: *Theory and models, Asynchronous interaction, Evaluation/methodology.*

INTRODUCTION

Extant literature on collaboration across borders in the Human Computer Interaction (HCI), Information Systems (IS), and International Management academic disciplines is focused on human actors and the IT artefacts that support direct human-to-human communication, interaction and

collaboration [1-4]. The core themes of the Collaboration across Borders (CABS) conference have a similar focus on human actors and the role of technology in bridging cultural, linguistic and geographic borders. While direct global interaction is important for distributed work and management, we believe that there is lack of understanding of indirect global interaction. Specifically, many application domains involve indirect interactions between human actors spanning different cultures, languages, and nations and they involve a wide variety of technologies (production, transport, information and communication, regulatory etc.). In many cases, such indirect global collaborations are characterized by economic and/or instrumental incentives and objectives instead of behavioral and/or interactional issues and concerns. In this paper, we seek to address such indirect global interactions that involve collaboration across borders involving different cultures, languages, technologies and nations. Specifically, we are analyzing the end-to-end supply chain of avocados from trees in Africa, avocados cross borders to grocery store shelves in the European Union.

International trade plays an important role in the economic growth, social welfare and human development of countries. International trade is characterized by an extremely complex eco-system of goods, actors, activities, technologies and rules. It involves interactions not only across national borders but also communications across diverse linguistic and cultural contexts. The domain of this revelatory case study is the international trade of fruit and vegetables form East Africa to the European Union (EU). By the invention and the use of refrigerated containers fruit and vegetables can keep high quality under long transports, even if the transport time with ship is weeks. This opens for new export possibilities for the East African countries and cheaper/better avocados for the EU consumer. Figure 1, which is adapted from the United Nations Centre for Trade Facilitation and Electronic Business (UN/CEFACT), presents a schematic overview of international trade.

Figure 1: The main roles of the actors and activities in international trade (Adapted from UN/CEFACT, 2001)

The importer and exporter are the two key actors. They agree to trade certain goods typically in exchange for a payment. However, in international trade, any trade will typically involve many service providers for the transportation of the goods, the monetary transactions and other related services. Additionally, the authorities will be involved in controlling the fruit or vegetables for health security, hazards, smuggling, collecting tariffs and fees when goods cross borders.

The two key issues for importers of fruits and vegetables in international trade is the quality of the product and the costs. The quality of the fruits and vegetables is strongly related to the lead time for getting the containers from the grower via the exporter, the importer and the retailer to the consumer [5-7]. As an exporter says: "*The vessel sails out weekly (from Mombasa, Kenya). If you miss that then you have the fruit stocked with you for another whole week and that means a lot of losses (of avocados) and a lot of money losses. You can take fruit (in reefers) to Europe in 25 days..*" This lead time is influenced by the established infrastructures and by the actors' (lack of) efficiency, especially in handling the barriers involved in crossing borders. Costs require a longer explanation.

Costs of international trade

There are mainly two determinants of the import trade cost for fruits and vegetables, the production price in the local export market (which is lower in East Africa than in Europe) and the cost associated with the international trade, i.e. the *transportation cost and cost related to crossing borders*.

Trade Cost €1.74

Local market price €1.00   International trade Cost €0.74

Transportation cost €0.21   Border related cost €0.53

Figure 2: Breakdown of Trade Cost in product price at local market and the trade cost for international trade, which is broken down in a part related to the physical transport and an administration part.

As illustrated in figure 2, crossing international borders presents costly barriers. The average additional cost of transportation itself adds 21% to the cost of the product (from exporter point of origin to importer warehouse having cleared customs and inspections in the importing country). However, the administration costs of cross border trading in the two or more countries involved from export to import country amounts to 53% of the value of the goods [8]. The total annual world-wide extra costs due to administrative burdens are estimated in the range 100-500 billion USD. Additionally the distribution via retailers to the consumers cost nearly the same as the product at local market price.

The reason for these border related costs are many, and for the transport of the goods (figure 1) include:

- Need for writing a number of documents for customs and inspection clearance (for each container there is a file of 20-30 paper based documents)

- Different version of documents for different actors in the ecosystem
- Number and time for the inspection(s) and control(s) - only some containers are selected
- Checking of documents
- Transferring of information from one document (in one IT system) to another
- Checking and correction of errors in documents
- Archiving of documents, often up to five years for future auditing

(There are additional issues related to the buy/sell and pay part of the international trade.)

Many of these issues are exacerbated due to problems related to different languages, currency, information, security, tariffs etc. The costs of international trade when crossing borders are a substantially supplement to the product cost of the fruit and vegetables for the importer. Furthermore, the trade cost associated with international trade of fruit and vegetables is higher than the average figures above. This is due to the fact that fruit and vegetables are transported in refrigerated containers which need energy to refrigerate and that authorities' demand for control of import of fruit and vegetables require more inspections and more documentation than for non-food goods. As such, energy costs and time spent on authorities control increase the cost for import of fruit and vegetables. Any increase in effectiveness will immediately result in higher prices for the exporter (which open up for export of new types of fruit and vegetables or other local goods e.g. flowers), lower prices for the consumer in the import country and/or higher margin for the trading industry. World Economic Forum (WEF) reports high variation in the cost of trade depending on the origin and the destination [9]. WEF estimates that improved trade facilitation to halfway of regional best practice has similar impact on global trade and Gross Domestic Product (GDP) as removing all tariffs, and that improved trade facilitation to halfway of global best practices with regard to reducing barriers, will result in growth of international trade and GDP by nearly 15% and 5% respectively [9]. Accordingly, reducing international trading cost can have a huge effect on the economic growth in both the exporting and the importing countries. Particularly in the developing countries, the growth in the export of fruit and vegetables can play a central role in improving the countries' economic conditions. A major problem for international trade of fruit and vegetables is that if the lead time gets too long then the product quality and thereby price is reduced significantly. Additionally, there seems to be high variation in lead time which makes the international trade of fruit and vegetables across borders quite risky.

The most concerning fact is that nobody has the complete picture of the process. Most information systems used are like isolated islands, created and maintained in order to serve the information needs of each of the 30-40 different actors involved in a typical trade of avocados. Even current inter-organizational information systems are often only used bilaterally with the immediate business partners. Further, these information systems are products of a local rationality; which may or may not serve the overall rationality of the trading ecosystem. We predict that information technology (IT) in the form of Inter-Organizational Systems (IOS) can play an important role. We find that there is potential for a large efficiency gain if there was a more effective exchange of documents (information) within an overarching global information infrastructure (II).

Research Question

It is clearly beyond the scope of this paper to deal with all of the critical issues in international cross border trade, and we shall delimit the scope of this paper to the following:

What are the critical procedural and administrative issues preventing efficient supply chain for international trade of fruit and vegetables, and how can they be addressed by utilizing modern information technology?

The rest of the paper is organized as follows. The theoretical framework section discusses Activity System Framework and Information Infrastructure, and presents a brief review of related extant literature. The methodology section presents details on the design of the case study, the description of the method used and the case study informants. The analysis section presents the findings from the empirical data. The list of critical issues and their probable causes are discussed next. Implications and limitations are discussed towards the end.

THEORETICAL FRAMEWORK

Activity Theory

In our view, the UN schematic of international trade described (Figure 1) as a system of only actors and activities is a rather simplistic view because the actors (e.g., the exporter) are geographically localized in their national community and are governed by the national rules. Further, they are using local technologies and equipment when handling the goods, related documents and information. Activity Theory Framework (ATF) helps take these elements into consideration and provides a conceptual vocabulary as well as theoretical mechanisms that are relevant and useful for the description of the part of the international trade that takes place in the individual geographical area (e.g. Kenya for the export). Instead of the standard ATF term of subject for human participants, we will use the term actor as it better emphasizes the actions contributing to completion of the activity.

Activity theory in general and Cultural Historical Activity Theory (CHAT) in particular have their origins in the Soviet Psychology of Vygotsky, Luria and colleagues [10-12]. Activity theory has been applied in multiple academic domains such as developmental psychology [13], educational psychology [14], learning sciences [15], human-computer interaction [16, 17], and information systems [18]. Activity Theory Framework [19] is built on the concept of system modeling by Engeström [20] where an activity consists of mutual link between three elements namely the actor, the object and the community. Activity Theory Framework

involves additionally three mediating elements: (a) the rules that mediate between the actor and the community, (b) the tools (/ equipment) which the actor uses in relation to the object, and (c) the division of labor which describe the structure (or lack of) for the community related to the object. The outcome of the activity is seen as a transformation process for the object. Figure 3 presents the basic structure of an activity.

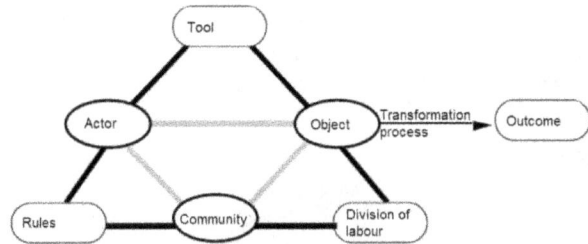

Figure 3: Basic structure of an activity with embedded the mediating relations modified after Kuutti [19] (with the term actor instead of subject)

Activities can be broken down into several actions and actions can be further broken down in many operations. Thus, the level of activity is comprised of actions which in turn are constituted by operations [19]. Each activity is aligned with a motive, the action with a goal and the operation with a condition. In our case, an activity can include actions of several actors each with their own motive (e.g. the exporter of fruit and vegetables, import of fruit and vegetables, and shipping goods in containers). The action is determined as the sum total of all the operations which an actor can perform in one continuous process independently of other actions involving others. We have limited our description to include only the operation(s) in an action that other actions depend on (e.g. an update by authorities of the status information for the container to "permission to remove" from customs area).

Information Infrastructure

Infrastructure is basic physical (and organizational) structures needed for facilitation and operation of a society / an organization and necessary for an economy to function [21]. The term typically refers to the technical structures that support a society, such as roads, bridges, water supply, sewers, electrical grids, telecommunications, and so forth, and can be defined as "the physical components of interrelated systems providing commodities and services essential to enable, sustain, or enhance societal living conditions" [22]. Infrastructures are characterized by nodes and means of connection as basis for activities, further that they are constantly evolving.

Regarding electronic infrastructures, the Software Engineering Institute (SEI) at Carnegie-Mellon University has identified the emergence of ultra-large-scale (ULS) systems [23]. They argue that these ULS systems will push far beyond the size of today's systems and systems of systems by every measure. They foresee that the scale of ULS systems presents challenges that are unlikely to be addressed adequately by incremental research within the established academic paradigms. In reply to the challenge put forward by SEI, some scholars (e.g., [24-26]) view the continuously increasing number and complexity of integrated information systems as information infrastructures (IIs), which is seen as a new type of IT artifact different from how information systems are presented in the literature (e.g. IIs has no life cycle since they already exists and is continuously evolving). Hanseth and Lyytinen [25] imply the increasingly integrated complexity of ULS systems [23] when defining an II as "*a shared, open (and unbounded), heterogeneous, and evolving socio-technical system consisting of a set of IT capabilities and their users, operations, and design communities*".

METHODOLOGY

We use a qualitative case study to address the research question. A case study investigates a contemporary phenomenon in depth and within its real-life context [27]. The case study method is especially relevant to our research problem since in international trade there are many more variables of interest than data points and therefore the results of the research relies on multiple sources of evidence with data convergence. A case study can potentially help to explain presumed phenomena in real-life interventions that are too complex for the survey or experimental research methods. Due to the complexity of the supply chain for international trade, we have selected only to focus on a specific trade lane for fruit and vegetables from East Africa to Europe. We have collected data in Kenya and in the Netherlands. Some of the data, especially on the exporting activity system, has been collected and reported in connection with a report for the World Economic Forum [28]. For the importing activity system, there are approximately 300 importers of fruit and vegetables in the Netherlands and they represent a great variation when examined in detail. Therefore, a set of representative importers have been selected for the case study. The General Secretary of the Dutch association of fruit and vegetable importers FrugiVenta has assisted in the selection of sites for visits, field observations and in-depth semi-structured interviews; and appointed the eight logistics experts for the focus group workshop. Besides exporter and importers visits, meetings and interviews have also been conducted with other actors such as the authorities, the terminal operator, logistic service provider and consulting companies regarding import declaration. The study is designed so that several actors contributed to its empirical data. Therefore, the overall results of the case study can be considered more robust according to Herriott & Firestone [27] and the research results will be more generally applicable. Of course, this remains to be verified by subsequent empirical research.

The case study reveals an extremely complex ecosystem. As such, to be able to communicate the findings, we have tried to find the right balance between abstraction and details. In what follows, we both present an overview of the process but also select important aspects for a more detailed and focused description. As stated earlier, the focus is on one trade lane for the import of fruit and vegetables: avocados from East

Africa to EU via the ports of Mombasa and of Rotterdam. Further, we only considered *the actors that can enable or prevent the container to be moved in the supply chain*. The total number of actors involved is estimated to be 30 – 40 different actors. The details of the activities and actions that the actors perform have been described at a high level of abstraction for activities and in greater detail only for the hand-over of communication action to another actor. Further the analytical focus has only been on the key documents (e.g. customs declaration) and a few key information items for the logistic coordination (e.g. estimated time of arrival). We hope that this balance between conceptual abstraction and operational detail will be informative to both academics and practitioners.

ANALYSIS
Activity Theory Framework

We applied ATF (Figure 3) for the international trade for fruit and vegetable, and identified the following dimensions for the geographical location as shown in Table 1: The *group of actors* include the farmer, the importer, the exporter, and different service providers; they are organized in *communities* in the form of various associations and organizations (e.g. the Fresh Producers Exporters Association in Kenya and the Dutch association FrugiVenta of importers of fruit and vegetable) and the authorities in the exporting country and the authorities in the importing country. The *object*s are the goods meaning the fruit and vegetables. The *transformation process* is the movement of the goods from the exporter to the importer via international shipping. The *rules* are the laws and regulations for international trade, and local laws and procedures in the individual country or region (e.g. Dutch and EU regulations, which applies for the actor group of the importers). The *tools* are the refrigerated container, the various means of transport, the information and documentation involved etc.; and the *division of work* includes the importer and the exporter's use of service providers with specialized capabilities for the movement of the containers with the fruit and vegetable, performing quality control of the fruits and vegetables, conducting inspections on behalf of the authorities, etc. Further, the authorities are the only actors allowed to release goods for export in the country of origin. In the country of destination, the authorities are the only actors that can allow the entrance of imported goods first into the customs area and then later allow the goods to pass out of the customs area and into the destination.

ATF is useful for describing the overall trade as consisting of three relatively independent activities, which in turn are decomposed into a tens of actions, which again are broken down into hundreds of operations carrying out by one (or a group) of individual(s). Only the object (specifically, fresh fruit and vegetables in refrigerated containers) and some related information are linking the activity systems of export, import and international shipping. Across the activity systems only the importer and the exporter interact, and typically the exporter and the importer respectively communicates with the shipping line often via a logistics service provider.

Activity Dimension	Export East Africa	International Shipping	Import Europe
Actors	Farmers, Exporters, Authorities, Service providers, Transporters	Terminal operators, Shipping lines	Importers, Authorities, Service providers as Transporter. Retail. Consumers.
Communities	Association of exporters in East Africa	Alliances of shipping lines	Association of importers of fruit and vegetables to the Netherlands
Objects	Fruit and vegetables in refrigerated containers with related documents and information	Refrigerated containers (with fruit and vegetables) with related documents and information	Fruit and vegetables in refrigerated containers with related documents and information
Tools / equipment	Local means of transports as trucks, local authorities information systems for export declarations, certificates, etc., local terminal operators information system	Straddle carriers, cranes, container ships, local port community information systems, EU authorities information system for ENS, shipping lines information system	Local means of transports as trucks, local authorities information systems for declarations, certificates, etc., local terminal operators information system
Rules	Exporting regulations in country of origin	International trade regulations, international seafarer rules, etc.	Import regulations in importing country and EU
Division of work	Farming, trading, packing, transport by truck, controlling and inspection	Transport, storage, and shipping	Trading, packing, transport by truck, controlling and inspection, and distribution

Table 1: Decomposition and categorization of the three activity systems of Export, Import, and International Shipping. Note only the Objects flow between the Activities and thereby transform across the system boundaries. All other dimensions are local and there are no relation between e.g. the rules in the export, import and shipping activity system. The focus of the shipper is to move containers and not the content. On the other hand, the focus of the importer and exporter is on the goods in the containers e.g. fruit and vegetables.

ATF provides valuable description of the part of the international trade that takes place in the exporting country e.g. Kenya and similar for the importing country e.g. The Netherlands. Our attempts to use ATF for the full trade lane including both the exporting, the importing countries and the shipping turned out to be problematic because the importer and the exporter are rather remote with limited contact. Further, the rules, the communities, the tools and to some extent the division of labor are different for the exporting and the importing country. Since the export and the import can be seen as distinct different activities with only the goods (and a few related documents) in common, then the ATF description is done separately for the each of them. Additionally, international shipping is a separate activity that represents the part of international trade that's the transport by ship from the port in the exporting country and the arrival to the port of destination in the importing country. This works out well because a special set of rules applies for international trade and international shipping, and that the relatively small number of actors have formed various alliances that use similar tools and a stable division of work to move containers around the globe. Therefore we end up with three relatively isolated activities described by ATF for export, shipping, and import as shown in Figure 4.

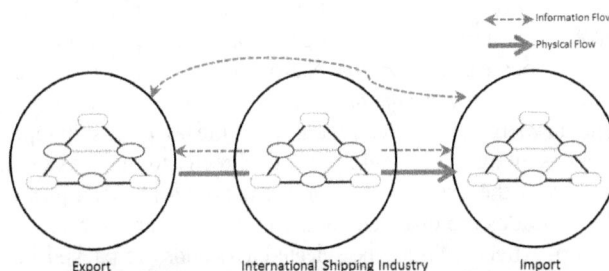

Figure 4: The ATF system of the exporter and the ATF system of the importer are linked across the borders by the international shipping industry. The three ATF systems are separated physically, geographically, and temporally; and linked via infrastructures.

We find that ATF is excellent at coping with activities in each geographical region, but inadequate in capturing a chain of activities across borders as in the physical supply chain for international trade. Additionally, ATF does not capture the absence of activities or delays (e.g. when the container is waiting for an activity) and waiting time is a major part of the lead time in the supply chain. ATF models have only one outcome linked to the object (Figure 2) and do not model inputs. The outcomes e.g. for the exporter in the international trade are the exported goods and in return, a payment, and vice-versa for the importer. Further, there are several documents and information exchanged between various actors (e.g. the exporter and the importer) which are another

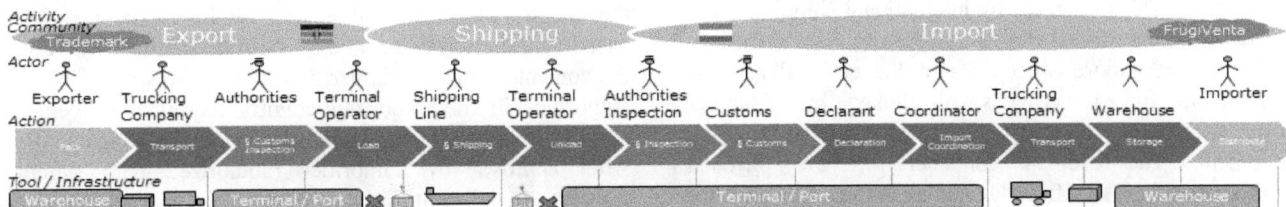

Figure 5: Physical infrastructure linking the national activities, the actors and the actions for international trade of avocados

type of output and input that are not easy to model using ATF. Therefore, the ATF seems best suited for description of the local aspect of international trade and not so well suited for the international aspect across borders. The general system theory by Bertalanffy [29] defines a system as the group of elements that have as few as possible connections to the environment, which is what we found out in the above analysis. The above analysis illustrates that the international trade can best be described by three separate activity descriptions utilizing the ATF. We propose to view these systems as interlinked with infrastructures. The boundaries between the three systems represent a major challenge and the crossing of the borders is the difficult part.

Infrastructures

Infrastructures can be divided into physical infrastructures and information infrastructures. Physical infrastructures serve the movement of equipment that moves people and objects (i.e. goods). Information infrastructures serves the communication of information and messages among actors and information systems. First the physical flow of the avocados will be described and then the related information will be described.

Physical Infrastructure

With regard to the physical flow, it starts in Kenya where the avocado is harvested by a large number of local farmers. A farmer located 70 km from Nairobi with ten avocado trees: *"Avocados are more profitable than the other things I grow"*. The farmers will typically transport the avocados in open pickups either via a local market or directly to the packaging facility of the exporter. During the handling phase, a part of the avocados are discarded and only the best are selected for export. After washing, the selected avocados are packed into separate carton boxes. The boxes are palletized and loaded to a refrigerated container at the packaging facility. The container will be transported approximately 500 km by truck to the port facility of Mombasa where the containers will be loaded on the vessel by the terminal operator and shipped to Rotterdam may be with one or more transshipment(s). After arrival to the port of Rotterdam the container will be unloaded by another terminal operator and later be transported to the importers warehouse for later distribution to the retail industry and later to the consumer.

The basic physical infrastructure is in place in the form of roads, shipping routes and tools, which are improving over time. Efficient physical infrastructures are in place in EU and are now being improved in some countries in East Africa. The physical infrastructure that enable efficient transport of the avocados from the exporter to the importer consists of trucks operated by local trucking companies, a network of national roads, and an extended routing network with deep sea container ships operated by international shipping lines. Several shipping lines offers service from East Africa to Europe. Furthermore, it consists of the national and the international linked networks, all linked by container terminals at ports with cranes and other container handling equipment. The use of containers in the physical infrastructure has significantly increased the efficiency for

handling of goods. In the case of East Africa, they have and continue to invest in establishing and improving the infrastructure both roads, rails and ports to facilitate the container transportation. The refrigerated containers can keep the fruit and vegetables fresh for weeks by storing them at a low temperature and adding a gas to prevent contact with oxygen. The trader states: *"This business would not be possible without the reefer (refrigerated container)"*. As such, the physical movement of fruit and vegetables from East Africa to Europe is possible and lead time is several weeks. Unfortunately, there is variation in the lead time which makes the business risky since the long lead time impacts the quality of the fruit and vegetables. For fruit and vegetables, the use of refrigerated containers and the existing infrastructure has enabled efficient movement of containers to new export markets and thereby opened new export businesses.

Information Infrastructure

Before international trade can take place, the exporter and the importer have to be connected. An association of exporters (e.g. Fresh Producer Exporters Association in Kenya) and an association of importers of fruit and vegetables (e.g. FrugiVenta in the Netherlands) can facilitate this. Representatives from the associations might meet at e.g. industry conferences (e.g. Fruit Logistica in Berlin every February). The importer and the exporter often never meet in person. Instead they exchange information about trade possibilities by various communication channels i.e. phone, fax, e-mail and ordinary mail. Their use of internet is limited since the few that have a website have it in their national language. At some point, an importer in The Netherlands in EU and an exporter from Kenya in East Africa agree to trade avocados. There are many ways they can arrange their trade. They will agree about the individual shipment, book the transport either directly with a shipping line or via an intermediary logistics service provider who will confirm the booking and then brings empty containers to the exporter. An example of the information flow related to international trade of fruit and vegetables (avocados) from East Africa to EU is illustrated in the Appendix.

There are a number of barriers before goods can be cleared for export which takes days. An exporter explains that the container has to leave Nairobi by Sunday afternoon by truck for Mombasa Port (500 km) to be able to catch the vessel departing Thursday. According to the rules in most countries, the exporter has to file an export declaration including a list of goods to the authorities in the country of origin (e.g. with description of the goods, quality, quantity, weight, etc.) and additional required information (e.g. Phytosanitary certificate for avocados). In most countries in Africa, the authorities in the country of origin will inspect all fruit and vegetables based on the information in the export declaration and verify the content of each container. Further, for import to EU, the authorities in the importing country require a movement certificate verified by the authorities in the exporting country. After approval by authorities (authorized with stamps, signatures and status change in the port community information system) in the exporting country, the terminal operator are allowed to load the declared goods in the containers on the vessel.

Additionally, before departure, the shipping line has to file an Entry Summary Declaration (ENS) to the authorities if the destination is within EU, the ENS has to be filled at least 24 hours prior to departure from the port in the country of origin. The shipping line sails the containers to the port of destination in EU, but might transit the containers and use several different modalities of transport, which requires additional documentation. Prior to the arrival of goods, the importer needs to file an import declaration with similar information as the export declaration and ENS, and provide additional documentation e.g. certificates. Typically, the importer will ask the exporter to provide the needed information and documentation, which then is used for import declaration. Upon arrival at the terminal, an operator will lift the container into the customs area in the port of destination only if the authorities has released the container to be unloaded. The authorities in EU will select containers for inspection and inform the carrier about this, who then informs the other actors. In the case of fruit and vegetables, the authorities or an authorized service provider most likely take samples for laboratory testing. Additionally, the customs informs the carrier if they selected the container for scanning to inspect and search for illicit contents (e.g. narcotics). Finally, the authorities will clear the goods and give "permission to remove" the container from customs area. Then the importer (or a service provider given this task) can contact a trucking company to order a truck and forward the permission to pick up the container and request the terminal operator to load the container on the truck for the last part of journey to the importer. The importers reports that the lead time from the vessel arrives in the port of Rotterdam until the reefers arrive in their warehouse typically takes 3 days and 5 days over weekends. At the importers warehouse, typically the fruit and vegetables will be quality controlled before they are distributed to retailers to finally reach the consumers. Additionally, the importer will provide product information e.g. for product quality for the retailers and the consumers.

As mentioned in the Methodology section, the above description focuses on selected operations in an action, which other actors later in the supply chain depend on. We find that this operation always seems to be a communication operation with some information by phone, fax, e-mail, or by updating an information system (e.g. file an import declaration). Without the information being properly communicated, the other actor will wait leading to delays.

The figure in the Appendix illustrates the information flow linking the activities of export, import and shipping in connection with the physical infrastructure for international trade of avocados. The major issues are peer to peer communication between the actors, manual retyping and copying of information, and different communication channels with limited access possibilities. A comprehensive illustration of the actions involved together with the flow of

selected and related documents and information in the Appendix shows that each actor tends to have their own information system(s). Regarding the flow of documents involved, many of them can be traced to their historical origin since many of the current electronic documents originally were paper documents e.g. the Bill of Lading (B/L). Although most of the documents and the information today too are in electronic form, we find that in our case, a majority of the information is retyped from one information system to another (e.g. for B/L is stated "as said" based on a packing list, which means that the actor did not verify the content visually). Paper version of certificates, declarations, and B/L still has to be presented to the authorities on request within 15 minutes. These are certificates in original version on official paper with stamps and signatures for every imported container. One certificate can cover a set of containers but there can only be one certificate per declaration. To avoid all containers in a shipment to be withheld by authorities, some importers ask the exporter to split a shipment (e.g. ten containers into ten shipments and thereby prepare ten export declaration). With multiple movement declarations instead of one, and a request for multiple certificates instead of one; the importer will have to prepare multiple import documents instead of one. It is a lot of work but the importer knows from experience that this might get more containers through the import clearance and much faster instead of awaiting clearance of all containers in a shipment at once.

The above analysis of the international trade shows that the three ATF systems and the concept of infrastructure can be used to understand the border crossing processes involving the exporter, the importer, and the shipping line. However AFT is not sufficient for the cross border analysis of international trade. For that purpose, we applied the notion of infrastructures, which not only connects the isolated AFT systems but also is part of the AFT systems where the tools / equipments utilize the infrastructure in accordance with the local rules and division of labor (the three mediation elements). This might be obvious since the originally meaning of the word infrastructure in English from 1887 was: "*the installations that form the basis for any operation or system*". The movement across borders of avocados depends on both the physical and informational infrastructures which enable the fruit and vegetables to be transported in a partially efficient way from origin to destination. Whereas the physical infrastructures already exist and continuously are being improved to become more efficient, the information infrastructure is rather messy with many different communication channels for primarily peer-to-peer messages, which is inefficient and error-prone with manual copy-and-paste of information The blurry information infrastructure is so fragmented and disconnected that it hardly comply to the definition of an information infrastructure (see Theoretical Framework Section). Our case study results show that an efficient information infrastructure is missing in reality.

Issues	Possible Causes
Communication between the actors is mostly done by phone (voice and sms) and e-mail, which are neither recorded nor structured information and therefore difficult to make visible and to share.	Those channels are fast and convenient to use when speed is required. The communication is, for historical reasons, primarily peer to peer using a range of communication channels / media. A range of various communication channels are being used.
None of the actors have real time knowledge.	Information recording is delayed by days or not recorded in information systems. The recorded information can only be accessed by the employees of the actor owning the information system.
Information is often delayed or even outdated.	Actors pass on information manually or by retyping / copying.
Variation in lead time decreases the quality of fruit and vegetables.	Lack of effective coordination planning due to disconnected information flows.
Planning information offered to the importer or their coordinator is error prone and not very accurate.	The service providers do not provide accurate logistic information e.g. estimated arrival time of the individual container set to the estimated time of departure for the ship from the port.
Importer or their logistics coordinator receive planning information with a delay of ½-1 day.	The planning information is delayed e.g. due to that the process is outsourced or not conveyed.
At several points in time neither the owner, the exporter nor the importer know where the container is.	Lack of logistic information. Information about the actual movement of goods in containers are communicated by phone and not recorded.
Error prone information can become a security issue for the authorities in the importing country	Information is retyped several times e.g. when the packing list becomes the B/L it is retyped or copied to several documents.

Issues	Possible Causes
Error prone information can become a security issue for the authorities in the importing country	Information is retyped several times e.g. when the packing list becomes the B/L it is retyped or copied to several documents.
Often containers have to await for information to arrive	The information systems are primarily standalone and serve only one actor e.g. the authorities system for filing declarations.
Different and inconsistent demands by export and import authorities (they request similar information but in each their form / format) therefore information is retyped by importer and shipping line.	Lack of international harmonized standards and local national implementation of standards in national information systems (often referred to as Single window system).
Original paper certificates from exporting country has to be send by the exporter to the importer by a courier to catch up with the shipment	Normally the authorities in the exporting haven't issued the certificates and they are not ready prior that the containers are shipped. The authorities in the importing country only accept the original paper certificate (with stamp and signatures) and do not accept or use modern electronic information.
It's a security risk when the authorities do not know who shipped the goods (crucial information in the authorities' security assessment).	For the type of shipping where a third party logistic service provider (3PL) arrange the shipping then they are not demanded and often not allowed (in EU) to reveal the real shipper i.e. the exporter.
Authorities might demand the shipping line to provide more information than required in the filed declaration.	Authorities are not satisfied with the information provided by the shipping line and request source documents. The quality of the information filed to the authorities is lacking e.g. due to the many retyping of the information (in average a B/L is changed more than 3-4 times after creation).

Table 2: Reported issues and possible causes.

CRITICAL ISSUES IN INTERNATIONAL TRADE

There are several suggestions that can improve the lead time for the individual process in the supply chain and thereby reduce the lead time of the supply chain. However, in general, each process is in itself efficient and the major part of the lead time is the waiting time where the fruits and vegetables in the refrigerated container await the next process or modality of transport. As stated, there is a significant variation in the lead time in the supply chain wherefore reliability is important. Exporter explains: *"Reliability in perishables (as fresh fruits) and in our business is extremely important because we are dealing with fruit so we have to get the fruits into Nairobi in time, we have to process in time, and we need the containers in time, to catch up with the vessel."* The physical transport of the fruits and vegetables is a chain of various processes with different means of transport and barriers by authorities. Some of the reasons for the variation in lead time are error prone information, missing communication, and lack of coordination due to lack of precise logistic information. An example is that the container(s) are held back until cleared by authorities who require certain documentation to be provided. Therefore, the timing of documentation is crucial. This includes

documentation for payment of dues, fees and tariffs. Also, the coordination, office hours and the timing of the shift of transport modality cause variation in the lead time (for instance, an importer reports: *"We knows the expected arrival of the vessel but never knows the exact unloading time or date of the (individual) container, we have to await that the logistic service provider tells us"* (who is informed by the carrier or checks the port community system directly).

The analysis of the information and documentation involved in international trade of fruit and vegetables from East Africa to EU shows a fragmented landscape of information and documents which are communicated by many different means of communication from telephone calls, faxes, e-mails to physical papers, etc. or can be accessed in certain information systems by actors having the right permissions. As mentioned before, lead time is critical for movement of fresh fruit and vegetables from farmer via exporter to importer and to the consumer. Too long lead time decreases the quality of the fruit and vegetables. This makes the business risky for the importer who might lose a shipment with several containers of fruit and vegetables (e.g. a shipment of five containers holds ½ million avocados). Several issues have been pointed out by the actors for international trade in interviews and focus groups. The list includes examples of issues (but is not exhaustive). Our main findings indicate that there is a well-established physical infrastructure which enables the efficient physical movement of fresh fruit and vegetables in refrigerated containers.

However:

1. Actors' communication is predominately peer-to-peer utilizing a range of different communication media /channels.
2. Current information infrastructure is costly and in-efficient which is creating long and varied lead times that directly and severely impact the quality of the fresh fruit and vegetables.
3. Lacking an efficient information infrastructure for efficient communication and coordination.

The utilized information infrastructure with multiple communication media/channels is a result of actors using what is available for them to use instead of carefully designed. Historically, ordinary mail was the mean of communication, which removed the need for the traders to travel in person. Later inventions such as telegraph, telex, telephone, fax, e-mail and EDI messages became effective substitutes for letters as a communication medium. New IT innovations provide efficient information infrastructures where information flows can be updated and viewed by many actors simultaneously in real time Examples in the consumer world are social collaborations on Facebook and Dropbox which utilize the internet as backbone infrastructure and involve human-to-human interactions across borders, geographical locations, time zones, and cultures. Emerging innovations in the field of Internet of Things (IoT) might be relevant for the containerized international trade enabling the containers to communicate about their actual condition and location. This could shift the communication processes away from actor-to-actor communication to sensors-to-human or even sensor-to-sensor communication, which might eliminate some of border crossing barriers and thereby improve the efficiency of the international trade. There is a need for researching how to design an efficient information infrastructure for international trade, which the traders and other actors potentially can benefit from using instead of or as a complement to the current used communication media / channels. Further, there is a need for researching to which degree existing local solutions being used (e.g. port community systems as Portbase in Rotterdam and single windows by authorities as Hongkong [30] and TradeNet in Singapore [31] can facilitate communication on a global scale.

CONCLUSION

To a great extent, the business model of a large group of service providers is based on the inefficiency in the international trade and they may therefore be reluctant to improve the situation. That said, the traders who are paying the trade costs and the authorities can change the rules of the game if they decide themselves or commission others to

design, develop, and implement joint efficient information infrastructures. Utilizing the established physical infrastructure this could mean a huge improvement in overall trade efficiency which potential could have a substantial impact on international trade and GDP. The document and information flow for international trade of avocados largely is not aided by applying modern technology. Collaboration among (some of the) organizations using electronic communication has primarily been based on electronic data interchange (EDI). This was originally researched in what was generally referred to as Inter-Organizational Systems (IOS) (e.g. [32]) and more recently as Information Infrastructure (II) (e.g. [25]). In most cases, IOS will have a positive effect on organizational performance. One major reason for this is that IOS impacts governance by shifting transactions from organizational hierarchies to markets and thereby lower external coordination or transaction costs [33]. The investment for IOS is significant especially for Small and Medium Enterprises in East Africa. Additionally their internal IS are rather limited which makes the IOS nearly impossible to implement. Therefore, the exporters and importers are reluctant to invest in IOS. Information infrastructures are by design based on shared source(s), open and unbounded [25]. IIs are supposedly less expensive than IOS based on EDI message exchange. Therefore a suggestion for improving the situation is to design an information infrastructure that is complementary to physical intercontinental infrastructure. This will potential make the collaboration across borders more efficient and potential increase collaboration across boundaries. By a proper implementation of an information infrastructure for the international trade between East Africa and EU many of the error-prone issues can be eliminated, the logistic planning and related alerts can be improved, the authorities can perform clearing prior to the arrival of the ship and the security control can focus on the most risky shipments. Further, the language and translation issues can be addressed. There are also issues where an II implementation will not have impact such currency exchange rate fluctuation issues. As pointed out by Carr [34], infrastructures are characterized by that they will be broadly shared and that they will become part of the general business infrastructure. We agree with the argument also brought forward by Henningsson and colleagues [35] that an information infrastructure potentially can improve the international trade. Therefore, our main recommendation based on our analysis of the empirical findings from the case study utilizing both system and infrastructure theory is to focus on the design, development, and implementation of a common information infrastructure that spans across borders and actors integrating the activity systems of exporters, imports and the shipping lines.

REFERENCES

[1] Vatrapu, R. Explaining culture: an outline of a theory of socio-technical interactions. *Proceedings of the 3rd ACM International Conference on Intercultural Collaboration (ICIC 2010)* 2010), 111-120.

[2] Setlock, L. D., Fussell, S. R. and Neuwirth, C. Taking it out of context: collaborating within and across cultures in face-to-face

settings and via instant messaging. *Proceedings of the 2004 ACM conference on Computer supported cooperative work*2004), 604-613.

[3] Vlaar, P. W., van Fenema, P. C. and Tiwari, V. Cocreating understanding and value in distributed work: How members of onsite and offshore vendor teams give, make, demand, and break sense. *MIS quarterly*, 32, 2 2008), 227-255.

[4] Werner, S. Recent developments in international management research: A review of 20 top management journals. *Journal of Management*, 28, 3 2002), 277-305.

[5] Stewart, G. Supply chain performance benchmarking study reveals keys to supply chain excellence. *Logistics Information Management*, 8, 2 1995), 38-44.

[6] Christopher, M. *Logistics and supply chain management.* Pearson UK, 2012.

[7] De Treville, S., Shapiro, R. D. and Hameri, A.-P. From supply chain to demand chain: the role of lead time reduction in improving demand chain performance. *Journal of Operations Management*, 21, 6 2004), 613-627.

[8] Anderson, J. E. and Van Wincoop, E. *Trade costs.* National Bureau of Economic Research, 2004.

[9] Group, W. E. F. i. c. w. T. B. C. Connected World. Transforming Travel, Transportation and Supply Chains. *World Economic Forum, Insight Report*2013).

[10] Vygotsky, L. *Mind in society.* Harvard University Press, 1930/1980.

[11] Vygotsky, L. *Thought and Language.* Massachusetts Institute of Technology, Cambridge, 1962.

[12] Roth, W. M. and Lee, Y. J. "Vygotsky's Neglected Legacy": Cultural-Historical Activity Theory. *Review of Educational Research*, 77, 2 2007), 186-232.

[13] Wertsch, J. *Vygotsky and the social formation of mind.* Harvard University Press, Cambridge, MA, USA, 1985.

[14] Jonassen, D. H. and Rohrer-Murphy, L. Activity theory as a framework for designing constructivist learning environments. *Educational Technology Research and Development*, 47, 1 1999), 61-79.

[15] Greeno, J. G. The situativity of knowing, learning, and research. *American psychologist*, 53, 1 1998), 5.

[16] Kaptelinin, V. *Acting with technology: Activity theory and interaction design.* Mit Press, 2006.

[17] Nardi, B. A. Activity Theory and Its Use Within Human-Computer Interaction. *Journal of the Learning Sciences*, 7, 2 1998), 257 - 261.

[18] Mursu, Á., Luukkonen, I., Toivanen, M. and Korpela, M. Activity Theory in information systems research and practice:

theoretical underpinnings for an information systems development model. *Information Research*, 12, 3 2007).

[19] Kuutti, K. *Activity theory as a potential framework for human-computer interaction research.* MIT Press, City, 1996.

[20] Engeström, Y. Learning by expanding: An activity-theoretical approach to developmental research1987).

[21] Sheffrin, S. M. Economics: Principles in action. *Upper Saddle River, New Jersey*, 74582003), 551.

[22] Fulmer, J. What in the world is infrastructure. *PEI Infrastructure investor*2009), 30-32.

[23] Feiler, P., Gabriel, R. P., Goodenough, J., Linger, R., Longstaff, T., Kazman, R., Klein, M., Northrop, L., Schmidt, D. and Sullivan, K. Ultra-large-scale systems: The software challenge of the future. *Software Engineering Institute*, 12006).

[24] Star, S. L. and Ruhleder, K. Steps toward an ecology of infrastructure: Design and access for large information spaces. *Information systems research*, 7, 1 1996), 111-134.

[25] Hanseth, O. and Lyytinen, K. Design theory for dynamic complexity in information infrastructures: the case of building internet. *Journal of Information Technology*, 25, 1 2010), 1-19.

[26] Tilson, D., Lyytinen, K. and Sørensen, C. Research commentary-digital infrastructures: the missing IS research agenda. *Information Systems Research*, 21, 4 2010), 748-759.

[27] Yin, R. K. *Case study research: Design and methods.* sage, 2009.

[28] Company, W. E. F. i. c. w. B. Enabling trade: From valuation to action. *Report*2014).

[29] Bertalanffy, L. v. *General system theory: Foundations, development, applications.* Braziller. New York, 1968.

[30] King, J. and Konsynski, B. R. *Hong Kong TradeLink: news from the second city.* Harvard Business School, 1990.

[31] King, J. L. and Konsynski, B. R. *Singapore TradeNet: a tale of one city.* Harvard Business School, 1995.

[32] Krcmar, H., Bjorn-Andersen, N. and O'Callaghan, R. *EDI in Europe: How it works in practice.* John Wiley & Sons, City, 1995.

[33] Robey, D., Im, G. and Wareham, J. D. Theoretical Foundations of Empirical Research on Interorganizational Systems: Assessing Past Contributions and Guiding Future Directions. *Journal of the Association for Information Systems*, 9, 9 2008).

[34] Carr, N. G. IT doesn't matter. *Harvard Business Review*2003), 5-12.

[35] Henningsson, S., Budel, R., Gal, U. and Tan, Y.-H. *Itaide information infrastructure (I3) framework.* Springer, City, 2011.

Uses and Benefits of Qualitative Approaches to Culture in Intercultural Collaboration Research

Sylvie Chevrier
University Paris-Est
Cité Descartes
77454 Marne la Vallée
France
sylvie.chevrier@u-pem.fr

Mary Yoko Brannen
Gustavson School of Business
University of Victoria
Victoria, BC V8W2Y2
Canada
maryyoko@uvic.ca

Carol Hansen
Georgia State University
PO BOX 3965
Atlanta, GA 30 302
United States
chansen@gsu.edu

Keywords
Intercultural collaboration, qualitative studies, story telling, organizational ethnography, content analysis, interpretive approach

ACM Classification Keywords
A.0 General Literature: GENERAL.

PANEL PROPOSAL
Cross-cultural research is mainly based upon the measurement of cross-cultural dimensions popularized by Hofstede (1980, 2001), Trompenaars (1993) or Schwartz (1994). These dimensions stemming from attitude scales are useful to compare national cultural differences on a general level but cannot adequately account for what happens when people actually meet and interact with each other.

For over twenty years, researchers have proposed alternative approaches drawing upon interpretive methods (d'Iribarne, 1989; Sackmann & Philipps, 2004). Beyond comparative studies, investigations were conducted into two types of cases: situations where management tools are used in another cultural context than the one from which they originated (D'Iribarne & Henry, 2007; Barmeyer & Davoine, 2011) and work interactions within multicultural organizations (Brannen & Salk, 2000; Chevrier, 2003; Moore, 2005).

In both kinds of situations, the objective is to see reality from the eyes of the actor and to grasp the meaning of their action; "it is to unravel and understand the world from the perspective of the acting persons situated in their own local context and therefore, understanding the society in which they live" (Romani, Sackmann & Primecz, 2011, p. 4).

Considering the importation of management tools, research has shown that the so called "best practices" have to take apositive meaning from the users' point of view if they are

CABS '14, August 21-22, 2014, Kyoto, Japan.
ACM 978-1-4503-2557-8/14/08.
http://dx.doi.org/10.1145/2631488.2631771

be actually used beyond ceremonial adoption (Yousfi, 2013). In international teams, common practices have to be negotiated to make sense to all members and to avoid conflicts or withdrawal attitudes. Therefore the meaning frames through which protagonists see the organizational world are worth looking at (D'Iribarne, 2009).

Interpretive researchers do not test hypotheses; as they investigate a real work setting, the contingent problems emerge and researchers unveil actors' meanings and eventually provide appropriate constructs.

Even if the situation is not generalizable, the results of an interpretive research may apply to a broad scope of situations. Contextualized observations made in specific cases can be transformed into evidence of the society as a whole when the logic or rationale for action in very different settings appears to take the same shape. Each case analysis brings light to the cultures of the societies under study and to intercultural interactions.

PANEL GOAL: PRESENTING QUALITATIVE METHODS TO BRING LIGHT ON SOCIETY CULTURES AND INTERCULTURAL INTERACTIONS

A large number of methodologies might be appropriate for interpretive research. The three panelists of this session will each discuss one methodology to provide new insights on cross-cultural collaboration through qualitative interpretive inquiry.

Mary Yoko Brannen: Strategic Ethnography and leveraging internal organizational insights for sustainable growth and renewal
Strategic ethnography adapts and extends ethnographic method to MNE strategy around leveraging local knowledge through insider/outsider eyes of multicultural teams. In this talk, Professor Brannen will discuss this new method from the lens of an in-depth study of retail giant, Tesco Plc's global operations. She will discuss three contributions of the study. Firstly, it offers a longitudinal field study of an actual multicultural team in practice with an organizational determined "real world" outcome measure, and, secondly, develops a clear definition of what is meant by "bicultural bridge" with three skill sets that make up the construct that are applied over three

organizationally relevant contexts for bicultural bridging, namely cognitive complexity, perceptual acuity and reflexivity. Finally, this study is methodologically innovative, in that the study was executed by a team of Asian in-house managers with no prior ethnographic skills. The academic team designed a custom-made training course including instruction in ethnographic research techniques. Further techniques to collate data gathered by the team had to be purpose-built and unique tools for the extraction and evaluation of key themes across data from a culturally diverse group had to be developed.

Sylvie Chevrier: Interpretive content analysis to highlight meaning frameworks

Interpretive content analysis can be used to unveil cultural frames of meaning of actors from different cultural backgrounds working in dispersed teams. When working at a distance, team members are often unaware that they do not give the same meaning to most basic management processes they are concerned with. This presentation will illustrate how qualitative research can provide insights about what decision-making or empowerment mean for employees from different countries. For instance measuring the power relationship index of a country induces managers to delegate more or less to employees. With qualitative understanding of what empowerment and decision-making mean, the question is no longer to know to what extent leaders should delegate but to find the specific conditions of delegation in various countries. This cultural understanding helps people to design management processes matching the requirements of partners from different cultures.

Carol Hansen: The potential of storytelling

To decipher the belief patterns that shape expectations that individuals in different societies and different organizations have about the means and ends of work, scholars have often employed techniques used by anthropologists. One such technique is to analyze stories about work as a cultural artifact (Boje, 2001, Martin, 1982, Schein, 1985). Carol Hansen will illustrate how stories act as a kind of cultural code (Hansen & Kahnweiler, 1993. An ontological notion of reality as a social construction suggests that tales reflect what people believe should be true and offer a vehicle for penetrating belief systems that are either difficult or impossible to articulate.   An additional and essential qualifier to the storytelling process (Martin, 1982) is that stories differ from other forms of communication as in the case of gossip, for example, because they express a moral; a lesson to be learned. Likewise, how informants define the key elements of a story, i.e. who is the hero or the villain and why, can reveal much about what is admired and what is to be avoided (Hansen & Kahnweiler, 1993).

Not only are stories entertaining, people tend to remember stories longer than other forms of transmission. Stories also provide a shortcut for new members to learn about the culture of their environment (Martin, 1982; Swap, Leonard,

Shields & Abrams, 2001). They equally aid in cross cultural collaboration by acting as a tool for communicating one's assumptions and for learning about those held by others in different organizations, and societies.

PANELISTS' BACKGROUND

Mary Yoko Brannen is the Jarislowsky East Asia (Japan) Chair at the Centre for Asia-Pacific Initiatives (CAPI) and Professor of International Business at the Peter B. Gustavson School of Business at the University of Victoria in British Columbia and serves as Deputy Editor of the Journal of International Business. She received her M.B.A. with emphasis in International Business and Ph.D. in Organizational Behavior with a minor in Cultural Anthropology from the University of Massachusetts at Amherst, and a B.A. from the University of California at Berkeley. She has taught at the Ross School of Business at the University of Michigan, the Lucas Graduate School of Business at San Jose State University, the Haas Business School at the University of California at Berkeley, Smith College, and Stanford University in the United States; Keio Business School in Tokyo, Japan, and Fudan University in Shanghai, China. Professor Brannen's expertise in cross-cultural management is evident in her research, consulting, teaching, and personal background. Born and raised in Japan, having studied in France and Spain, and having worked as a cross-cultural consultant for over 25 years to various Fortune 100 companies, she brings a multi-faceted, deep knowledge of today's complex cultural business environment. Her consulting specialty is in helping multinational firms realize their global strategic initiatives by aligning, integrating and deploying critical organizational resources. Professor Brannen's current research projects include research on knowledge sharing across distance and differentiated contexts, directing a global think tank focusing on biculturals and people of mixed cultural origins as the new workplace demographic, and developing strategic ethnography as a method by which global companies can realize sustainable competitive advantage.

Sylvie Chevrier is professor of management at Université de Paris-Est at Marne-la-Vallée (France). She is deputy Director of the IRG (Institut de Recherche en Gestion) research center and responsible for a master program in Human Resource Management and International Staffing. She obtained a PhD in management from the University du Québec à Montreal (Canada) and her main research interests focus on the management of cross-cultural teams. She published several articles and books on cross-cultural management presenting qualitative research on multicultural teams including members from Europe, Asia, Africa and America.

Specializing in organizational culture and ethnographic research methods, **Carol Hansen** is emerita at Georgia

State University, Atlanta, Georgia (USA) with experience in both the private and public sectors. Her various roles include research professor, branch chief at the United States Department of State and research consultant to universities and corporations. She conducted research in North and West Africa and in Western Europe and she has been a visiting professor in business and psychology at the Universities of Paris I and Paris-Est, Lausanne, Strasbourg, Mainz, and Valencia. Her award winning publications include two books, numerous book chapters and over 40 articles and conference proceedings. She was a Fulbright scholar to India and she obtained her Ph.D. from the University of North Carolina at Chapel Hill. chansen@gsu.edu

REFERENCES

1. Barmeyer, C., and Davoine, E. (2011). The intercultural challenges in the transfer of codes of conduct from the US to Europe, in Primecz, H., Romani, L. and Sackmann, S., *Cross-cultural Management in Practice. Culture and Negotiated Meanings*, Edward Elgar, 53-63.

2. Boje, D. (2001). *Narrative Methods for Organizational and Communication Research*. Newbury Park, CA: Sage.

3. Brannen MY. and Salk, JE. (2000). Partnering across Borders: negotiating organizational culture in a German-Japanese joint-venture, *Human Relations*, 53(4), 451-87.

4. Chevrier, S. (2003), « Cross-cultural Management in Multinational Project Groups » *Journal of World Business*, n°140, 1-9.

5. Hansen, C. and Kahnweiler, W. (1993). Storytelling: An instrument for understanding the dynamics of corporate relationships. *Human Relations*, 46(12), 1391-1409.

6. Hofstede, G. (1980). *Culture's Consequences: International Differences in Work related Values*, Beverly Hills, CA: Sage.

7. Hofstede, G. (2001) *Culture's Consequences: Comparing Values, Behaviors, Institutions and Organizations Across Nations*, 2nd ed., Thousand Oaks, CA:Sage.

8. D'Iribarne, P. (1989). *La logique de l'honneur* [the logic of honor], Paris: Seuil.

9. D'Iribarne, P. and Henry, A. (2007). *Successful companies in the Developing World: Managing in synergy with cultures*, Paris: Agence Française de Développement.

10. D'Iribarne, P. (2009). National Cultures and roganizations in search of a theory: an interpretative approach, *International Journal of Cross-Cultural Management*, 9(3), 309-21.

11. Martin, J. (1982). Stories and scripts in organizational settings. In A. M. Isen ed. *Cognitive Social Psychology*, 235-305. New York, NY: Elsevier.

12. Moore, F. (2005). *Transnational business cultures. Life and Work in a Multinational Corporation*, Hants, Ashgate.

13. Primecz, H., Romani, L. and Sackmann, S. (2011). *Cross-cultural Management in Practice. Culture and Negotiated Meanings*, Edward Elgar

14. Sackmann S. and Philipps, M. (2004) Contextual Influences on Culture. Research: Shifting Assumptions for New Workplace Realities, in *International Journal of Cross-cultural management*, 4(3), 371-392.

15. Schein, E. H. (1985) *Organizational Culture and Leadership*. San Francisco, CA: Jossey Bass.

16. Schwarz, S.H. (1994). Beyond individualism/collectivism: New cultural dimensions of values, in U. Kim H.C. Triandis, C. Kagitcibasi, SC. Choi, and G. Yoon (eds), *Individualism and Collectivism: Theory, Method and Applications*, London: Sage, 85-119.

17. Swap, W., Leonard, D., Sields, M. & Abrams, L., (2001) Using mentoring and storytelling to transfer knowledge in the workplace. *Journal of Management Information Systems*, 18(1), 95-114.

18. Trompenaars, F. (1993). *Riding the waves of culture. Understanding Cultural Diversity in Business*, London: The Economists Book.

19. Yousfi, H. (2013). Rethinking Hybridity in Post Colonial Contexts: What changes and what persists? The Tunisian case of Poulina, *Organization Studies*, 1-29.

10,000 Miles Across the Room?
Emergent Coordination in Multiparty Collaboration

Greetje Corporaal
VU University Amsterdam
De Boelelaan 1081
1081 HV Amsterdam, NL
g.f.corporaal@vu.nl

Dick de Gilder
VU University Amsterdam
De Boelelaan 1081
1081 HV Amsterdam, NL
tc.de.gilder@vu.nl

Julie Ferguson
VU University Amsterdam
De Boelelaan 1081
1081 HV Amsterdam, NL
j.ferguson@vu.nl

Peter Groenewegen
VU University Amsterdam
De Boelelaan 1081
1081 HV Amsterdam, NL
p.groenewegen@vu.nl

ABSTRACT

This paper addresses cross-boundary coordination in a multiparty collaboration. So far, collaboration among among multiple dispersed parties has received scant attention in research on cross-boundary coordination. Building on this gap, this study analyzes an extreme case of inter-organizational collaboration between four geographically dispersed groups of engineers from subsidiaries of a Japanese multinational and an American engineering contractor. We explain how coordination is achieved among multiple parties. In our study, diverse boundaries posed challenges to the execution of work tasks being performed. In response, collaborating parties developed four organizing processes for coordinating their task-related activities, comprising information sharing, task negotiation, task execution and task integration. We suggest that together, these processes constitute a dynamic coordinating structure that is developed and enacted in parties' everyday collaborating and coordinating activities, which may enable but can also impede the successful execution of joint work tasks.

Author Keywords: Cross-boundary coordination; Multiparty collaboration; Process

ACM Classification Keywords: H.5.3 Group and Organization Interfaces: Computer-supported cooperative work; J.4 Social and Behavioral Sciences: Sociology

INTRODUCTION

This paper addresses the challenges of geographically dispersed multiparty collaboration between diverse parties. Specifically, we investigate the organizing processes that emerge in such collaborations that enable the coordination of dispersed parties' interrelated work tasks. Multiparty collaborations often face persistent problems. Collaborating parties need to build upon the existing coordinating mechanisms within the boundaries of their own organization, while also developing new ones across them. A critical organizational challenge is understanding how interdependent work tasks can be successfully integrated across a variety of boundaries while keeping coordination costs at a minimum [1, 2]. To address this challenge, a better understanding is required of how individual project members can establish a solid basis toward the coordination of work tasks across various boundaries. In this study, we zoom in on a collaboration between geographically dispersed engineers in Japan, China, Belgium and the Netherlands, and address the question: How do dispersed parties achieve coordination across boundaries in a multiparty collaboration? We focus on the emergent coordination processes in dispersed, multiparty collaborations, and explain how a coordinating structure emerged from and was enacted in everyday collaborating and coordinating activities. Herewith, we contribute to our understanding of dispersed inter-organizational collaboration and cross-boundary coordination.

Conceptual Background:
Cross-Boundary Coordination Between Multiple Parties

We define coordination as a temporal and contextualised process of managing interdependent work tasks with the aim of realising a collective performance [3]. Within Organization Studies, the topic of coordination has a longstanding heritage. Early studies emphasized that organizational work can be coordinated through control, hierarchy and rule- or program based systems [4]. A recent stream of research has started to focus on more informal or 'emergent' coordination, viewing the management and integration of interdependent work tasks as an ongoing accomplishment [3]. This perspective on coordination is less concerned with optimizing organizational structures and instead studies its emergent and dynamic aspects and contextually situated nature as a social practice [5].

CABS '14, August 21-22, 2014, Kyoto, Japan.
ACM 978-1-4503-2557-8/14/08.
http://dx.doi.org/10.1145/2631488.2631493

The challenges of effectively coordinating work tasks continues to be of relevance to both scholars and professionals, since organizations increasingly engage their members forms of collaboration across various boundaries, creating various discontinuities [6]. Yet, little research has addressed the specific coordination challenges emerging from collaborations across organizational and other boundaries. This requires a better understanding of how organizations can develop a capability in dealing constructively with differences between the involved parties (i.e. practices, interests and competencies) and effectively coordinating their multiple interdependent relations. We therefore analyze and explain how cross-boundary coordination is accomplished in inter-organizational collaboration among multiple parties and across various boundaries.

Research Setting and Methods

We conducted an in-depth case study of a multiparty collaboration in an engineering project, the No Project (a pseudonym). The No project is a collaboration between four geographically dispersed parties, consisting of engineers from subsidiaries of a Japanese multinational (MNC), MCorp (pseudonym), and an American engineering contractor, Ancone (pseudonym). Our field research was aimed at understanding the everyday work activities of members of the No Project. Data were collected between May 2012 and May 2013 by the paper's first author (henceforth field researcher). Data were collected in China, Japan, Belgium and the Netherlands, mostly through in-depth, semi-structured interviews (N=20; table 1), and supplemented with project documents, field notes and business press accounts. We identified the boundaries, which were perceived as requiring coordination, the collaboration and coordination activities among and between the multiple, dispersed parties involved in the project, and the interrelations in these activities. Data analysis was conducted by means of Atlas ti and further interpretive analysis, identifying the most significant patterns.

Results

During the data collection process, we were aware of the challenges of dispersed collaboration posed by the boundaries of time-space, organizational, and technology differences as well as challenges due to relational boundaries between collaborating members. In our study however, the distance between Europe and Asia and high political tensions between Japan and China at the time, posed little challenges for the project. While the collaboration between the Japanese part of Mirai Corp and Chinese part of Ancone went surprisingly well, our findings show that most collaboration difficulties were actually encountered between the Belgian and Dutch engineers, who worked in the same office most of the time. This unsuspected localization of problems and tensions in the collaboration could not be explained by these explicit boundaries. We therefore analyzed participants descriptions of more implicit (perceived) boundaries they encountered in their everyday work activities and derived

from the organizations' embeddedness in different local realities (knowledge and relational boundaries) and the parties' different roles and responsibilities in the collaboration (task boundaries).

We further sought to explain these counterintuitive findings by analyzing the 'collaborating' and 'coordinating' activities that were enacted to enable collaboration across these boundaries, and to what extent these activities were shared across the collaborating parties. We made a distinction between knowledge coordinating activities (e.g. activities related to sharing knowledge), task coordinating activities (e.g. activities related to managing the execution of work tasks) and relational coordinating activities (e.g. activities related to managing relationships). Together, these activities formed different organizing processes that parties engaged in to coordinate their multiple relations across various boundaries and emerged over the course of the collaboration. Parties engaged in information sharing (i.e. activities related to the sharing of information between parties), task negotiation (i.e. activities related to the discussion and negotiation of work tasks between parties), task execution (i.e. activities related to carrying out work tasks), and task integration (i.e. activities engaged in to integrate to work tasks of different parties).

Discussion & Conclusion

We provided insight into the social processes underlying dispersed collaboration among multiple parties and across various boundaries. We argue that the described organizing processes constitute an emergent and dynamic coordinating structure, which explains how cross-boundary coordination is achieved in the complex context of dispersed, multiparty projects. Herewith we contribute to debate on boundaries by describing how various emergent (perceived) boundaries manifest themselves in multiparty collaboration as posing significant coordination challenges and therefore requiring coordination. Yet, when effectively coordinated, these boundaries may also enable successful task execution. We further contribute to the coordination literature by developing a process model, comprising four parallel organizing processes of information sharing, task negotiation, task execution, and task integration.

References
[1]   Carlile, P.R. A pragmatic view of knowledge and boundaries: Boundary objects in new product development. Organization Science, 13, 4 (2002), 442-455.
[2]   Cummings, J. N. and Kiesler, S. Collaborative research across disciplinary and organizational boundaries. Social Studies of Science, 35 (2005), 703-722.
[3]   Faraj, S. and Xiao, Y. Coordination in fast-response organizations. Management Science, 52 (2006), 1155-1169.
[4]   March, J.G. & Simon H.A. Organizations. Wiley, New York (1958).
[5]   O'Mahony, S. & Bechky, B.A. Boundary organizations: Enabling collaboration among unexpected allies. Administrative Science Quarterly, 53, 3 (2008)., 422-459.
[6]   Watson-Manheim MB, Chudoba KM, Crowston K Perceived discontinuities and constructed continuities in virtual work. Inform. Systems J. 22, 1 (2012), 29-52.

To Be Like You to Be Liked by You: Cultural Effects on Adjusting Awareness Information Gathering Behavior

Nanyi Bi
Dept of Communication
Cornell University
Ithaca NY 14850 USA
nb333@cornell.edu

Susan R. Fussell
Dept of Communication
Cornell University
Ithaca NY 14850 USA
sfussell@cornell.edu

Jeremy Birnholtz
Dept of Communication Studies
Northwestern University
Evanston IL 60208 USA
jeremyb@northwestern.edu

ABSTRACT
Behavioral accommodation, the adjustment of one's own behavior to match that of other people, is prevalent in human communication, but people differ in the extent to which they accommodate each other. This paper presents a laboratory study examining how cultural background affects behavioral accommodation in awareness information gathering behaviors. Results suggested that members of collectivistic cultures (e.g., China) adjusted their behaviors to match those of their partners, when they were working with someone from other culture, whereas members of individualistic cultures (e.g.: the United States) did not accommodate when in the same situation. Our results suggest that accommodation exists even in online collaborations where no linguistic elements are involved, but this existence is affected by one's cultural background.

Author Keywords
Accommodation; adjustment; culture; awareness information; liking.

ACM Classification Keywords
H.5.3. [Group and Organization Interfaces]: Computer-supported cooperative work.

INTRODUCTION
Accommodation behavior has been defined in various ways, but most of them refer to the process in which one changes one's verbal and nonverbal behaviors to match that of others [45]. It is an important factor in many aspects of human communication [15], because it can foster a positive interpersonal relationship [43], increase feelings of similarity, affiliation, rapport, and liking (e.g., [27]; for a review, see [29]). Behavioral accommodation can also sometimes make people more cooperative [21] and easily persuaded [49], and it can facilitate tasks like negotiation [32]. People also report that it is smoother and more enjoyable to communicate with those who accommodate to match their linguistic style than with those who do not [44].

Behavioral accommodation is highly prevalent in everyday life. When interacting face-to-face, people accommodate each other in numerous aspects. Linguistically, communicators change their accents, speech rate, word choice, utterance duration and syntax to match those of a conversational partner [6, 12, 17, 18]. Communicators also modify nonverbal behaviors such as gaze or frequency of head nods, sometimes without even realizing it [14, 21, 25].

Compared to the large body of research on behavioral accommodation in face-to-face settings, fewer have investigated similar behaviors online. Although the lack of audio and visual cues limits the communication of nonverbal behaviors such as nodding, people still accommodate each other linguistically, in terms of word and phrase choices, especially those that express politeness or emotions [8, 36, 39, 40]. The extent to which online communicators accommodate each other's nonlinguistic behavior has been less studied, and is one of the goals of the current research.

While behavioral accommodation is common, individual level factors such as people's cultural background have been shown to influence the extent to which people accommodate [9, 16]. For example, in an online text-based brainstorming task, Wang et al. [50] found that Americans in same culture pairs (i.e., both from the same culture) were more responsive to each others' messages than Chinese participants in same culture pairs. In mixed culture pairs (i.e., participants were from different cultures), Chinese participants accommodated their partners' levels of responsiveness by increasing their responsiveness to match that of the Americans. However, there was no evidence that Americans reduced their responsiveness to accommodate their Chinese partners. van Baaren et al. [48] similarly report that Japanese participants adjusted their face-rubbing and foot-shaking behavior to match that of a confederate to a much greater extent than did American participants. These results suggest that there may be cultural differences in accommodation, though to our knowledge these differences have yet to be examined in the context of online non-linguistic behaviors, which is also one goal of the current study.

In the current study, we are interested in examining whether and how people from different cultures accommodate each other in terms of a specific online nonverbal behavior: awareness information gathering behavior. Awareness gathering behaviors are the actions by which a person gains information about their collaborator's presence and activities [19]. For example, peeking in someone's office or checking their Instant Messaging status would be types of awareness information gathering behaviors. In our study, we examine awareness gathering in the context of a prototype collaboration tool called OpenMessenger [5], which allows geographically distributed collaborators to examine each other's task progress, while at the same time makes such behavior visible to the person whose awareness information is gathered as well. Because awareness information gathering behavior conveys certain communicative intentions (e.g., to initiate a conversation) even without words, it is an interesting arena for examining cultural effects on behavioral accommodation.

In the remainder of this paper, we first present the theoretical motivation for our study, and then outline our hypotheses and the experimental design we used to examine the effects of one's own and a partner's cultural background on adjusting one's awareness information behavior. As we will show in the results section, there are differences both in the rates at which people from different cultures perform awareness checks and in the extent to which they adapt their awareness checking behavior to match that of a partner from a different culture. We conclude with implications for theories of behavioral accommodation and designs of tools to support intercultural collaboration.

BACKGROUND
In this section, we review literatures in three fields: behavioral accommodation, cultural dimensions, and the awareness information gathering behaviors.

Behavioral accommodation
Behavioral accommodation is an important aspect of communication behavior. It has been labeled in various ways in different theories, like accommodation, mimicry, reciprocity, synchrony, or style matching [45]. Despite of the different foci on intentionality, and on verbal vs. nonverbal behaviors, in essence these terms all refer to a modification of one's behavior to match that of a partner. (for a review, see [45]). For this paper's purpose, we will refer to this type of adjustment as *behavioral accommodation*.

Behavioral accommodation in offline and online settings
Giles [17] defined accommodation as a process in which people reduce their communicative differences with their interactants and achieve a converging effect. It is highly common in everyday life. Chartrand et al. [14] proposed that it is so common that "people automatically behave as they perceive" (p. 334). Evidence abounds in the accommodation in face-to-face settings. People accommodate other's speech style [17], facial expressions

[1], postures and mannerism [27], idiosyncratic movements [2], and sometimes emotion and mood [42] as well.

Evidence also suggests that behavioral accommodation is prevalent in some other cultures apart from the American. For example, van Baaren et al. [48] found that both Japanese and American participants adjusted their own face-rubbing and foot-shaking behaviors to match those of a confederate (but to different extents).

Such accommodation does not only occur in face-to-face interaction, but also in online settings. Bunz and Campbell [8] investigated politeness accommodation in email use and found people reciprocated with politeness markers (e.g., phrases like "please" or "thank you") when they received it; and they tended to be more polite in replies when the received email contained structural politeness elements, such as use of salutation (e.g., Dear [recipient's name]) and closing remarks (e.g., "Regards" at the end of the email).

Riordan et al. [36] found that when conversing via instant messenger, interlocutors have a tendency to converge in terms of the length and duration of contributions, no matter whether they have interaction histories before.

Influencing factors of accommodation
Despite of its prevalence, people differ in the extents to which they accommodate due to a variety of factors. For example, Lakin et al. [28] found that, motivated by the desire of belongingness, an excluded member of a group accommodate more than an included one, and they are more likely to mimic an in-group member's behavior rather than an out-group one's.

The perceived social power difference between a target and oneself affects the extent to which people accommodate themselves in that people with lower social status are more likely to accommodate to those with higher status [17].

Miles et al. [35] found that the social impression makes a difference for accommodation as well, in that people are more likely to mimic a punctate partner rather than a tardy one.

Previous interaction history makes a difference too. Riordan et al. [36] contrasted friends and strangers and found that the linguistic convergence is more manifest in friend-pairs than in stranger-pairs.

Giles [17] suggested that people sometimes over-accommodate due to their subjective sense of the need to accommodate. However, these accommodative acts may miscarry the intention when perceived by the target of accommodation. It's complicated in that it depends on whether you are in the out-group or not (see more details later).

Giles [17] also proposed that people sometimes choose to non-accommodate or under-accommodate to diverge their behaviors from other interactants. Symmetrical accommodation strengthens interpersonal relations; by the same token, a mutually non-accommodative interaction is likely to worsen those relations.

Social consequences of behavioral accommodation
Lakin et al. [29] cited evidence in evolutionary psychology [11] that accommodation or mimicry has its evolutionary significance, in that by mimicking other people's behavior, one is more likely to avoid being ostracized from a group, which, in an environment that was difficult for an individual to navigate, was a crucial factor for survival. They [29] further proposed in the current society, accommodating other people verbally and nonverbally also serves as glue for social relations in that it fosters positive interpersonal likings.

The bi-directional relationship between liking and behavioral accommodation has received much attention from research. Byrne [10] argues that this happens through a similarity-attraction link: People prefer others who are like themselves more so than those who are not. Quite a few studies support this conclusion. For example, Chartrand and Bargh [13] found that people developed more liking toward strangers who mimicked them more. Hove and Risen [22] also found that people felt more affiliated with strangers who synchronized their movements with themselves than those who did not. Buller and Aune [7] found that speech rate similarity could increase intimacy and immediacy, which was, in turn, linked to greater compliance in the context of help requests.

Scissor et al. [38] measured repetition of words, word phrases (excluding numbers, connecting words, etc.) and abbreviations to examine the linguistic mimicry in IM chat. In their experiment, participants who mimicked each other in the same chat session trusted each other more than those who mimicked less.

However, there is also evidence suggesting the liking developed from behavioral accommodation only stands when the interactants have the same group identity; in other words, such a correlation does not hold if the mimicker thinks the mimickee is an out-group member. Likowski et al. [30] found the mimickee liked the in-group mimicker more than the out-group one, even though the two were both mimicking the behavior of the mimickee. The mimickee actually liked the out-group member who does not mimic more than the one who does mimic.

Behavioral accommodation, especially language style matching, according to Ireland and Henderson [25], may also lead to impasse in negotiations, because negotiators were less focused on the task itself. They also found accommodation at different stages of a negotiation task matters, in that accommodation in later stages predicts a more positive relationship than that in earlier stages.

In another study about online communication, Scissor et al. [39] found that certain types of similarity from accommodation may lead to lower level of trust. Those similarities include more use of negative emotions and words relating to money.

In general, accommodation prevails in both online and offline settings, in both verbal and nonverbal behaviors. In some cases, accommodation between people may increase the affiliation, rapport, and social attraction they feel from each other; but in other cases, especially when the accommodator is perceived as an out-group member or when they mimic negative emotions, accommodation may lead to the socially negative consequences. However, most of the studies above focus on the North American population instead of people from other cultures, which, as van Baaren et al. [48] and Wang et al. [50, 51] have suggested, makes a difference when it comes to behavioral accommodation.

Cultural dimensions
Cultures differ from each other in several important ways. Cultures vary along the dimension of individualism and collectivism (e.g., [22]). Members of individualistic cultures are more focused on self and their direct family, whereas members of collectivist cultures are more focused on the groups to which they belong.

A related cultural difference is the emphasis a culture places on maintaining social relationship with others versus completing task efficiently. Triandis [47] found people from individualistic cultures (e.g., United States, Canada) focus more on task efficiency than on relationship development and maintenance. When facing conflicts between task completion and interpersonal relationship issues, they tend to complete the task rather than maintain their relationships. In contrast, members of collectivist cultures (e.g., China, Japan) prioritize relationship maintenance more than task efficiency. This difference is also reflected in various workplace settings [20, 24, 26, 37, 38, 41, 46, 47].

Individualism and collectivism are also related to different chronically dominant self-construals in different cultures. Markus and Kitayama [33] contend that people in individualistic cultures have a more independent self-construal as they are more likely to identify themselves as individuals with their own significant inner attributes, whereas people in collectivistic cultures have a more interdependent self-construal as they are more likely to identify themselves as part of certain groups and/or families.

Wang and colleagues [50, 51] found that Chinese participants are more likely than Americans to change their behavior to match that of other cultures. In their study, American participants generated significantly more conversational content than Chinese participants when they were paired with someone from their own culture. However, Chinese participants became significantly more talkative when they were paired with an American collaborator than when they were paired with a Chinese one, whereas Americans did not vary in talkativeness as a function of the cultural background of their partner. This suggests that Chinese participants are more likely to accommodate than American participants.

van Baaren et al. [48] proposed a similar hypothesis that people with an interdependent self-construal are more prone to mimicry than those with an independent self-construal. In their experiment, in which mimicry was operationalized as foot shaking and face-rubbing, they found that people who were primed to have a more independent self-construal conducted significantly less mimicry than people in the control session (not primed) and even more so than people whose interdependent self-construal was primed. They also replicated the same experiment on Japanese and American participants, whom they considered to have a chronic interdependent and independent self-construal, respectively. The results showed that Japanese performed more mimicry than Americans, further supporting the cultural effects on behavioral accommodation.

Accommodation in Awareness Behaviors

While previous work on behavioral accommodation has looked at verbal language and nonverbal face-to-face behaviors, we conjecture that other types of behaviors that occur in interaction may also lend themselves to accommodation. In particular, we focus on actions people take to maintain awareness of what their partners are doing [19], such as peeking into someone's office in face-to-face settings or seeking details about others online.

Mutually visible awareness information gathering behavior helps time the initiation of interaction, in that even if the person whose awareness information is being gathered is busy and not available for most interruptions, he/she has relative more control over the incoming communication requests – he/she can choose to respond to specific people in certain cases (e.g., urgent task) even if he/she is busy. However, since such behavior is visible to both parties at the same time, it bears the social cost of annoying or interrupting people [4].

In a previous study, Bi et al. [3] found that awareness information, due to its tradeoff between task performance and relationship maintenance, is gathered differently in terms of frequency for Americans and Chinese participants. Specifically, Chinese participants conducted significantly fewer awareness checks than their American counterparts within a certain period of time. This was true in stranger as well as friend pairs. Bi and colleagues reasoned that this difference stemmed from cultural differences in task vs. relationship orientation [38]. Because those of Chinese cultural background tend to be more relationship-oriented than those of American background, Chinese participants were less likely to intrude on their partners to gather awareness information even though it would have benefited their personal task performance. In contrast, Americans, who tend to be more task-oriented, conducted awareness

checks because they were important for getting the work done.

Bi et al.'s [3] study compared culturally homogeneous pairs; in other words, the collaborators were both from the same culture, either American or Chinese. Based on the literature review about behavioral accommodation, we asked whether participants would change their behavior when they are paired with someone not from their culture.

THE PRESENT STUDY

In regards to the preceding review and questions, we proposed a series of hypotheses and ran a laboratory experiment to answer them. This section describes the specific hypotheses, research questions, and the methodological details.

Hypotheses

The first hypothesis addresses the cultural effect on the awareness information checks. Based on the previous work, we believed that awareness checks would be more frequent among Americans than among Chinese, because the task-oriented cultural background will encourage the Americans to conduct the awareness checks, which is beneficial for task completion, whereas the relationship-oriented cultural background would discourage the Chinese from doing so, since they were aware that the collaborator could see their awareness checks and might be annoyed if those checks were too frequent. We therefore hypothesized that:

H1: American participants will conduct awareness checks more frequently than Chinese participants.

The second set of hypotheses address the effects of culture on behavioral accommodation of participants' awareness checks. Previous work [50, 51] has shown that Chinese are more likely to adjust their behaviors than Americans, because the interdependent self-construal makes the former more sensitive to the environmental cues than the latter, and therefore are more likely to respond to it by adjusting their own behaviors. Combining with the results from the study about awareness checks difference between American and Chinese pairs that Americans conduct more checks than Chinese do [3], we hypothesized that:

H2a: Chinese participants will conduct awareness checks more frequently when they work with an American partner than when they work with a Chinese partner.

H2b: American participants will conduct awareness checks less frequently when they work with a Chinese partner than when they work with an American partner.

H2c: The adjustment in the awareness checks frequency will be bigger for Chinese participants than for American participants.

The last hypothesis deals with the correlation between the behavioral accommodation level and the social liking between collaborators. As reviewed previously, past research have indicated at least two possibilities, that behavioral accommodation either increases the liking or decreases it. To date, most studies have indicated that a higher level of accommodation will induce the target of accommodation to like the accommodator more. Therefore we hypothesized that:

H3: The more similar the awareness checks frequencies are between the collaborators, the more they will like their partner.

We were also interested in knowing when this adjustment, should it exist, starts, and to what extent it affects the awareness information gathering behaviors of Chinese participants. Therefore we asked:

RQ1: How does accommodation, if it occur, vary across the time of the interaction?

Design
We used a between-participant design, in which we recruited participants from both American and Chinese cultures separately, and paired them with each other. Each participant had the same chance to be paired with an American or a Chinese, and thus we had three different cultural compositions: American-American, Chinese-Chinese, and American-Chinese pairs.

We had those participants work together on a series of tasks that were similar in nature; it usually took them around one hour to complete the whole experiment.

Participants
We recruited 50 participants at a large university in the northeastern United States (36% male; 52% Americans, 48% Chinese; 28% undergraduates, the rest were graduate students). The Chinese participants were all international students who were born in Mainland China, and had been in the States for fewer than five years.

Those 50 participants were formed into 25 pairs, among which there were 9 American-American pairs, 8 Chinese-Chinese pairs, and 8 American-Chinese pairs. We also made sure they were paired with someone of their same academic level (i.e., undergraduate and undergraduate, graduate and graduate) to ensure equal power status. All the participants had no previous interaction before the experiment.

Tasks and tool
The task used for this study was designed to replicate a real-world scenario in which a person has shared and individual tasks that are interdependent in a complex way, and in which incentives for shared and individual tasks are mixed. The goal of the task was for the participants to collaborate on completing five jigsaw puzzles on the computers, each of which was further divided into six smaller sections that were completed one by one. Each participant needed to finish three of the six sections.

The puzzle section was solved in a "puzzle window" (see Figure 1), which consisted of the puzzle itself and a space for the pile of puzzle pieces. Participants solved the puzzle sections by dragging the pieces from the pile area (right) and snapping them into the grid on the left.

To create interdependency in the task, participants could only start a new puzzle section after the partner had also finished his/her own section. Those who completed a section faster than their partner were offered an opportunity to earn additional points – and a potential cash bonus for themselves – by accessing and playing solo "shape games".

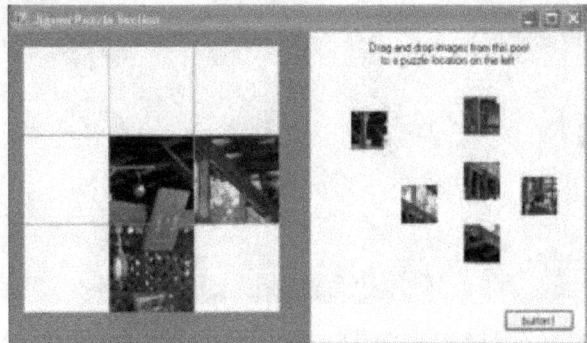

Figure 1. Puzzle interface, with the puzzle section (left) and the pile of pieces (right)

Every time the participants finished a puzzle section faster than their partner, a dialog box popped up and asked them whether they wanted to play the shape game or not with options of "Yes" and "No" If they chose "Yes", they proceeded to the shape game; if they chose "No", no points were deducted, but they were not able to play any shape games until after the next time they finished the puzzle section faster than their partner.

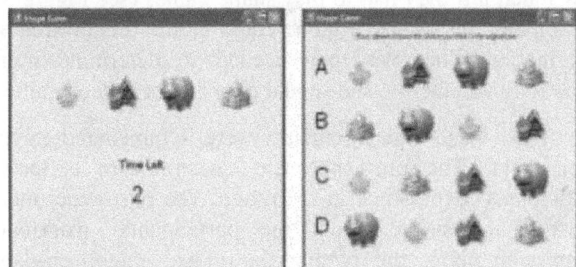

Figure 2. Shape game interfaces, with the initial sequence (left) and the set of choices (right)

Participants were shown a sequence of ordinary objects when they played the shape game. This sequence disappeared in 5 seconds. The participants had to identify the original sequence from four options (see Figure 2) to earn the points. For each shape game successfully completed, the participant got 1 point; but if their partner finished the jigsaw puzzle section while the participant was still playing a shape game, the participant lost 5 points. Points were used to determine the cash bonus received at the end of the experiment. In this way, there was a clear incentive to use awareness information to estimate available time for shape games.

To gather awareness information about their partner's task progress, participants used OpenMessenger (OM), a prototype developed by Birnholtz et al. [5], to view the number of puzzle pieces their partner had correctly placed.

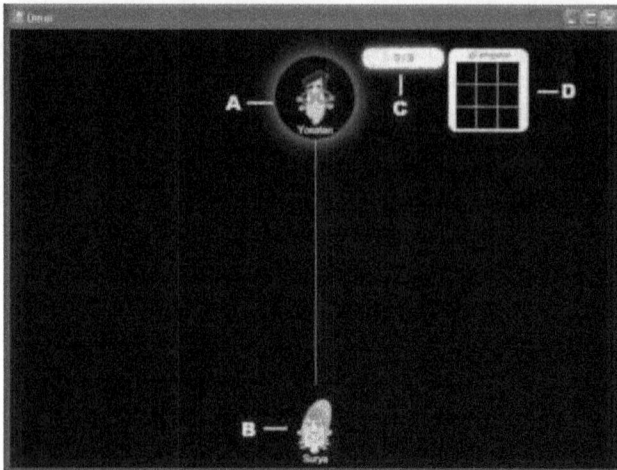

Figure 3. The projected awareness window including: (A) the partner's avatar, (B) the participant's avatar, (C) the number of correctly placed piece puzzles, and (D) the location of correctly placed puzzle pieces

The number of correctly placed puzzle pieces was an indicator of how far along one's partner was on the puzzle task and how much time the participant had to play shape games. By hovering the mouse cursor over the avatar on top, which represented their partner, participants would see the number of puzzle pieces correctly placed by the partner. This information was used to help the participant decide how much left they had to play shape games (see Figure 3). Participants in the shape game could gather this awareness information whenever they needed to determine more accurately whether he/she should play another shape game.

Two paper-based questionnaires were administered in the experiment. The pre-experiment questionnaire collected participants' experience in IM usage. The post-experiment questionnaire asked about the participants' workload, impression about the partner, individualism/collectivism, evaluation of self-performance, task/relationship orientation, and demographic information.

Procedures

Participants came to the laboratory alone and were paired up with another participant. Before the experiment started, we made sure that the participants had never met each other before. Then we had each participant write down his/her last name and place of birth (including the city and country) on a piece of paper, and exchange this information with each other, so they knew whether their partner shared the same cultural background with themselves.

Participants were then seated in two corners of the laboratory, facing different directions and separated by dividers to make sure they could not see each other. They

wore noise-cancelling headphones to reduce ambient sounds.

The participants were first shown a short instructional video introducing the puzzle, shape game tasks and the financial incentive. The video also explained the scoring scheme and its connection to the cash bonus. The participants were told explicitly that they would earn 1 point for each shape game they played correctly and that a wrong answer would mean a 1-point loss. Most importantly, if their partner finished their puzzle section while they were still playing a shape game, they would lose 5 points. The final total points would be used to determine cash bonuses, with more points meaning a larger cash bonus.

This scoring scheme was designed to motivate participants' awareness information gathering behaviors, as they needed to get information about their partner's progress on the puzzles in order to gain more points and avoid losses. In other words, it was to the participants' advantage to know how far along their partner was on the puzzle task, so they could estimate whether there would be enough time to play shape games to earn points without being cut off and thereby losing points. They were instructed to use OM to collect such information.

After the instructions but before starting the tasks, participants completed a practice session, including a simple puzzle section and one shape game that asked them to gather awareness information from their partner, to familiarize themselves with the game rules and the OM system.

Measures

Awareness checks

Counts of awareness checks per puzzle section were extracted from the OM log files. Because the raw number of checks was correlated with the amount of time available to participants for these checks, we first used the logs to determine how much time was available. Participants only had time for shape games, and thus only had reason to perform the awareness checks, if they finished their section of the puzzle before their partner did. This means that only one of the two participants could engage in shape games in a given puzzle section. We determined which partner had time for shape games, and how much time was available, for each section. We then used the total amount of time available to the participant across all puzzles and sections as the denominator to compute our rate of awareness checks. The resulting value was positively skewed so we used a log transformation prior to analysis.

Liking

We adopted the sub-scale from the Interpersonal Attraction Scale [34] to measure the social attraction of participants. Scores on five questions pertaining to participants' desire to interact socially with their partners (e.g., "I would like to have a friendly chat with him/her") were averaged to create a social attraction measure (Cronbach's α = .87).

RESULTS

H1 predicted that Americans, being more task-oriented, would conduct the awareness checks more frequently than the relationship-oriented Chinese. We tested this hypothesis using a mixed model ANOVA in which participants were random factors, and puzzle number, participants' own cultural background, and partner's cultural background were fixed factors. Note that mixed method analyses can result in non-integer degrees of freedom [31]. We found that, in the overall sample, one's own cultural background affects the frequency of awareness checks, in that Americans (M = 2.39, SE = .16) conducted awareness checks significantly more frequently than their Chinese counterparts (M =1.85, SE = .16; F [1, 51.32] = 5.548, p = .02). This is consistent with previous findings that awareness checks are more frequent in American participants than in Chinese, probably because the American culture emphasizes task completion and performance more so than Chinese culture, which prioritizes relationship maintenance. Therefore H1 is supported.

H2a predicted that Chinese participants would conduct awareness checks more frequently when they were paired with an American than when they were paired with a Chinese, while H2b predicted that Americans would conduct less awareness checks when their partner was Chinese than when the partner was American. We tested these hypotheses using a mixed model ANOVA of the same form as for H1 above. As Figure 4 shows, we found that Chinese participants paired with an American partner conducted significantly more awareness checks (M = 2.19, SE = .26) than those who had a Chinese partner (M = 1.52, SE = .19; F [1, 51.32] = 4.26, p = .04), but did not find a significant difference for the American participants. Therefore H2a is supported but H2b is rejected.

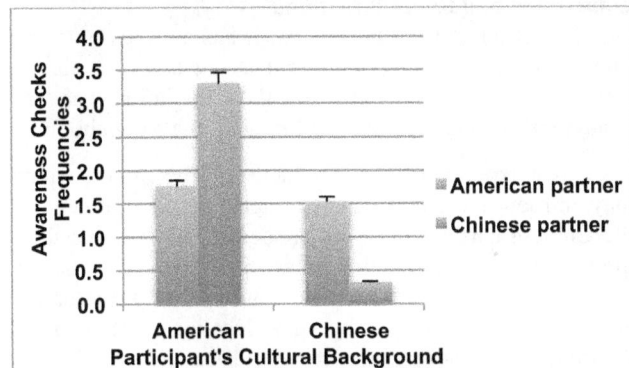

Figure 4. Average awareness checks frequency for Americans and Chinese with different partners

H2c predicted that the Chinese participants would accommodate more so than Americans in culturally heterogeneous pairs (i.e., AC pairs). According to H2a and H2b, Chinese did change whereas Americans did not, and we can conclude H2c is also supported, in that Chinese showed accommodation, whereas Americans did not.

H3 predicted that the more one accommodate the partner, the more the partner would like the participant. The bivariate correlation analysis shows there was a negative correlation between the difference of the awareness checks and the social attraction that approached significance (r [44] = -.27, p = .08), meaning if the difference was smaller, and the two collaborators were similar in their awareness checks frequency, they would tend to like each other more. This offers some preliminary yet insufficient support for the argument about accommodation leads to more liking.

The literature also suggests an important boundary condition for the liking and behavioral accommodation is the group identity. Therefore it is likely that the accommodation has different effects for groups with different cultural composition. We examined the correlation between liking and cultural composition in the sub-groups (AA, CC and AC), but did not find any significant correlation or trend.

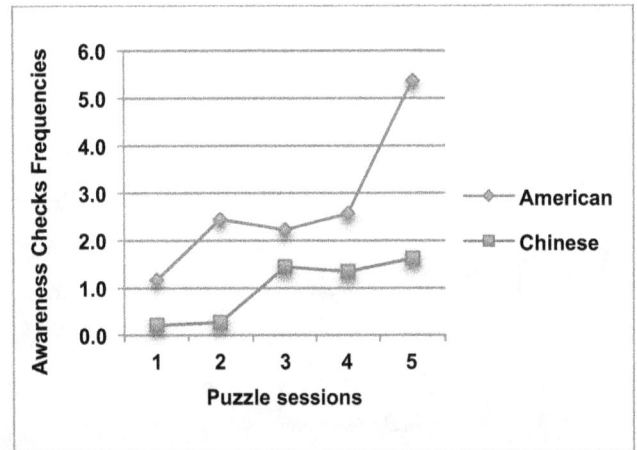

Figure 5. Average awareness checks frequencies for Americans and Chinese in each puzzle

RQ1 asked how the accommodation plays out across time. To examine this, we first looked at the data by running univariate ANOVAs for the five puzzle trials respectively. As Figure 5 shows, in the first puzzle, Americans (M = 2.10, SE = .27) conducted awareness checks more frequently than Chinese (M = 1.34, SE = .25) (F [1, 41] = 4.36, p = .04). The same thing occurred in the second puzzle as well: American's (M = 2.46, SE = .23) awareness checks frequency was still significantly higher than the Chinese's (M = 1.37, SE = .26) (F [1, 40] = 9.80, p < .01). However, from the third puzzle onward, the awareness checks frequency did not show a significant difference between cultures; neither did the Chinese participants surpass their American counterparts in the later puzzles (F [1, 38] = .28, $n.s.$ for the third puzzle; F [1, 40] = 1.46, $n.s.$ for the fourth puzzle; F [1, 39] = 1.31, $n.s.$ for the fifth puzzle). So we can conclude that such accommodation allows the Chinese user to adjust their awareness checks frequency to a similar level of Americans.

To further examine the effects of collaboration time on specific cultural groups, we ran a univariate ANOVA for the four subsets of sample separately (AA, CC, AC, and CA pairs, the first letter in each group representing the participant's background we examined). As Figure 6 shows, American-American pairs did not increase their awareness checks across time. This is also true for Americans who were paired with a Chinese partner, as well as Chinese-Chinese pairs. However, for Chinese participants with American partners, puzzle session has a main effect: in the first (M = 1.30, SE = .34) and second puzzles (M = 1.42, SE = .40), the awareness checks frequency are significantly lower than the ones in the next three puzzle sessions.

This result suggests Chinese participants who were partnered with an American increased their awareness checks frequency as they progressed on the task, and this increase only exists in this particular subset, not others.

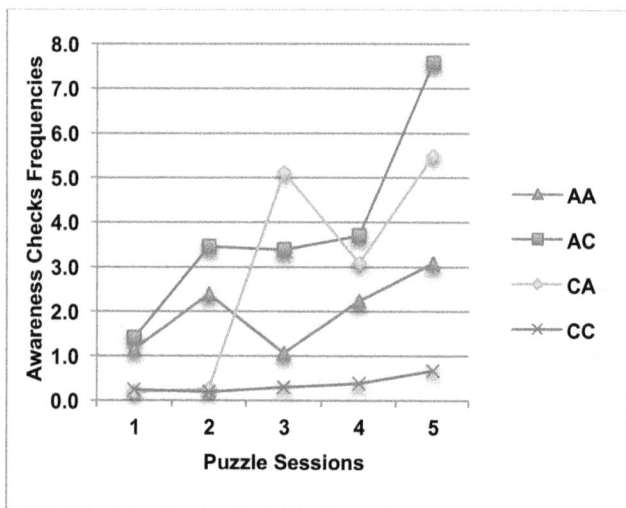

Figure 6. Average awareness checks frequencies for different groups in different puzzle sections

We also looked at only the culturally heterogeneous pairs only, and we found that there is no difference between American and Chinese participants from the first puzzle session. This suggests that the change started in the very beginning of their collaboration; a reasonable assumption is that it might have occurred within the three puzzle sections during the first session. However, due to insufficient data in the first session, we were unable to confirm this possibility.

DISCUSSION

In this study, we found that there are cultural differences in the awareness information gathering behavior between Americans and Chinese, in that (1) in general, Americans conduct awareness checks more frequently than Chinese, and (2) Chinese accommodate more than Americans when they work with someone from a different culture. We also found a trend between social attraction and accommodation that the more alike the participants' awareness checks frequencies are, the more likely they find each other

socially attracted, even though they did not know each other before.

The finding about cultural difference in the adjustment of awareness checks frequencies provides empirical evidence about the existence of behavioral accommodation online, in a nonverbal context. Previous research has identified accommodation in word choice and other linguistic behaviors [36, 39, 40] via email and instant messenger, but not in nonverbal ones. Our study suggests it does exist in awareness information gathering behavior, but is only conducted by Chinese participants. This finding is also consistent with previous work that suggest [50, 51] Chinese, being more sensitive to the environmental cues, are more likely than Americans to accommodate when working with someone from a different culture.

We also found very preliminary evidence for the correlation between liking and behavioral accommodation in that people tend to like those who are in behavioral synchrony with themselves than those who are not. This is not only consistent with some previous literatures about such a positive correlation, but also indicates that in a work-related environment, unlike negative emotions or money-related words in Scissor et al's [39] study, more similarity in awareness information gathering behavior tend to foster positive social consequences rather than negative ones. On one hand, for designers, it offers more motivation to engineer the awareness tools in a way that visualizes the difference and encourages the collaborators to minimize such difference by accommodating each other; on the other hand, it suggests that for two cultures that also differ in awareness checks frequencies but may be less likely to accommodate with each other, such behavioral difference of awareness checks may lead to problems involving distrust, dislike and feeling not affiliated.

Limitations and future directions

One limitation of the study is that it has a relatively small sample size (n = 50). With more data, we might be able to find more robust evidence for the correlation between behavioral accommodation and liking of one's collaborator.

Also, our experiment was conducted in the States, which may introduce the confounding factor of environment. If the Chinese participants were unconsciously influenced by the notion that they should "do as the Romans do when in Rome", their behavioral accommodation may be interpreted as partially influenced by the location and cultural environment they are in. It would be helpful if this experiment were replicated in a Chinese-dominant context to eliminate the possible confounding factors of environment.

CONCLUSION

In summary, although previous finding has suggested that Americans conducted awareness checks more frequently than Chinese, we found that, when paired with an American, Chinese participants adjusted their awareness information gathering behavior to match that of their collaborators'. It is consistent with the literature that suggests Chinese, being more sensitive to the social cues, are more likely to accommodate their behavior than Americans. The study also examined the liking generated from the behavioral accommodation and offers preliminary yet insufficient evidence for such a correlation.

ACKNOWLEDGMENTS

We thank the National Science Foundation (OCI #0942658) for support. Any opinion, findings, and conclusions or recommendations expressed in this material are those of the authors and do not necessarily reflect the views of the National Science Foundation. We thank Allie Miller, Ben Jacoby, Danny Sullivan, John Schultz, Matt LePage, and Patrice Lawless for their assistance with this work.

REFERENCES

1. Bavelas, J. B., Alex, B., Lemery, C. and Mullett, J. "I show how you feel": Motor mimicry as a communicative act. *Journal of Personality and Social Psychology*, *50*, 2 (1986), 322-329.

2. Bavelas, J. B., Black, A., Chovil, N., Lemery, C. and Mullett, J. Form and function in motor mimicry: Topographic evidence that the primary function is communicative. *Human Communication Research*, *14*, 3 (1988), 275-299.

3. Bi, N., Birnholtz, J. P. and Fussell, S. Intercultural awareness: Cultural and relational effects on awareness information gathering behavior. In *Proc. iConference* (2014), 426-443.

4. Birnholtz, J. P., Bi, N. and Fussell, S. Do you see that I see? Effects of perceived visibility on awareness checking behavior. In *Proc. ACM Special Interest Group on Computer-Human Interaction* (2012), 1765-1774.

5. Birnholtz, J. P., Gutwin, C., Ramos, G. and Watson, M. OpenMessenger: Gradual initiation of interaction for distributed workgroups. In *Proc. CHI* (2008), 1661-1664.

6. Bock, J. K. Syntactic persistence in language production. *Cognitive Psychology*, *18*, (1986), 355-387.

7. Buller, D. B. and Aune, R. K. The effects of speech rate similarity on compliance: Application of communication accommodation theory. *Western Journal of Communication*, *56*, Winter (1992), 37-53.

8. Bunz, U. and Campbell, S. W. Politeness accommodation in electronic mail. *Communication Research Reports*, *21*, 1 (2004), 11-25.

9. Burgoon, J. K. and Hubbard, A. S. E. Cross-cultural and intercultural applications of expectancy violations theory and interaction adaptation theory. In W. B. Gudykunst ed. *Theorizing about Intercultural Communication*, Sage, 149-172.

10. Byrne, D. *The Attraction Paradigm*. Academic Press, New York, 1971.

11. Caporael, L. R. Evolutionary psychology: Toward a unifying theory and a hybrid science. *Annual Review of Psychology*, *52*, (2001), 607-628.

12. Cappella, J. N. and Planalp, S. Talk and silence sequences in informal conversations III: Interspeaker influence. *Human Communication Research*, *7*, 2 (1981), 117-132.

13. Chartrand, T. L. and Bargh, J. A. The chameleon effect: The perception-behavior link and social interaction. *Journal of Personality and Social Psychology*, *76*, 6 (1999), 893-910.

14. Chartrand, T. L., Maddux, W. W. and Lakin, J. L. Beyond the perception-behavior link: The ubiquitous utility and motivational moderators of nonconscious mimicry. In R. R. Hassin, J. S. Uleman and J. A. Bargh eds. *The New Unconscious*, Oxford University Press, 334-361.

15. Chartrand, T. L. and van Baaren, R. Human Mimicry *Advances in Experimental Social Psychology*, 219-274.

16. Gallois, C., Ogay, T. and Giles, H. Communication Accommodation Theory. In W. B. Gudykunst ed. *Theorizing about Intercultural Communication*, Sage, 121-148.

17. Giles, H. Communication Accommodation Theory. In L. A. Baxter and D. O. Braithwaite eds. *Engaging Theories in Interpersonal Communication: Multiple Perspectives*, Sage, 161-173.

18. Gregory, S. W., Dagan, K. and Webster, S. Evaluating the relation of vocal accommodation in conversation partners' fundamental frequencies to perceptions of communication quality. *Journal of Nonverbal Behavior*, *21*, 1 (1997), 23-41.

19. Gross, T., Stary, C. and Totter, A. User-centered awareness in computer-supported cooperative work-systems: Structured embedding of findings from social sciences. *International Journal of Human-Computer Interaction*, *18*, (2005), 323-360.

20. Hamid, P. N. Self-monitoring, locus of control, and social encounters of Chinese and New Zealand students. *Journal of Cross-Cultural Psychology*, *25*, 3 (1994), 353-368.

21. Heyes, C. What can imitation do for cooperation? In B. Calcott, R. Joyce and K. Sterelny eds. *Signaling, Commitment, & Emotion*, MIT Press.

22. Hofstede, G. (1991). *Cultures and Organizations: Software of the Mind*. New York: McGraw Hill.

23. Hove, M. J. and Risen, J. L. It's all in the timing: Interpersonal synchrony increases affiliation. *Social Cognition*, *27*, 6 (2009), 949-960.

24. Hu, H. and Jasper, C. R. A cross-cultural examination of the effects of social perception styles on store image formation. *Journal of Business Research*, *60*, 3 (2007), 222-230.

25. Ireland, M. E. and Henderson, M. D. Language style matching, engagement, and impasse in negotiations.

Negotiation and conflict management research, 7, 1 (2014), 1-16.

26. Krishna, S., Sahay, S. and Walsham, G. Managing cross-cultural issues in global software outsourcing. *Communications of the ACM, 47,* 4 (2004), 62-66.

27. LaFrance, M. and Broadbent, M. Group rapport: Posture sharing as a nonverbal indicator. *Group & Organization Management, 1,* (1976), 328-333.

28. Lakin, J. L., Chartrand, T. L. and Arkin, R. M. I am too just like you: Nonconscious mimicry as an automatic behavioral response to social exclusion. *Psychol Sci, 19,* 8 (2008), 816-822.

29. Lakin, J. L., Jefferis, V. E., Cheng, C. M. and Chartrand, T. L. The chameleon effect as social glue: Evidence for the evolutionary significance of nonconscious mimicry. *Journal of Nonverbal Behavior, 27,* 3 (2003), 145-162.

30. Likowski, K. U., Schubert, T. W., Fleischmann, B., Landgraf, J. and Volk, A. Positive effects of mimicry are limited to the ingroup (2008).

31. Littell, R. Milliken, G. A., Stroup, W. W., & Wolfinger, R. D. (1996). *SAS System for Mixed Models.* Cary, NC: SAS Institute.

32. Maddux, W. W., Mullen, E. and Galinsky, A. D. Chameleons bake bigger pies and take bigger pieces: Strategic behavioral mimicry facilitates negotiation outcomes. *Journal of Experimental Social Psychology, 44,* (2008), 461-468.

33. Markus, H. R. and Kitayama, S. Culture and the self: Implications for cognition, emotion, and motivation. *Psychological Review, 98,* 2 (1991), 224-253.

34. McCroskey, J. C. and McCain, T. A. The measurement of interpersonal attraction. *Speech Monographs, 41,* August (1974), 261-266.

35. Miles, L. K., Griffiths, J. L., Richardson, M. J. and Macrae, C. N. Too late to coordinate: Contextual influences on behavioral synchrony. *European Journal of Social Psychology,* (2009), n/a-n/a.

36. Riordan, M. A., Markman, K. M. and Stewart, C. O. Communication accommodation in instant messaging: An examination of temporal convergence. *Journal of Language and Social Psychology, 32,* 1 (2012), 84-95.

37. Ruble, D. N. and Nakamura, C. Y. Task orientation versus social orientation in young children and their attention to relevant social cues. *Child Development, 43,* 2 (1972), 471-480.

38. Schuster, C. P. and Copeland, M. J. *Global Business Practices: Adapting for Success.* Thompson Higher Education, Mason, OH, 2006.

39. Scissors, L. E., Gill, A. J., Geraghty, K. and Gergle, D. In CMC we trust: The role of similarity. In *Proc. CHI* (2009), 527-536.

40. Scissors, L. E., Gill, A. J. and Gergle, D. Linguistic mimicry and trust in text-based CMC. In *Proc. CSCW* (2008), 277-280.

41. Shell, R. *Bargaining for Advantage: Negotiating Strategies for Reasonable People.* Viking, New York, 1999.

42. Snyder, M. and Tanke, E. D. Social perception and interpersonal behavior: On the self-fulfilling nature of social stereotypes. *Journal of Personality and Social Psychology, 35,* 9 (1977), 656-666.

43. Stel, M. and Vonk, R. Mimicry in social interaction: Benefits for mimickers, mimickees, and their interaction. *British Journal of Psychology, 101,* (2010), 311-323.

44. Tanner, R. J., Ferraro, R., Chartrand, T. L., Bettman, J. R. and van Baaren, R. Of chameleons and consumption: The impact of mimicry on choice and preferences. *Journal of Consumer Research, 34,* (2008), 754-766.

45. Toma, C. Towards a conceptual convergence: An examination of interpersonal adaptation. *Communication Quarterly,* (In press), 38.

46. Triandis, H. C. *Culture and Social Behavior.* McGraw Hill, New York, 1995.

47. Triandis, H. C., Bontempo, R. and Villareal, M. J. Individualism and collectivism: Cross-cultural perspectives on self-ingroup relationships. *Journal of Personality and Social Psychology, 54,* 2 (1988), 323-338.

48. van Baaren, R. B., Maddux, W. W., Chartrand, T. L., de Bouter, C. and van Knippenberg, A. It takes two to mimic: Behavioral consequences of self-construals. *Journal of Personality and Social Psychology, 84,* 5 (2003), 1093-1102.

49. van Swol, L. M. The effects of nonverbal mirroring on perceived persuasiveness, agreement with an imitator, and reciprocity in a group discussion. *Communication Research, 30,* (2003), 461-480.

50. Wang, H.-c. and Fussell, S. Cultural adaptation of conversational style in intercultural computer-mediated group brainstorming. In *Proc. IWIC* (2009), 317-320.

51. Wang, H.-c., Fussell, S. and Setlock, L. D. Cultural difference and adaptation of communication styles in computer-mediated group brainstorming. In *Proc. ACM SIGCHI* (2009).

Verbal Cues of Involvement in Dyadic Same-culture and Cross-culture Instant Messaging Conversations

Duyen T. Nguyen
Human Computer Interaction Institute
Carnegie Mellon University
tdnguyen@andrew.cmu.edu

Susan R. Fussell
Department of Communication
Cornell University
sfussell@cornell.edu

ABSTRACT

This paper explores how people in same-culture and cross-culture pairs use verbal cues to express involvement in dyadic text-based Instant Messaging (IM) conversations. We report an experimental study with same-culture and cross-culture pairs of American and Chinese participants, in which we manipulated the participants' level of involvement in IM conversations using a distraction task (an online game). We found that American and Chinese participants used verbal involvement cues, such as cognitive words and definite articles, differently to express involvement. Our results provide suggestions for improving international, multicultural team collaboration using computer-mediated communication (CMC) tools.

Author Keywords

Involvement; CMC; conversation; communication processes; verbal cues; intercultural collaboration

ACM Classification Keywords

H5.3 Group and Organization Interfaces: Computer-supported cooperative work

General Terms

Experimentation; Human Factors

INTRODUCTION

Conversational involvement is defined as the extent to which participants are immersed and engaged with their partners and with the ongoing dialog [7], and can be perceived from both the non-verbal and verbal cues an interactant exhibits. An uninvolved interactant may be viewed negatively by his or her conversational partners. Many people find conversations with uninvolved partners less satisfying than those with highly involved partners [3], as suggested in the phrase "it's like I'm talking to myself". For two people working together on a team, involvement in conversations is thus especially important, as the level of involvement of a team member in work-related discussion

influences the teammate's impressions of him or her, their interpersonal relationships, and their willingness to collaborate [3, 16].

With the rising popularity and various benefits of global collaboration today, multinational work teams, consisting of members from different cultures and speaking different languages collaborate via computer-mediated communication (CMC) channels more and more, due to the low cost and high efficiency in coordinating meetings [11]. While in face-to-face interaction non-verbal behaviors, such as direct eye contact, animated facial expressions, or forward lean, are important for the expression and interpretation of involvement [17, 22], in most text-based CMC, such audio and video cues are not supported. Without these non-verbal cues, however, several studies found that participants can still express emotions, status, and even involvement [26, 19]. Nguyen & Fussell [19] found that in text-based IM conversations, subtle verbal cues such as the high frequency of assent words and low frequency of singular first-person pronouns (e.g., "I", "me") are significant indications of involvement. For example, in an experimental study, conversationalists who used many assent words and few "I" pronouns reported being more involved in the IM conversation [19]. They were also rated as being more involved than those who used few assent words and many "I" pronouns by third-person observers, who watched a screen recording of the conversation.

However, most studies of conversational involvement have not considered cultural differences in communication styles that may influence the use of involvement cues [21, 5]. For example, the use of "I" vs. "we" pronouns has been shown to differ across cultures [31]. In addition, verbal cues such as the word "yeah" can be interpreted differently by members of different cultures [33]. Given such culture differences in communication styles, the results about the verbal indicators of involvement from previous studies with mostly North American participants may not apply to participants from other cultures such as China or Japan. Moreover, very few studies examined how verbal involvement cues are used in intercultural pairs in which a North American participant converses with an East Asian participant. This study aims to bridge this important literature gap.

We begin with an overview of the concept of interaction involvement, verbal cues of involvement, and cultural differences in the usage of these verbal cues. We then outline our research questions and hypotheses and present an empirical study examining the expression of involvement in IM conversations between two same-culture or cross-culture American and Chinese partners collaborating on a decision making task. As we will show, American and Chinese participants used certain verbal cues of involvement differently when talking to a partner from the same versus a different culture. The results of our study contribute to the development of CMC theories and carry implications for the design of communication tools to support remote intercultural collaboration.

BACKGROUND

Scholars have taken various perspectives on involvement in social interactions, defining involvement as a cognitive dimension of an inherent trait [7], or as a communication process measured by behavioral indicators (e.g. nonverbal behaviors, facial expressions, tone of voice) [23]. Despite differences between these approaches, most scholars conclude that interaction involvement consists of both an individual component (e.g., one's own ability to focus) and a changing, adaptive component under the influence of the partners, the media, the conversational task, and the social context surrounding the conversation [5, 6]. Moreover, the dedication of cognitive attention is an important component of interaction involvement [7]. In today's workplace where many people use IM to discuss serious work-related issues, multitasking during an IM conversation is common [11]. Such multitasking may steer the interactant's cognitive attention away from the partner and the ongoing IM conversation, reducing the interactant's involvement. Based on this, we manipulated the participants' level of involvement in our experiment using a distraction task, mimicking actual multitasking situations common in today's workplace.

Expression and interpretation of involvement cues in IM

Besides non-verbal cues of involvement, studies of face-to-face interaction have looked at the relationship between certain verbal cues such as the use of pronouns and interaction involvement [17]. Camden & Verba [4] found that the level of involvement of a speaker in an ongoing face-to-face conversation could be inferred from three linguistic features of the speaker's speech: (a) the number of intensifiers (related to certainty words) vs. qualifiers (related to hedge words); (b) the number of personal ("I", "we") vs. impersonal ("you", "they") pronouns; and (c) the number of definite vs. indefinite articles. Another study suggested that highly involved dyads used fewer personal pronouns ("I", "me"), and more relational pronouns ("we", "us", etc.), than less involved dyads [4]. Moreover, the use of definite articles (e.g., "the", "this", or "that") increases as a speaker becomes more cognitively involved with the topic of the (face-to-face) conversation [4]. In text-based IM conversations, Nguyen & Fussell [19] found that participants said fewer "I" pronouns, more assent words,

more cognitive words, and more definite articles when they were highly involved than when they were less involved due to multitasking.

The above studies explained their results based on previous research about the use of "I" pronouns, assent words, cognitive words, and definite articles. First, reference to oneself through the use of many "I" pronouns indicates an inward orientation to one's own thoughts and feeling, rather than an outward attention to, and connection with, the partner [24]. Therefore, high number of personal pronouns indicates a lack of focus towards the conversation. On the other hand, agreements in decision-making discussion express participants' acceptance of each others' utterances as correct or true. Agreements thus can reflect a speaker's attention to, and active processing of, a partner's messages [12, 29]. Words expressing agreements (e.g., "yes", "true", "right") were thus suggested to be an indicator of attention, and in turn, involvement in a conversation [29]. In the decision-making discussions in Nguyen & Fussell's study [19], thoughtful contributions to the dialog indicate active cognitive focus on the content of the conversation, and therefore, high involvement. Such thoughtful contributions often contain words expressing thinking, assumption, or speculation such as "think", "suppose", "guess", "presume" that are used to form arguments in the decision-making process [27]. Lastly, definite articles are used to refer to thoughts, objects, images, or people that the conversation partners can identify [1], based on common ground or mutual knowledge [8]. Therefore the use of definite articles also indicates attention to the partner, and thus involvement in the dialog.

In summary, previous studies found that the number of "I" pronouns, assent words, cognitive words and definite articles a participant said are good verbal indicators of that participant's involvement in conversations. However, these previous studies did not consider cultural differences in the way people use various verbal cues such as pronouns, which other studies have found both in face to face and in IM conversations [e.g. 31, 32]. The expression of involvement also depends on cultural norms and styles [5]. We turn to the literature about cultural differences in the use of the above verbal cues of involvement next.

Cultural differences in the use of verbal involvement cues

Culture differences in communication styles have been widely studied. People from Western cultures are often said to be more individualistic, and thus emphasize the independence of individuals, whereas people from Eastern cultures such as China or Japan are often described as collectivistic, emphasizing the interconnectedness of individuals in the context of social behavior and interactions [13]. Moreover, people from Western cultures such as North America tend to adopt a direct, low-context style of communication, stating their opinions and thoughts explicitly and verbally, with little reliance on non-verbal cues such as facial expression [10, 9]. On the other hand, people from Eastern cultures such as China or Japan tend to adopt an indirect, high-context style, deriving meanings not only from the explicit, verbal content, but also from the communication context such as the relationship between speakers, and relying on the non-verbal cues such as facial expression or body language for the expression and interpretation of meaning [10, 9].

In CMC environments, studies have found evidence of cultural differences in the verbal communication styles and strategies of participants from Western cultures and those from Eastern cultures. Setlock, Fussell, & Newirth [30] examined various features of language use in audio and video conferencing of American-American (AA) pairs, American-Chinese (AC) pairs, and Chinese-Chinese (CC) pairs doing a decision making task together. They found that CC pairs used more "we" pronouns than other pairs. Stewart, Setlock, & Fussell [30] examined the argumentation styles of AA, AC, and CC pairs in text-based IM conversations and found that Chinese participants tended to use more reasoning activities (providing reasons for their claims) in their conversations than American participants.

These studies however did not consider different levels, or states of involvement that participants had during their conversations. The use of verbal cues to convey involvement in interactions might be different for speakers from different cultures [5, 21]. Regarding the use of pronouns, previous studies suggested that "I" pronouns are used more frequently by members of individualistic, Western cultures such as those from North America as these cultures promote individual identity, while the inclusive "we" pronouns are used more by members of collectivistic, Eastern culture such as those from China who tend to view themselves as members of a collective [30, 31]. Consequently, we expect that American participants will rely on "I" pronouns to express involvement in conversation more than Chinese participants.

H1: American participants will use "I" pronouns to express different levels of involvement in text-based IM conversations more than Chinese participants.

In terms of assent words, Stewart et al. [32] found that in IM conversations, American participants tended to use more convergent markers (to express agreement) than Chinese participants. We hypothesize that:

H2: American participants will use assent words to express different levels of involvement in text-based IM conversations more than Chinese participants.

Setlock, Fussell, & Quinones [31] found that same-culture American pairs used more words related to thinking and reasoning such as "expect" and "assume" than same-culture Chinese pairs or cross-culture pairs in IM conversations. We hypothesize that:

H3: American participants will use cognitive words to express different levels of involvement in text-based IM conversations more than Chinese participants.

Lastly, few studies have compared the use of definite articles between American participants and Chinese participants in conversations, much less in text-based IM conversations. Therefore, we ask:

RQ1: How do American participants and Chinese participants differ in the way they use definite articles to express involvement in a text-based IM conversation?

METHOD

To test our hypotheses and research question, we conducted an experiment in which same-culture and cross-culture pairs of American and Chinese participants discussed a business idea using only text chat. During their 20-minute discussion, we manipulated each participant's level of involvement using a distraction task such that there were five minutes during which both participants were highly involved, five minutes during which one participant was highly involved and the other was distracted, five minutes during which the other participant was highly involved and the first distracted, and five minutes during which both were distracted. After each five-minute period, participants answered questionnaires measuring their level of involvement, other communication process outcomes such as emotions or understanding, and other variables.

Participants

Participants consisted of 60 students (41 undergraduate students, 47 females) studying at a large American university. There were 30 North American participants born in the United States (29) or Canada (one) and speak English as their native language. Of the North American participants, 28 were Caucasian and two were Asian. There are 30 Chinese participants born in China (25), Taiwan (three), or Hong Kong (two), and speak Mandarin as their native language. Participants were recruited for course credit or $10 compensation. Each participant was paired randomly with a partner from the same culture or from a different culture, resulting in three combinations: 10 Chinese-Chinese (CC) pairs, 10 American-American (AA) pairs, and 10 American-Chinese (AC) pairs. Participants in a pair did not know each other prior to the experiment.

Materials

Task. Pairs of participants discussed a business proposal for 20 minutes. The proposal is for a new on-campus outlet of a popular ice-cream brand. All of the participants in this study knew the ice-cream brand and the typical set-up of an outlet of this brand. In our scenario, the owner of the ice-cream brand, in response to higher demand from the student population, wanted to open a new shop on the university campus. Eight on-campus locations were under consideration. The participants needed to discuss with their partners to choose one of these eight locations for the new outlet. Each pair needed to consider the locations carefully, listing at least five pros and five cons for every location, keeping in mind aspects such as: the personas of the customers who most frequent that location, costs of opening an outlet at that location, benefits and drawbacks to the student community, etc. To keep the participants engaged in the discussion for the whole 20 minutes, the experimenter recommended that they discuss the pros and cons of two locations every 5 minutes in the order these locations were listed, and then choose the best location to recommend to the owner of the ice-cream brand. To keep them engaged in the discussion, pairs were told they would have to write a final report together after their 20-minute discussion listing the pros and cons of each location and indicating their choice. However, we did not make them write the report.

Distraction task. To manipulate the level of involvement of participants during their conversation, we used a distraction task in the form of an online computer game. At some points during the 20-minute discussion, each participant in a pair had to play this game while he or she was chatting, paying equal attention to the game and to the conversation. The game was thus introduced to distract the participants from the conversation, resulting in lower level of involvement than that in the full involvement condition, where participants only focused on chatting.

The game was a memory puzzle, in which players had to uncover 18 matching pairs of common food items. A maximum of two food items can be uncovered at a time. If the two items do not match, they will be covered again. The player had to uncover two identical items at the same time, and had to successfully uncover all 18 pairs of food item within the time limit. The game is available online at http://www.agame.com/game/tasty-food-memory.html.
When participants were in the distracted condition, they had to play the game continuously for five minutes. If a game ended before 5 minutes were up, the experimenter asked the participant to restart and play the game again.

Communication processes survey. Every five minutes during the discussion, each participant was asked to pause everything he or she was doing and fill out a short online survey. Since the discussion task was 20 minutes in total, each participant completed four such surveys in each experiment.

The survey contains six 7-point Likert scale questions about the participants' self-reported level of involvement in the conversation. We asked two questions about how involved participants were, and how involved they think their partners were, in the last 5 minutes (1=not involved at all, 7=very involved). The next four questions were adapted from Cegala's [7] Interaction Involvement Scale to measure the participants' level of involvement during the last 5-minute portion of the conversation. These four questions were chosen based on the result of a pilot test (see Table 1).

Post task survey. After the 20-minute discussion was over, participant completed an online post-task survey that collected demographic information.

Equipment
Both participants used identical Mac Book Pro laptops, running Mac OS X Lion, with pre-installed "Messages" software, an IM client that can be configured for Google Talk chat servers. Participants chatted with their partners using the "Messages" program without any audio or video, and played the computer game on Safari web browser. A computer program written in Apple Script was used to control the flow of the experiment. It would pop-up messages asking the participants to pause the discussion and the game, bring the communication process survey to the front, and prompt the participants to fill out this survey every 5 minutes during the 20-minute discussion. At the end of the discussion, the computer program would prompt participants to fill out the post-task questionnaire.

Procedure
Two participants were invited to the lab, and asked to sit down at two workstations, separated by a large divider. The experimenter then introduced the study, and briefed participants on how to use the chat program, how to play the game, and explained the discussion task. The participants were then asked to read more detailed instructions on the computer. Both participants practiced the game until they understood it before starting discussion.

At the beginning of the discussion, and every five minute during the 20 minutes discussion, the experimenter would randomly ask each of the participant in the pair to either play (low involvement, or L condition), or not to play (high involvement, or H condition) the computer game while they were chatting, with equal attention to the game and the discussion. To give the participants an incentive to pay attention to both the game and the discussion equally, the experimenter told the participants that apart from the $8 basic compensation they would get for the experiment, they had a chance to earn a maximum of $2 bonus based on their game scores and the quality of their discussion. The experimenter randomized the order of the L and the H conditions; so that for four segments (each segment lasting 5 minutes) of the 20-minute discussion, there would be one segment in which both participants in a pair were in the L condition (playing the game while chatting), one segment in which both of them were in the H condition (not playing the game), and two segments in which one of them were in the L condition, and the other in the H condition.

After every 5-minute segment during the 20-minute discussion, both participants stopped all their activities to answer the communication process survey and to receive instructions from the experimenter (about whether to play the game) for the next 5-minute segment. In all these four segments, the participants discussed the pros and cons of eight locations to open a new outlet of an ice cream brand,

and chose the best location. The experimenter suggested that they discussed two locations during each segment, but the participants could opt to lead their discussion their own way, as long as they finished the task given. All pairs conversed until they were out of time. After four segments, participants were asked to fill out the post-task survey. We then carefully debriefed the participants. We asked them about the workload during the whole experiment. While participants commented that playing the game while talking was hard and distracting, they did not think that such experimental tasks were too difficult. Finally, all participants were thanked, and given $10 for their participation, regardless of their performance on the final report or on the game.

Measures
We collected two types of measurements from the experiments. First, from the communication process survey participants filled out every 5 minutes, we collected measurements about their self-reported involvement in the conversation. Second, from the logs of IM chat sessions, we counted the number of different linguistic cues such as "I" pronouns that each participant used during their conversations, using TAWC, an adaptation of Pennebaker & Francis's LIWC [25], developed by Kramer et al. [14]. These two sets of measurements will be used as dependent variables in later statistical analyses.

Involvement during the conversation
We used 4 items from Cegala's Interaction Involvement Scale (IIS) [7] with some adaptation to suit the context of the study (see Table 1). These four items formed a reliable scale (Cronbach's α = .78) so scores were averaged to compute the level of involvement.

Items	1=Very rarely, almost never 7=Very frequently, almost always
1	During the previous 5 minutes of the conversation, I carefully observed how my partner responded to me.
2	During the previous 5 minutes of the conversation, I was sensitive to my partner's hidden or subtle meanings.
3	During the previous 5 minutes of the conversation, I pretended to be listening to my partner while in fact I was thinking about something else.
4	During the previous 5 minutes of the conversation, I was preoccupied and did not pay complete attention to my partner.

Table 1. Four items adapted from Cegala's involvement scale.

We also asked participants to answer a single question about how involved or committed they were (self's involvement), and their partners were (partners' involvement) in the conversation (1=not at all involved, 7=very much involved). The ratings were negatively

skewed. For these measures, log and other conventional transformations did not improve the normality of the data. Instead we used a histogram of the level of involvement to recode the data into three categories (1 to 4 =1, 4 to 6=2, and 7=3), roughly corresponding to low involvement, average involvement, and high involvement.

Verbal cues to involvement
Based on the results of Nguyen & Fussell [19] regarding the verbal cues of involvement in text-based IM conversations, we are only interested in the use of personal pronouns, assent words, definite articles, and cognitive words in this study. We counted the number of these verbal cues to involvement in the transcript of the participants' IM chat session. The word counts were computed using TAWC [14]. The raw word counts were negatively skewed, and thus the logs of the raw count were used in statistical analyses.

Personal pronouns. Personal pronouns are those that refer to the individual self, such as "I", "me", or "mine". We generated a list of personal pronouns based on the dictionary created by Pennebaker & Francis [25], and also taking into account the corpus from our data, to include possible misspelled words or abbreviations with the same meaning that participants typed in their conversation.

Assent words. We counted the number of words expressing consent to an idea stated before it based on the dictionary by Pennebaker & Francis [25].

Definite articles. The list of definite articles such as "the", "this", "that" was generated based on the dictionary created by Pennebaker & Francis [25].

Cognitive mechanism words. We also counted the number of words expressing thinking, reasoning, contemplating, speculation, or reflection based on the dictionary by Pennebaker & Francis [25].

RESULTS
We report the results in two parts: 1) a manipulation check to make sure the distraction task lower participants' level of involvement in the conversation 2) the use of verbal involvement cues in IM conversations between pairs of cross-culture, and same-culture American and Chinese partners in two involvement conditions. The first part includes analyses of participants' level of involvement on a 7-point Likert scale, measured every 5 minutes of their conversation in two conditions: high involvement (without distraction task) and low involvement (with distraction task). The second part includes analyses on the word counts of different categories for each participant in pairs of different culture combinations, in the two involvement conditions.

Manipulation Check
To make sure that the distraction task successfully lowered the participants' level of involvement, we conducted a

mixed model ANOVA on self-reported involvement as measured by 4 items adapted from Cegala's IIS [7] (R^2=.79). The fixed factors are the speaker condition and partner condition (both either low involvement with distraction task or high involvement without distraction). The random factors are the pairs, participants, and time order. Since we collected ratings at 4 different points of time, this time variable has value 1 to 4, 1 being the first 5-minute of the 20 minute discussion, and 4 being the last 5-minute segment.

We controlled for the involvement of the partner in these analyses since involvement is an interactive process, in which the two speakers mutually influence the involvement of each other [23]. The results indicated that the manipulation worked. Participants reported being significantly less involved (F[1, 145.30]=456.51, p<.0001) in the low-involvement condition (M=5.61, SE=.11, 95% CI [5.46, 5.76]) than in the high-involvement condition (M=3.46, SE=.11, 95% CI [3.28, 3.67]) (Cohen's D=2.22).

Participants' ratings of partners' involvement. We asked participants to rate their partners' level of involvement and understanding every 5 minutes (1=lowest to 3 = highest, after recoding to adjust for normality). We then conducted a mixed model ANOVA of the same form on the speaker's ratings of their partner's involvement (R^2=.63) and understanding (R^2=.62). We found that speakers rated their partners significantly higher in involvement (F[1, 114.6]=35.60, p<.0001) when the partners were in the high involvement condition (M=2.16, SE=.06, 95% CI [2.04, 2.28]) than in the low involvement condition (M=1.98, SE=.06, 95% CI [1.86, 2.10]) (Cohen's D=.27).

Word count per minute. We analyzed the total number of words said by participants every minute, for each 5-minute segment of their conversation, in the two involvement conditions. We expected that people in the high involvement condition would be more responsive than in the low involvement condition, as indicated in the number of words they said per minute. We conducted a mixed model ANOVA, with speakers' (participants') involvement condition, and partners' involvement condition as the fixed effects, and pair, participants, and time as the random effect on the total number of words said every 1 minute (R^2=.62). We found that participants spoke significantly more words per minute (F[1,142.50]=80.77, p<.0001) when they were highly involved (M=23.42, SE=.89, 95% CI [21.85, 25.01]) than when they were less involved (M=16.18, SE=.89, 95% CI [14.88, 17.49]) (Cohen's D=.90).

Cultural differences in the use of verbal involvement cues

H1 to H3, and RQ1 refer to the difference in the way American and Chinese participants in same-culture and cross-culture American and Chinese pairs used verbal involvement cues such as "I" pronouns and assent words differently in their IM conversations. To test these hypotheses and answer this question, we conducted mixed model ANOVAs. Participants' culture, the partners' culture, the two involvement conditions, and the interactions between these three variables were the fixed effects. Pair, participant, and time were the random effects. The dependent variables are the log of the counts of "I" pronouns, assent words, definite articles, and cognitive words every 5 minutes. We also control for the total number of word said during the 5 minutes. We included the correlation among these word counts in Table 2, and the means and SE of these word counts in Table 3. Differences in the ways American participants and Chinese participants used verbal cues to express different level of involvement can be observed through significant interaction effects of participants' culture and involvement conditions on the number of verbal cues uttered.

	"I"	Assent	Def. Art.	Cog. words	Word rate
"I" Pronouns	1				
Assent words	.035	1			
Definite Articles	.082	.215	1		
Cognitive words	.364**	.261**	.437**	1	
Words per 5 mins	.206**	.232**	.566**	.367**	1

**. Correlation is significant at the 0.01 level (2-tailed)

Table 2. Correlations of different categories of word counts.

Word category	Involvement condition	
	High	Low
"I" pronouns	M=2.58 (SE=.27)	M=3.52 (SE=.27)
Definite articles	M=6.02 (SE=.32)	M=4.70 (SE=.32)
Assent words	M=3.72 (SE=.23)	M=2.43 (SE=.23)
Cognitive words	M=10.74 (SE=.42)	M=7.91 (SE=.42)

Table 3. The means and standard errors of the number of words in different categories each participant uttered every 5 minutes in the two involvement conditions.

"I" pronouns. A mixed-model ANOVA of the form outlined above on the log of the number of "I" pronouns every 5 minutes (R^2=.51) showed no main effects of participants' culture (F[1, 56.63]=1.56, p=.21), and partners' culture (F[1, 54.22]<1, n.s) on the number of "I" pronouns a participant said every 5 minutes. We found a main effect of involvement condition (F[1, 181.2]=18.10, p<.01), showing that participants said fewer "I" pronouns in the high involvement condition than the low involvement condition (Cohen's D=.29, see Table 3). But we found no significant interaction effects. H1 was not supported.

Assent words. We conducted a mixed model ANOVA of the form outlined above on the log number of assent words said every 5 minutes (R^2=.39). We found a significant main effect of participants' culture (F[1, 52.05]=4.61, p=.03). Chinese participants said significantly more assent words (M=3.2, SE=21, 95% CI [2.76, 3.63]) than American participants (M=2.54, SE=.22, 95% CI [2.14, 3.01]) (Cohen's D=.28). There is also a significant main effect of involvement condition (F[1, 182.8]=16.31, p<.001). Participants said significantly more assent words in the high involvement condition than in the low involvement condition (Cohen's D=.55, see Table 3). We found no significant interaction effect. Thus, H2 was not supported

Cognitive words. A mixed model ANOVA of the form outlined above on the log number of cognitive words every 5 minutes (R^2=.23) showed a significant main effect of involvement condition (F[1, 184.7]=4.38, p=.03). Participants said significantly more assent words in the high involvement condition than the low involvement condition (Cohen's D=.54, see Table 3). We also found a near significant interaction effect of participants' and partners' culture (F[1, 26.94]=3.15, p=.08). We conducted one planned post-hoc test between the log number of cognitive words said by participants in same-culture pairs and by those in cross-culture pairs. We found that participants said marginally (F[1, 26.94]=3.16, p=.08) more cognitive words in same-culture pairs (M=9.01, SE=.63, 95% CI [7.75, 10.27]) than in cross-culture pairs (M=9.58, SE=.41 95% CI [8.67, 10.29]) (Cohen's D=.10) (see Figure 1).

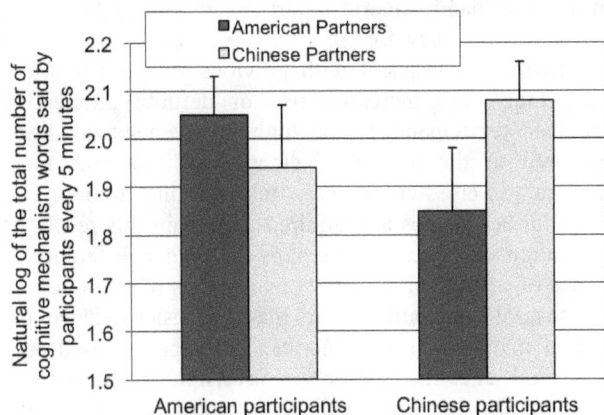

Figure 1. Log number of cognitive words said every 5 minutes for pairs of different cultural combinations: AA, AC, and CC.

We also found a significant interaction effect of participants' culture and involvement condition (F[1, 177]=5.23, p=.02). A post-hoc Tukey HSD contrast revealed that only the difference between the high involvement and the low involvement condition for the Chinese participants was significant at α=.05. Chinese participants said significantly more cognitive words in the high involvement condition (M=10.41, SE=.60, 95% CI [9.22, 11.62]) than in the low involvement condition (M=6.50, SE=.56, 95% CI [5.37, 7.63]) (Cohen's D=.87).

Contrary to H3, For the American participants, the difference between the high involvement condition (M=11.06, SE=.67, 95% CI [9.75, 12.38]) and the low involvement condition (M=9.33, SE=.78, 95% CI [7.77, 10.89]) was not significant according to the Tukey HSD contrast (see Figure 2).

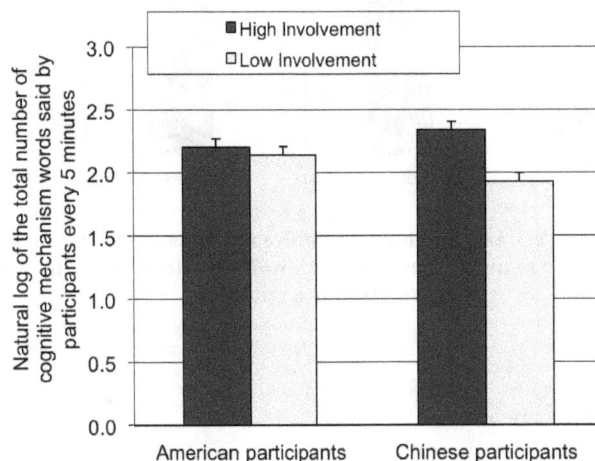

Figure 2. Log number of cognitive words said every 5 minutes by American and Chinese participants in two conditions.

Definite articles. To answer RQ1, we conducted another mixed model ANOVA of the form outlined above on the log number of definite articles said every 5 minutes (R^2=63). We found a significant main effect of involvement condition (F[1, 180.40]=5.40, p=.02). Participants said significant more definite articles in the high involvement condition than in the low involvement condition (Cohen's D=.54, see Table 3). We found a significant interaction effect of partners' culture and involvement condition (F[1, 175.5]=5.84, p=.02). A Tukey HSD contrast revealed that only the difference between the high and low involvement condition for the Chinese partners was significant at α=.05. Participants said significantly more definite articles in the high involvement condition (M=6.80, SE=.58, 95% CI [5.63, 7.96]) than in the low involvement condition (M=4.30, SE=.45, 95% CI [3.36, 5.17]) when they worked with a Chinese partner (Cohen's D=.60). When participants worked with an American partner, the difference between the high involvement condition (M=7.25, SE=.67, 95% CI [5.89, 8.60]) and the low involvement condition (M=5.13, SE=.46, 95% CI [4.20, 6.05]) was not significant (see Figure 3).

We also found a significant three way interaction effect of participants' culture, partners' culture, and involvement condition (F[1, 175.3]=5.32, p=.02). A Tukey HSD contrast showed that only for American participants working with Chinese partners, the difference in total number of definite articles said in 5 minutes between the high involvement condition (M=9.85, SE=1.21, 95% CI [7.30, 12.39]) and the low involvement condition (M=4.55, SE=1.05, 95% CI [2.33, 6.76]) was significant (Cohen's D=1.03). All other comparisons were not (see Figure 4).

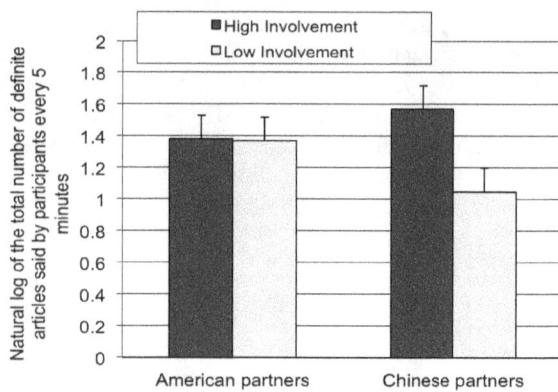

Figure 3. Log number of cognitive words participants said every 5 minutes when they work with American and Chinese partners in two conditions.

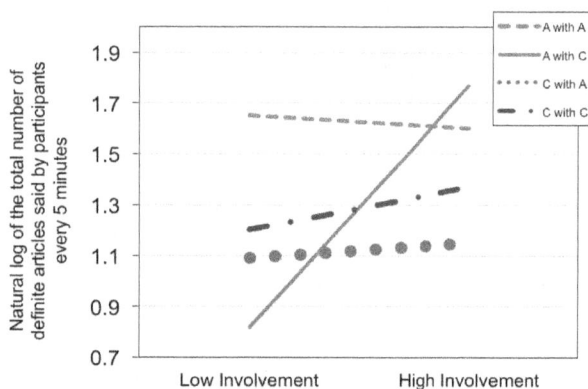

Figure 4. Log number of cognitive words participants said every 5 minutes for different cultural combinations in two conditions.

DISCUSSION

In general, our results show that participants used "I" pronouns, assent words, cognitive words, and definite articles differently when highly involved and when less involved, consistent with previous studies [20]. More importantly, we found several cultural differences not only in the way American and Chinese participants used verbal cues in general, but also when they are highly involved or less involved. First, we found that Chinese participants used significantly more assent words than American. One explanation is that Chinese participants are relationship-oriented and tend to avoid conflicts and preserve harmony [34] through words of agreement. Some studies found that Chinese participants sometimes responded with assent words even when they disagreed [30, 18]. Another explanation is that Chinese participants tend to use assent words not to signal agreement, but as a form of back-channel responses to signal acknowledgement to the partners more than American participants [33].

Second, we found that participants said marginally more cognitive words in same-culture pairs than in cross-culture pairs. This result is consistent with Nguyen & Fussell's

[19] finding that in cross-culture pairs participants tended to say fewer opinions in a problem-solving task. It is possible that participants feel more comfortable expressing their ideas when talking to a partner from the same culture. This result call attention to a challenge in intercultural collaboration when multi-cultural team members tend to hold back their thoughts despite the need for a variety of perspectives or approaches in a team discussion.

Third, we found several evidences that Chinese and American participants used verbal cues to express involvement differently. Contrary to our expectation, Chinese participants significantly changed their frequency of cognitive words between the high and low involvement conditions, but not American participants. It is possible that while American participants used more cognitive words in general than Chinese participants [31], the difference in the frequency of cognitive words said by American participants between the high and low involvement conditions is less perceptible. Therefore, cognitive words might play a smaller role in the expression and interpretation of involvement for American participants than for Chinese participants.

We also found for Chinese participants the use of definite articles did not change significantly between the two involvement conditions. This result may be due to the fact that Chinese participants who speak English as their second language tend to omit articles in their English sentences because of the lack of articles in Mandarin [28].

On the other hand, American participants changed their use of articles when they are highly involved and when they are less involved, consistent with previous studies [4]. More interestingly, the increased use of definite articles by American participants in the high involvement condition compared to the low involvement condition was more significant in cross-culture pairs than in same-culture pairs. While further studies are required to explain this result, its implication is interesting. Perhaps the bigger difference in the use of definite articles in conversations of cross-culture pairs than of same-culture pairs makes it easier to detect the level of involvement of American participants based only on textual cues in text-only conversations. Nguyen & Fussell's [20] findings call for reconsideration of the presumed primary importance of non-verbal cues to involvement in face-to-face conversations [3], as simple verbal cues may be enough for participants to express and detect level of involvement in text-based IM conversations. Our result adds to this finding by implying that the role of simple verbal cues in the expression of involvement becomes even more significant when IM conversations happen in cross-culture pairs or teams.

Our results also help explain the findings from previous studies, which found that participants reported higher negative emotions in intercultural IM conversations [19, 18]. Nguyen & Fussell [18] found that such negative emotions emerged when one member mistakenly perceived the other member as less dedicated to the team task, based solely on what was said in the IM conversation. Our results further suggested that because American participants and Chinese participants express and interpret involvement cues differently, there is higher risk of misunderstanding about the state of involvement of team members in intercultural teams. This may explain why frustration arose in cross-culture IM conversations, where there is a lack of audio and visual cues to provide more awareness about each team members' activities.

Lastly, our results also call into attention an important confounding factor in many lab studies about cross-culture conversations. Most such studies did not consider the level of involvement of their multicultural participants and how involvement may influence participants' communicative behaviors. There are cultural differences in the way participants in different countries perform and pay attention during lab experiments (e.g., East Asian participants tend to be more serious and focused than North American ones). Our results further show that American and Chinese participants exhibited different communicative behaviors when their level of involvement varied. Therefore, future experimental studies of intercultural conversations should be aware of the potential impacts of involvement on the communication process under investigation.

DESIGN IMPLICATIONS
In intercultural teamwork, IM is a popular, quick, and easy communication solution [11]. We found that participants from different cultures had different verbal styles of conveying conversational involvement. Members of intercultural team may face difficulties in understanding teammates' involvement, which may lead to frustration and negative experience. In the context of increasing multitasking at work, our result suggests the need to increase team members' awareness of the activities of others during a team discussion via IM. Several tools have been designed to support attention and awareness in conversations using non-verbal and verbal cues, such as the GroupMeter system [15], or Conversation Clock [1]. Tools similar to these can be developed to display an aggregate visualization of the team members' involvement in a conversation based on verbal cues.

Moreover, while it is possible to detect people's involvement in a text-based IM conversation based on several verbal cues as studies suggested [20], our results also call attention to the varying significance of these cues when applied to people from different cultures. We found that for Chinese participants article use may not be a good indicator of involvement, but cognitive word use is. The opposite applies to American participants. Designers of future tools that rely on verbal cues to detect involvement in team conversation may need to consider these differences when designing for work teams from different cultures, or for multicultural teams.

LIMITATIONS & FUTURE DIRECTIONS
Our paper is not without limitations. We only study dyads, while group interaction is more common for remote intercultural collaboration. We only studied American and Chinese participants while real intercultural collaboration involve people from many more countries. Lastly, our small sample size might have limited the power of some results.

In future studies, we intend to code agreements, disagreements and relational messages. This coding scheme takes into account the conversational context to classify idea units based on their meanings, instead of mere word counts. Future studies may also record the IM chat window of participants' conversations to capture the speed of response for analysis. Lastly, future research can investigate conversations in more realistic team settings such as at actual workplaces, or can even allow all participants to use their native language to communicate with one another.

CONCLUSION
Our study examined the cultural differences in the use of verbal involvement cues in text-based IM conversations between American and Chinese participants. We conducted an experiment using same-culture and cross-culture pairs of American and Chinese participants discussing a decision making task via IM. Our results showed that American and Chinese participants used several involvement cues, such as cognitive words and definite articles, differently. Our study sheds light on an important communication process in intercultural CMC, and carries implications for the design of CMC tools to enhance collaboration among dispersed multicultural team members.

ACKNOWLEDGMENTS
This work was funded in part by NSF grant #0803482. We thank Leslie Setlock and the anonymous reviewers for their feedback on past revisions of the paper.

REFERENCES
1. Bergstrom, T., & Karahalios, K. (2007). Seeing More: Visualizing Audio Cues. *Proc. INTERACT '07*, 29-42.
2. Birner, B., & Ward, G. (2012). Uniqueness, familiarity, and the definite article in English. In *Proceedings of the Annual Meeting of the Berkeley Linguistics Society, 20* (1), 93-102.
3. Burgoon, J. K., & Le Poire, B. (1999). Nonverbal cues and interpersonal judgments: Participants and observer perceptions of intimacy, dominance, composure, and formality. *Communication Monographs, 66,* 105-124.
4. Camden, C, & Verba, S. (1986). Communication and consciousness: Applications in marketing. *Western Journal of Speech Communication, 50,* 64-73.
5. Cappella, J. N. (1983). Conversational involvement: Approaching and avoiding others. In J. M. Wiemann & R. P. Harrison (Eds.), *Nonverbal interaction* (pp. 113-148). Newbury Park, CA: Sage.

6. Cegala, D. J. (1989). A study of selected linguistic components of involvement in interaction. *Western Journal of Speech Communication, 53,* 311-326.

7. Cegala, D. J. (1981). Interaction involvement: A cognitive dimension of communicative competence. *Communication Education, 30, 2,* 109-121.

8. Clark, H. H., & Marshall, C. R. (2002). Definite reference and mutual knowledge. *Psycholinguistics: critical concepts in psychology, 3,* 414-460 .

9. Gudykunst, W. B., Matsumoto, Y., Ting-Toomey, S., Nishida, T., Kim, K., & Heyman, S. (1996). The influence of cultural individualism-collectivism, self construals, and individual values on communication styles across cultures. *Human Communication Research,* 22, 510.

10. Hall, E. T. (1976). *Beyond culture.* Garden City, N.Y.: Anchor Press.

11. Isaacs, E., Walendowski, A., Whittaker, S., Schiano, D., & Kamm, C. (2002). The character, functions, and styles of instant messaging in the workplace. In *Proc. CSCW '02,* 11-20.

12. Jones, E., Gallois, C., Callan, V., & Barker, M. (1999). Strategies of accommodation: Development of a coding system for conversational interaction. *Journal of Language and Social Psychology, 18,* 123-152.

13. Kim, M.-S., Hunter, J. E., Miyahara, A., Horvarth, A.-M., Bresnahan, M., & Yoon, H.-J. (1996). Individual vs. culture-level dimensions of individualism and collectivism: Effects of preferred conversational styles. *Communication Monographs, 63,* 29–49.

14. Kramer, A.D.I, Fussell, S. R., & Setlock, L. D. (2004) Text analysis as a tool for analyzing conversation in online support groups. *CHI 2004 Late Breaking Results.*

15. Leshed, G., Perez, D., Hancock, J., Cosley, D., Birnholtz, J., Lee, S., McLeod, P., & Gay, G. (2009). Visualizing real-time language-based feedback on teamwork behavior in computer-mediated groups. In *Proc. of CHI'09,* 537-546.

16. McLeod, P.L., & Kettner-Polley, R.B. (2004). Contributions of psychodynamic theories to understanding small groups. *Small Group Research, 35(3),* 333-361.

17. Mehrabian, A. (1967). Attitudes inferred from non-immediacy of verbal communications. *Journal of Verbal Learning and Verbal Behavior, 6,* 294-305.

18. Nguyen, D. T., & Fussell, S. R. (2012). How did you feel during our conversation? Retrospective analysis of intercultural and same-culture Instant Messaging conversations. *Proc. CSCW'12,* 117-126.

19. Nguyen, D. T. & Fussell, S. R. (2013). Effects of message content on cognitive and affective processes in cross-culture and same-culture instant messaging conversations. *Proc. CSCW'13,* 19-31.

20. Nguyen, D. T., & Fussell, S. R. (in press). Lexical Cues of Interaction Involvement in Dyadic Instant Messaging Conversation. In press in *Discourse Processes.*

21. Norton, R. W. (1983). *Communication styles: Theory, applications and methods.* Beverly Hills, CA: Sage.

22. Otsuka, K., Yamato, I., Takemae, Y., & Murase, H. (2006). Quantifying interpersonal influence in face-to-face conversations based on visual attention patterns. *CHI '06 Extended Abstracts,* 1175-1180.

23. Patterson, M. L. (1983). *Nonverbal behavior: A functional perspective.* New York: Springer-Verlag.

24. Pennebaker, J. W. (2011). *The secret life of pronouns.* New York: Bloomsbury Press.

25. Pennebaker, J.W., & Francis, M.E. (1999). *Linguistic Inquiry and Word Count: LIWC [software program for text analysis].* Lawrence Erlbaum Associates.

26. Pirzadeh, A. & Pfaff, M. (2012). Expression of emotion in IM. In *Proc. of CSCW '12,* 199-202.

27. Resnick, L., M. Salmon, C. Zeitz, S. Wathen and M. Holowchak (1993). Reasoning in Conversation. *Cognition and Instruction, 11,* 347-364.

28. Robertson, D. (2000). Variability in the use of the English article system by Chinese learners of English. *Second Language Research, 16, 2,* 135-172.

29. Scheerhorn, D. R. (1991). Politeness in decision-making. *Research on Language and Social Interaction, 25,* 253-273.

30. Setlock, L. D., Fussell, S. R., & Neuwirth, C. (2004). Taking it out of context: Collaborating within and across cultures in face-to-face settings and via instant messaging. Proc. CSCW'04, 604-613.

31. Setlock, L. D., Quinones, P. A., & Fussell, S. R. (2007). Does culture interact with media richness? The effects of audio vs. video conferencing on Chinese and American dyads. *Proceedings of HICSS 2007.*

32. Stewart, C. O., Setlock, L. D., & Fussell, S. R. (2007). Conversational argumentation in decision-making: Differences across cultures and communication media. *Discourse Processes, 44,* 113-139.

33. Tao, H. Y., & Thompson, S. A. (1991). English backchannels in Mandarin conversations: A case study of superstratum pragmatic "interference". *Journal of Pragmatics, 16,* 209–233.

34. Walls, J. (1993). Global networking for local development: Task focus and relationship focus in cross culture communication. In L. M. Harasim (Ed.), *Global networks: Computers and international communication.* Cambridge, MA: MIT Press.

Cross Cultural Research, Innovation and Design in 2050

Apala Lahiri Chavan
Global Chief of Technical Staff, HFI
CEO - Institute of Customer Experience
http://ice.humanfactors.com/index.html
apala@humanfactors.com

ABSTRACT

Cross Cultural Research, Innovation and Design has been my passion for many years and I never thought I would have a question like this! But as I have been envisioning what the future of user experience is going to be like, I am beginning to wonder if there will be 'cross cultural' anything left in 2050? Will we live in a universe where trans-humans and humanoid robots make up the population? A universe where we have 'evolved' to become much more powerful as individuals but very homogenous and hence the concept of 'across cultures' will cease to exist? OR, will 2050 see the opposite reality, where every single human / trans-human / humanoid robot is different and hence cross-cultural research, innovation and design will be the most sought after discipline?

Author Keywords

Cross cultural design; future visualization; future trends; user experience

ACM Classification Keywords

J.4 Social and Behavioral Sciences

BIO

Apala is a world-renowned expert on cross cultural design and contextual innovation. Her innovative and pioneering techniques have benefitted global giants such as HP Labs, Adidas, Nokia, Sony Ericsson, NCR, and Intel, among others. She is also the recipient of the International Audi Design Award.

She is also a dynamic and creative instructor and author. Her keynote talks on contextual innovation, ecosystem research, internationalization, and designing for emerging markets have received acclaim in USA, Canada, Europe, India, and China. She has developed a vast array of data-gathering techniques such as Bollywood Method, Bizarre Bazaar, and Funky Facilitator, which help understand the user experience in diverse cultural and economic environments. She and her team pioneered the "Ecosystem Chart" that organizes vast amounts of ethnographic data into a coherent model.

Apala also specializes in creating UX strategy for organizations that are looking at creating breakthrough user experience for their customers and other stakeholders. Some of her recent projects include:

- UX strategy for cross channel integration of one of the largest banks in South Africa.
- Ecosystem research and innovation strategy for a large German appliance maker.
- Research, innovation and design for the in home entertainment domain in India, China and USA.
- Ecosystem research about cell phones for the Indian market for a large Finnish mobile phone maker.
- Microcredit system, managing small loans to farmers and small businesses, with operators who could only read numbers, not text for MIT Media Lab Asia.
- Researching media applications in rural markets for an American technology company.
- Applying handwriting recognition in small businesses in India.
- Unusual applications for ATM machines.
- Identifying latent needs in emerging markets for a US based home medical equipment company, used in the therapy process.
- Innovation and strategy for Inclusive banking in Kenya.
- Innovation and strategy for mobile banking in South Africa.

Apala has been with HFI since 1999 as Managing Director, HFI India, and VP, HFI Asia, Chief Oracle and Innovator before assuming her current role. In addition to her usability certifications (CUA and CXA), Apala holds an MSc with distinction in User Interface Design from London Guildhall University. She is also a TEDx speaker. Her TEDx Talk is titled 'Three Laws of UX':

https://www.youtube.com/watch?v=MiwjplU6kAc

CABS'14, August 21-22, 2014, Kyoto, Japan.
ACM 978-1-4503-2557-8/14/08.
http://dx.doi.org/10.1145/2631488.2637431

TransDocument: Exposing Sentence Structure for Efficient Translingual Communication

Takeo Igarashi

Computer Science Department, The University of Tokyo

7-3-1 Hongo, Bunkyo, Tokyo, JAPAN

takeo@acm.org

ABSTRACT

Machine translation systems are effective for translating relatively short sentences, but they often return incomprehensible results when applied to long sentences with complicated dependency structures. We therefore propose to expose sentence structure to writers and readers to facilitate translingual communication via imperfect machine translation systems. The writer encodes his or her message into a structured text, which is a collection of sentence fragments organized in a hierarchical structure. The system then translates these fragments individually, using a standard machine translation system. The structure itself is preserved. The reader reads the structured text in the target language. In this paper, we present an interactive text-editing system that supports the writing and reading of such structured texts. We also run a small scale user study to investigate the potential of the proposed method, and the result suggests that the structure information can be helpful in improving the understandability of machine translation results.

Author Keywords

Natural language; machine translation; translingual communication; sentence structure; text editor.

ACM Classification Keywords

H. Information Systems; H.4 INFORMATION SYSTEMS APPLICATIONS; H.4.3 Communications Applications

INTRODUCTION

Machine translation has progressed significantly in recent years, mainly due to the availability of a large corpus and appropriate statistical methods to utilize it. Various commercial machine translation systems are available, including those freely available on the internet, such as Microsoft Translator and Google Translator. However, these systems have not yet been perfected, making communications using machine translation remains difficult [1, 11]. They work well for short sentences, but often return a

meaningless sequence of words when applied to a long sentence. This is because they are not very good at analyzing the structure of the original sentence. They can reliably carry out word or phrase level translations, but structure inference remains a significant challenge in machine translation (this is the author's subjective observation by using existing commercial services). Sentence structure is difficult to handle by statistical methods alone, since it is often necessary to consider the semantics of a sentence.

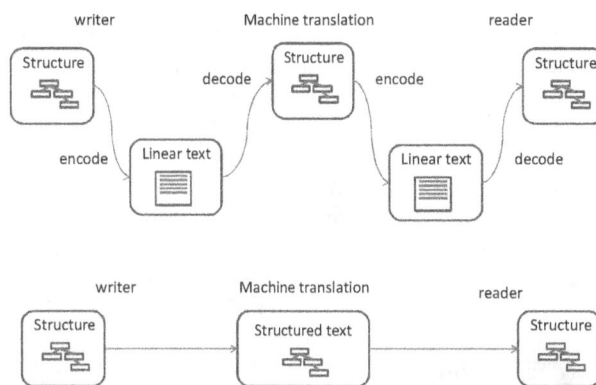

Figure 1. Standard machine translation involves encoding and decoding of structure information (top). Our method bypasses this difficulty by exposing the structure to the users (bottom).

We therefore propose to expose sentence structure to writers and readers to support translingual communication using imperfect machine translation systems. Figure 1 illustrates the basic idea. A standard machine translation system takes a linear text written in the source language as input, decodes its structure, and then returns a linear text written in the target language, encoding the structure into it (Figure 1, top). However, the decoding and encoding of a structure may both be erroneous. We propose to avoid this decoding and encoding process by having the writer explicitly specify the sentence structure, and enabling the reader to see the structure information (Figure 1, bottom). Since the sentence structure is presumably already in the writer's mind before writing a linear sentence (this claim is the authors' subjective hypothesis and not supported by any study), explicitly specifying that structure should not entail too much overhead for the writer. Similarly, the reader must infer the sentence structure from a linear text in order to understand it, so explicitly displaying the structure might be helpful to the reader as well.

This paper presents a system for facilitating multi-lingual communication using machine translation by having the writer to explicitly specify sentence structure and presenting it to the reader. Specifically, the writer decomposes an input sentence into sentence fragments and specifies its dependency structure via interactive editing. The system then translates the sentence fragments independently using a standard machine translation, and presents the result to the reader the dependency structure.

We also explain the design process for the current prototype system, including alternative designs we considered during the process. We then report the results of a user study. Five Japanese speakers composed structured sentences in Japanese, and five English speakers read the structured sentences translated into English, and rated their usefulness. The results show that the readers found the structured sentences to be useful in most cases, although the variance was large.

Our current target is translation from Japanese to English, but the basic idea is not limited to this combination. The technique might be particularly useful for one-to-many language translation. In the present study, we also assumed that the writers did not understand the target language, and so we did not expose the translation results to the writers. However, if a writer does have some understanding of the target language, it might be better to share the translation results with the writer for verification or modification. We intend to explore these possibilities in future research.

RELATED WORK

All traditional machine translation systems take a linear natural language text as input and return a linear text as output [4]. They use an internal hierarchical structure as an intermediate representation, but such structure information is not usually exposed to the end users. Some systems ask the user to provide structure information to accurately translate a text [2], but the output is still a linear text, and the user must carefully decompose the text according to predefined rules. Some systems facilitate manual translation by showing the predicted results of machine translation procedures [6]. Our approach is unique, in that we expose sentence structure to both a reader and a writer, as a new form of computer-supported human-human communication.

Controlled natural language [9] is a technique for increasing the accuracy of machine translation by imposing various restrictions on the input text. The input text is written according to specific rules, using a subset of the grammar or vocabulary of the natural language. This approach has been successfully employed in certain fields, such as the aerospace industry, where it is necessary to translate a large number of manuals. However, texts must be very carefully written according to the rules. Our method is more flexible, since the structure is presented directly to the readers without being

processed by the machine, thus eliminating the constraints of strict machine-oriented rules.

An interesting technique for checking the correctness of a machine translation without reading the text in the target language is back translation [8]. In this approach, translation results are retranslated into the original language and presented to the writer. If the back translation results properly convey the intention of the original sentences, one can assume that the translation results are also successful. If the back translation results are completely wrong, it is quite probable that the translation results are also wrong. However, this technique only indicates the existence of problems, and provides no information on how to remedy them. The writer is then obliged to test various versions of the original sentences until the back translation results become satisfactory. Our procedure allows the writer to actively address the problem by giving structure to the original text.

Our method is motivated to some extent by hypertexts [3], in that text representation is enhanced by adding nonlinear structures. However, the granularity and purpose of these structures are very different. Hypertexts define relationships among document fragments to facilitate navigation in a large document, whereas our technique defines relationships among sentence fragments as an aid to understanding a machine translation of a sentence. Our work is also inspired by various computational supports for text writing and reading, such as interactive front end systems for inputting complex characters (IME), auto completion and listing in code editors (e.g., Eclipse and Visual Studio), and spell checkers in document editors (e.g., Microsoft Word). Another inspiration comes from natural language command line interface with rich visual feedback [7]. Similarly, we try to enhance communication using natural language with rich user interaction.

THE TRANSDOCUMENT SYSTEM

Figure 2 shows the overall communication process using our system. The system functions as a structured text editor and viewer. The writer composes a structured sentence in the source language. This structured sentence is a set of hierarchically organized sentence fragments. The system then individually translates the sentence fragments into the target language using a standard machine translation technique, and the reader reads the structured sentence in the target language.

A structured sentence is represented as a tree consisting of hierarchically organized nodes, each of which represents a sentence fragment. Figure 3 shows an example. The root node is a special abstract node that represents the entire sentence. Its immediate children (called 1st level nodes) represent fragments (phrases or clauses) of the sentence. A node in the tree (other than the root and its immediate children) represents a phrase or clause that gives additional information about the parent node. For example, a relative clause is a child of the noun it modifies. The children of a node constitute an ordered set.

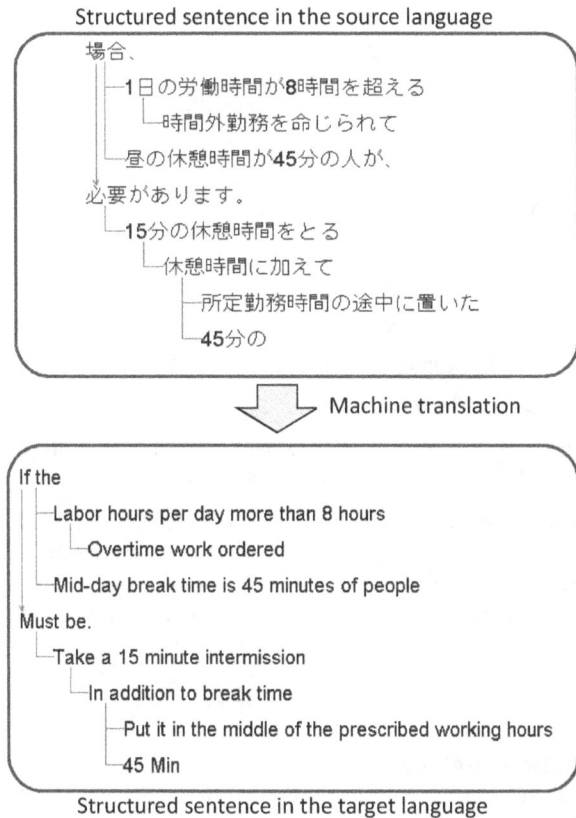

When reading a structured sentence, the reader first reads the 1st level nodes in the given order to understand the basic structure of the sentence. The reader then recursively reads the child nodes of each node to obtain further information about the node.

Note that the structure is not strictly defined in a grammatical sense. The structures are intentionally designed to be simple and flexible. The writers use the hierarchical structure in their own way, so that the meaning of the sentence is clearly delivered to the reader after the machine translation is applied to each node. The structure itself is not analyzed or modified by the computer, so there is no need to follow strict, inflexible rules, as in controlled languages or programming languages.

Sending sentence fragments into machine translation instead of whole sentence reduces errors caused by the system wrongly analyzing the global structure of the sentence. For example, given a sentence "the girl who looks at a dog who is barking," the system might wrongly relate "who is barking" to "the girl". This can be avoided if the user specifies the structure. On the other hand, splitting a sentence into fragments might be disadvantageous for machine translation because it cannot leverage semantic context. Context can be very useful for disambiguation of a word. We believe that this can be alleviated by sharing the context information from the original sentence when translating individual sentence fragments, but it is left as a future work.

Editing Structured Sentences

Here we describe the behavior of the editor in detail. The current prototype system is designed to compose a single sentence as a structured text, and it is an object of future research to develop a fully functional text editor that supports long text with multiple sentences. The user creates a structured text (such as the example shown in Figure 3), using the keyboard and mouse. The basic operations are similar to those of a hierarchical document editor, such as an XML editor and outliner programs. A notable feature is that our system supports fluent, gesture-like mouse operations for editing hierarchical structures. The user can quickly experiment with assorted hierarchical structure variations, using simple drag-and-drop operations, which greatly facilitates finding an appropriate structure by trial and error.

Editing starts with a blank canvas. The user either copies and pastes a sentence from an existing source or types a new sentence, as in standard text editors. The user then presses the Enter key to split a sentence at the cursor position (Figure 4, top). The text that follows the cursor position becomes a new node, and is appended to the tree as a sibling of the original node.

After splitting the original sentence into meaningful chunks, represented as nodes, the user can add a hierarchical structure to the nodes. Pressing the Tab key makes the selected node (on which the cursor is located) a child of the preceding sibling (Figure 4, bottom). Repeatedly pressing the Tab key

Figure 2. Translingual communication using the TransDocument system. The original Japanese sentence is shown at the bottom. Manual translation of the original Japanese sentence is "*In the event where one needs to work more than 8 hours a day, whose designated lunch break time is 45 minutes, he/she has to take an extra 15 minutes' break on top of the 45 minutes' break to be taken in-between his/her designated working hours.*".

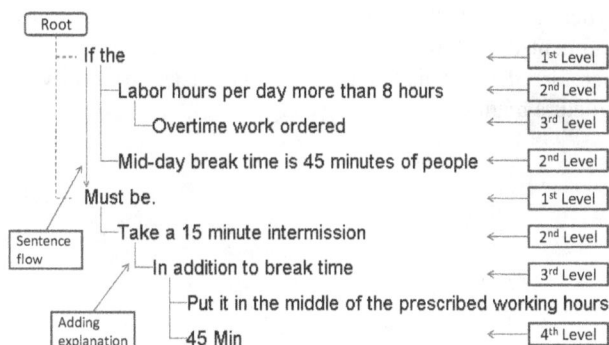

Figure 3. Composition of a structured sentence.

moves the node downwards in the tree (moving it to the right on the screen). Pressing the Backspace key at the beginning of a block reverses the procedure. The selected node is moved upwards in the tree (to the left on the screen), making it a sibling of the parent.

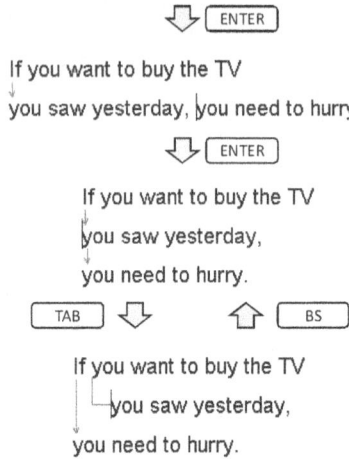

Figure 4. Keyboard operations for editing a structured sentence.

The user can also edit the structure by using the right mouse button. Pressing and holding the right mouse button on a node grabs the node. The user then drags the node to the left or right to move the node upwards or downwards in the tree (Figure 5, left). The user can also drag the node vertically to change the order (Figure 5, right).

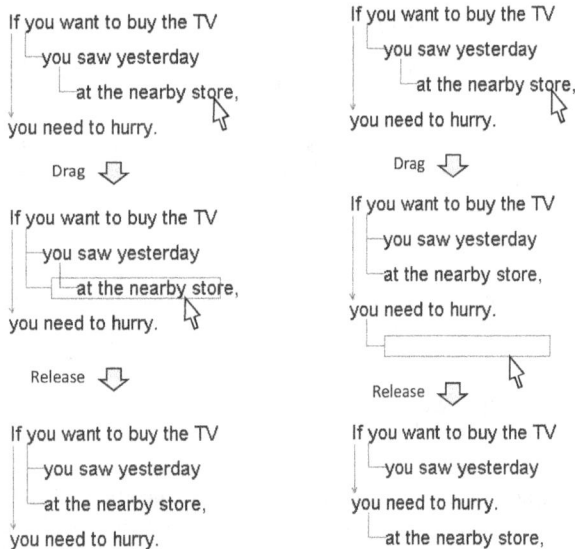

Figure 5. Mouse operations for editing a structured sentence. Horizontal dragging changes the horizontal position (left) and vertical dragging changes the vertical position (right) of a node in the tree.

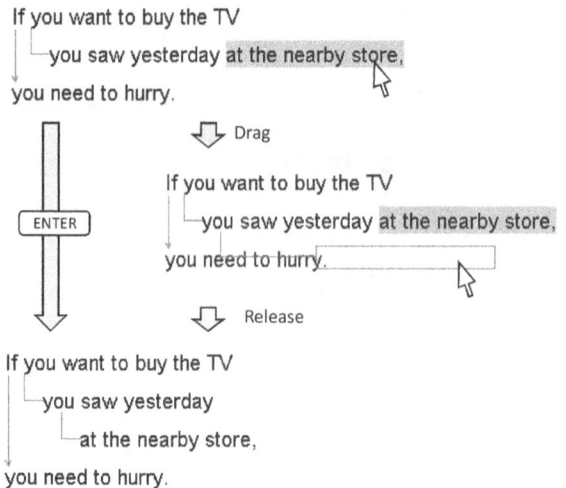

Figure 6. Converting part of a node into a new node with keyboard (left) and mouse operations (right).

The user can select (highlight) part of a text, and then drag the selected text (Figure 6) to create a new node. The selection is performed as in a standard text editor, by dragging the cursor with left mouse button or using the arrow keys with the Shift key held down. The selected text is removed from the original node. The user can also create a new child node by pressing Enter after selecting part of a text.

DESIGN ITERATIONS

We arrived at the current design by following an iterative design process. Here we briefly explain the alternative designs considered during the process, and why we chose the current design.

Automatically Inferred Sentence Structure

We initially tried to use sentence structures that were automatically analyzed by existing natural language processing techniques. We tested a dependency analysis tool for Japanese, known as KNP[1] [5], which decomposes a sentence into words and displays the relationship between the words. An example is shown in Figure 7. We tested this on several sentences, but found that the structure is too fine-grained for use as a human-friendly communication tool. It inevitably introduces errors, making it necessary for the writer to read the results carefully. However, reading fragmented text is very tedious and time consuming. We therefore decided that it is faster and easier to specify the structure manually.

---

[1] http://nlp.ist.i.kyoto-u.ac.jp/EN/index.php?KNP

年間———
　契約等で——┐
　　既に———┤
　　契約———┤
　　締結し、<P>———┐
反復的に——┐　　│
　給付を———┤　│
　受けている<P>—PARA——┐
　　　取引に———┐
　　　についは、——┤
　現状の———┐　　│
　　まま———┤　│
　取引———┐　│
　　継続で———┤
　　　差し支え<P>——┤
　　ありません。<P>—PARA

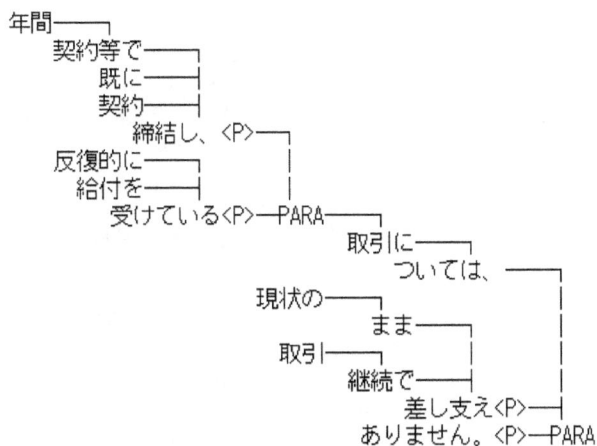

Figure 7. Structural information provided by KNP, a dependency relationship analyzer for Japanese texts.

Unconstrained Canvas

A possible approach to composing a graphical representation is to allow the user to freely place nodes on a 2D canvas, as in drawing systems (e.g., PowerPoint) or mind-map systems. Figure 8 shows an example. We did not implement this concept, and the figure is only a mock-up image. This approach is more expressive, in that the writer can make intelligent use of the layout to clarify the message. For example, it might be useful to place important components near the center and trivial components at the periphery.

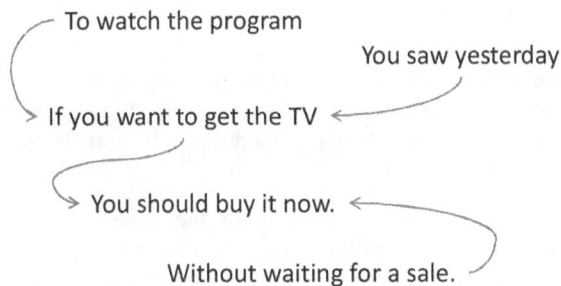

To watch the program

You saw yesterday

If you want to get the TV

You should buy it now.

Without waiting for a sale.

Figure 8. Structural information drawn on an unconstrained canvas, as in Mindmap.

However, after experimenting with several sentences, we concluded that this approach is too flexible and requires too many mouse operations, since the user must explicitly specify the location of each node. It also became clear that this approach requires too much space. Another concern was that the intention of the writer might not be correctly communicated to the reader without a common agreement on how to use the layout.

We decided, therefore, on a more constrained layout approach. A constrained approach significantly simplifies the interface, making it possible to manipulate the layout using only a keyboard, as in a standard outline editor. A constrained approach also clarifies the meaning of the layout, resulting in a more compact layout than a freestyle approach.

Annotating the Original Text with Brackets

Another design we experimented with was to ask the writer to annotate the original sentence with brackets explaining the recursive containment structure of the sentence. Figure 9 shows an example. This technique can be viewed as an enhancement of the use of commas in a natural language. A comma represents a boundary between sentence fragments, but cannot indicate a containment structure. On the other hand, a bracket can explicitly represent the start or finish of a containment structure. We also anticipated that inserting brackets in a text would be simpler than drawing a graph on a canvas, since it can be accomplished using a standard text editor, and requires no special canvas.

We implemented a working prototype system and experimented with various sentences. The system worked reasonably well, but we found that a containment structure is inadequate for representing a dependency structure. Suppose a relative clause A is modifying a word B that immediately follows A. Simply placing brackets before and after A is not sufficient to indicate that A is modifying B, since the word order varies depending on the language. If A is modifying B, A precedes B in Japanese, but A follows B in English. It is possible to reorder the sequence automatically, but this is a difficult machine translation problem, which should be avoided to reduce the uncertainty in the process. This observation led us to the next approach, in which the user explicitly specifies which word to modify.

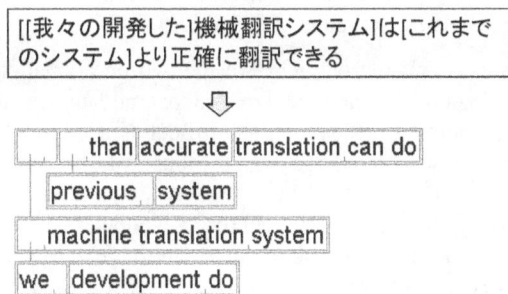

[[我々の開発した]機械翻訳システム]は[これまでのシステム]より正確に翻訳できる

⇩

| | than | accurate | translation | can do |

previous | system

machine translation system

we | development | do

Figure 9. The user annotates a natural language text with brackets to encode a hierarchical containment structure (top), and the system renders the structure graphically.

Specifying the Target Being Modified

In this design, the writer is requested to explicitly specify which word or phrase a sentence fragment (such as a relative clause) is modifying. Figure 10 shows an example. We initially tried to accomplish this by simply inserting some characters in the text (as in the previous approach), but it was difficult to find an intuitive representation. Accordingly, we decided to introduce mouse and keyboard editing operations similar to those of our current design.

As for transactions
　　　　├─which have already entered into annual contracts
　　　　└─and the benefit of which have been received
　　　　　　　　　　　　└─repetitively,
the transactions can be continued
　　　　　　　　└─as they are in the current states.

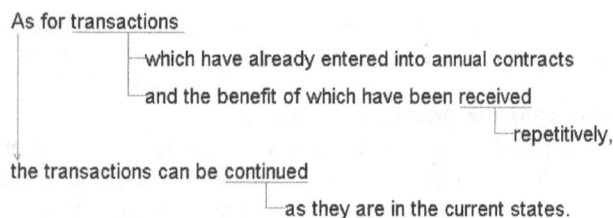

Figure 10. Specifying the target word or phrase being modified. Each link indicates which word or phrase is modifying which.

Once again, we implemented a working prototype of this approach and tested it on various sentences. The new procedure worked better than the previous design, but the user operations proved to be too complicated. The user was required to select both a modifier fragment and a modifying fragment for each instance, thus necessitating relatively complicated operations. We also observed that if each sentence fragment is small enough, it is not really necessary to explicitly specify which word or phrase in the fragment is being modified. We concluded that simply displaying the dependency relationships among sentence fragments is adequate for inferring the meaning of a sentence, and this is the current design.

USER STUDY

We conducted a small-scale user study to investigate the effectiveness of the approach using our prototype implementation. We also try to obtain informal insights for further development of the system. However, a rigorous evaluation to systematically verify the effectiveness of the method is beyond the scope of this paper.

There are several reasons why we focused on a small-scale study at this point. Writing and reading natural language texts is time consuming, which makes it difficult to acquire a large sample of test users. Moreover, because of the potential learning effect, test users cannot be reused, compounding the difficulty of obtaining a large sample. Nevertheless, since the variances among users and sentences are large, many users and sentences are necessary to obtain statistically reliable results. Since the system is still at an early prototypical stage, and the design is not yet finalized, such a costly large-scale study is not justified at this point.

The test consisted of a writing task and a reading task. For the writing task, the participants added structure to a plain Japanese sentence using our system. For the reading task, the participants examined a machine translation with structure information, and evaluated the usefulness of the structure information as an aid to understanding the sentence. Strictly speaking, the writing task here is actually structuring task or annotating task. However, we decided to call it writing task here because the structuring task is supposed to be performed by the writer in our target application scenario. We tested structuring task only because we need to use common original sentences for comparison.

We prepared 26 Japanese sentences for the study, sampled from messages recently posted to the internal bulletin board system of a university department. Since our method is designed to facilitate the understanding of relatively long sentences with complicated structures, we manually collected relatively long sentences, excluding those that included long proper nouns. We also removed e-mail addresses appearing in these sentences. We also tried to sample sentences with wide variety of meanings and structures.

We did not measure machine translation quality of the structured text because these is no established method exist for structure text. Existing measurements, such as TER/WER (translation/word error rate) [10], only work for linear texts. It is possible to apply such a method to fragmented sentences, but it cannot measure the benefit of user-defined structure information in the multi-lingual communication process.

Writing Task

We recruited five volunteers for the writing task, all of whom were male graduate students at the local university. They major in computer science but not natural language processing. Four of them were native Japanese speakers. One participant (#3) was Korean, but he has lived in Japan for more than 6 years, and is fluent in Japanese. No compensation was given. The test lasted approximately 1 to 1.5 hours.

Figure 11 shows a screenshot of the system we used for the writing task. The top pane shows the original Japanese sentence and the bottom pane shows the structured sentence being edited. The participants worked exclusively on the Japanese sentences, and saw no English translations while performing their tasks, under the assumption that they were entirely unfamiliar with the target language. We asked them to simply change the structure, and did not ask them to edit the content.

We first explained the purpose of the study, namely to manually add structural information to a Japanese sentence to facilitate the understanding of a machine translation. We then explained how to use the system to add structure to a sentence. We showed the participants how to add structure to the first three sentences, and asked them to perform the same operation on the rest of the sentences. For the next three sentences, we continued to provide help and answer questions when necessary. The main task then commenced, and the participants completed the remaining 20 sentences without our assistance. The data were taken from these 20 sentences. All participants worked on the same 26 sentences in the same order.

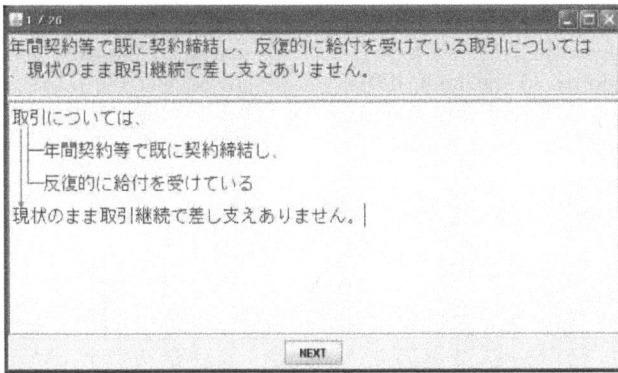

年間契約等で既に契約締結し、反復的に給付を受けている取引については
　現状のまま取引継続で差し支えありません。

取引については、
　└年間契約等で既に契約締結し、
　└反復的に給付を受けている
現状のまま取引継続で差し支えありません。

NEXT

Figure 11. Screenshot of the system used for the writing task. The top pane shows the original linear text and the bottom pane shows the structured text being edited.

Figure 12 shows the time spent on the writing task. The variances among participants and sentences were both very large. The average time per sentence was 171 seconds, but spent less time in the later sentences (average was 217 seconds for the first 5 sentences and 116 seconds for the last 5 sentences). We also asked a professional translator to translate the same 20 sentences, and he reported that he spent roughly 10 minutes on each sentence. This shows that the time spent adding structure may be shorter than the time required for manual translation.

The participants reported that they were not very sure how to add structure to a sentence in the beginning, but gradually decided on a strategy for the later sentences, thus reducing the time expenditure.

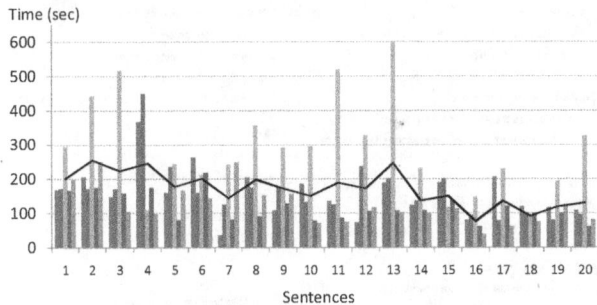

Figure 12. Time spent on each sentence in the writing task. The colors represent participant IDs. Black line indicates the average.

Reading Task
We recruited five different volunteers for the reading task, all of whom were foreign male graduate students and post-docs working on research projects in Japan. They were from Brazil, Netherland, Denmark, Austria, and Korea. Two of them had been studying Japanese for several months, while the others had no reading knowledge of the language.

We employed the same 26 sentences used in the writing task, and prepared three different translations for each of them. The first was a standard machine translation (we used Microsoft translator[2]). The second was a manual translation provided by a professional service (at approximately 400 yen per sentence). The third was a machine translation of the structured text. Each block of structured text was translated independently. There were five translated structured sentences for each sentence created by the writing task participants and one of them was presented to a reading task participant.

The reading task participants used the first six sentences for practice, and worked on the remaining 20 sentences as their main task, in the same order as in the writing task. The writer-reader sentence assignment was balanced as much as possible. The writers composed a total of $5 \times 20 = 100$ structured sentences, and each of these was used only once in the reading task. A single reader worked on four structured sentences composed by each writer.

Figure 13 shows a screenshot of the program we used for the reading task. For each sentence, the participant was first presented with a machine translation, and was asked to infer the meaning of the sentence. The user then pressed the "next" button and the structured sentence appeared below. We explained that the structured sentence had been manually created by a human being, and that the structure shows the hierarchical dependency relationships among the sentence fragments. We then asked him to infer the meaning of the sentence, taking the structure into account. The participant pressed the "next" button again, and the manual translation of the sentence was displayed, together with a scoring panel, as shown in the figure. We asked the participant to rate the usefulness of the structured text as an aid to understanding the machine translation, using the scoring panel.

We also experimented with a head-to-head comparison of plain and structured sentences, using a between-sentence method. In other words, a participant read half the sentences as plain sentences and the remaining half as structured sentences. However, the variance among sentences was too large to obtain meaningful results. Since we can assume that the original plain sentences are also available in practice, we decided to measure the *added* value of providing structured sentences on top of plain sentences.

---

[2] http://www.microsofttranslator.com/tools/

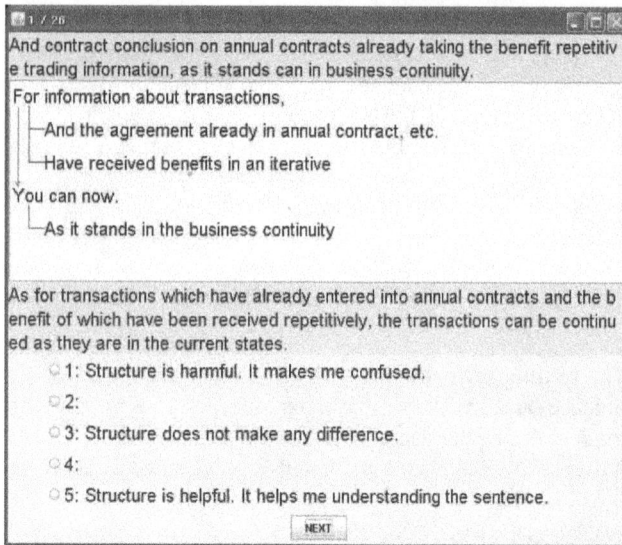

Figure 13. Screenshot of the system used for the reading task. The topmost pane shows the machine translation of the original linear text. The second pane shows the structured text created from the machine translation. The third pane shows the manual translation. The bottom pane shows the radio buttons used for scoring. These panes appear successively as the user presses the "next" button. The manual translation and scoring pane appear simultaneously.

Figure 14 shows the time spent reading the machine translations and their structures. The average time spent was 52 seconds, with a standard deviation of 20 seconds. The variations among participants and sentences were large. A slight learning effect can be seen, with less time spent for the later sentences (average was 57 seconds for the first 5 sentences and 39 seconds for the last 5 sentences).

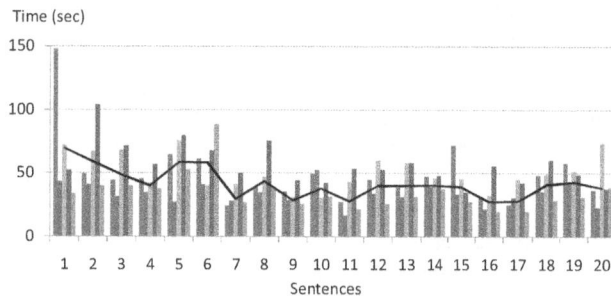

Figure 14. Time spent on each sentence in the reading task (machine translation and structured sentence). The colors represent participant IDs. Black line indicates the average.

Figure 15 shows the scores registered by the participants. The variation was large but scores higher than 3 are more frequent than scores lower than 3. We analyzed the data with one-sided one-sample t-test with null hypothesis of average being 3 and significance level being 0.05. When t-test is applied to the set of 20 samples for each participant, the average was significantly higher than 3 for the subject 3, 4, and 5, while the average was not significantly lower than 3 for any subject. When t-test is applied to the set of 5 samples for each sentence, the average was significantly higher than 3

for the sentence 3, 4, 5, 9, and 20, while the average was not significantly lower than 3 for any sentence. The same test applied to the total 100 samples showed that the score is significantly higher than 3 (majority is 3, but there are more 4 and 5 compared to 2 and 1).

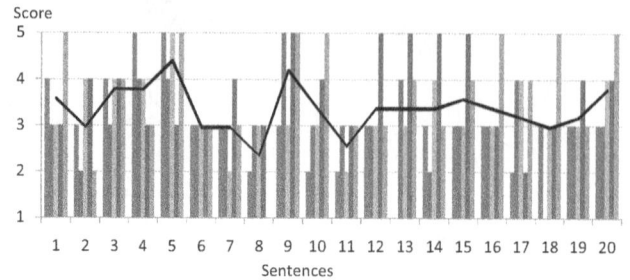

Figure 15. Scores given by the five participants in the reading task. A higher score indicates that the structure was helpful and a lower score indicates that the structure was harmful. Black line indicates the average.

Let us take a closer look at some of the results. Figure 16 shows the structured sentences created for the sentence #5. This is a good example in which the structure is not properly captured in machine translation while structured sentence conveys the meaning well regardless of small individual differences among the writers. Figure 17 shows those for the sentence #8. This is a case where structured sentences were not very helpful. Here, the structures created by the writing task participants were diverse, which probably means that the original Japanese sentence was ambiguous. As a result, structured sentences did not work better than standard machine translation.

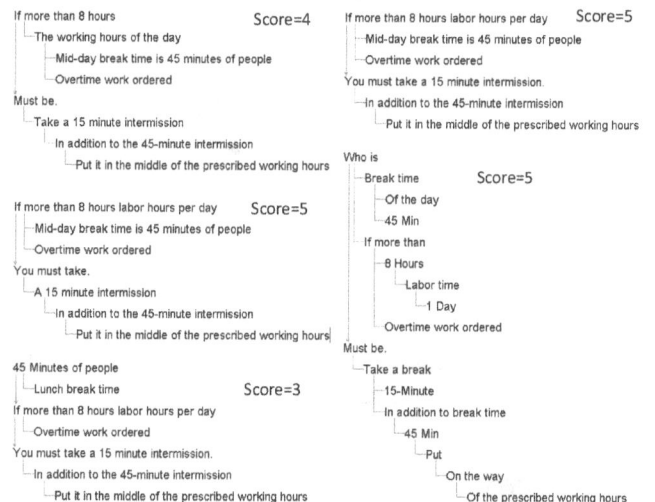

Machine translation: "Mid-day break time is 45 minutes, but overtime must take a 15 minute intermission as well as put in the middle of the prescribed working hours if ordered work day labor time exceeds 8 hours, 45 minutes of break time.."

Figure 16. Structured sentences created by the writing task participants for sentence #5. The original Japanese text and manual translation is given in Figure 3. Scores were given by the reading task participants.

```
If the representative institutions        Score=3      When to apply for this competition,       Score=3
  ├─ Therefore, the                                       ├─ If the representative institutions
  ├─ When to apply for this competition                        └─ In the application by the Consortium format, etc.
  ├─ In the application by the Consortium format, etc.   Please consult us.
Please consult us.                                          └─ First of all departments apply Office representative
  └─ First of all departments apply Office representative

Therefore, the                            Score=1      Therefore, the
First of all consult applicants clerical Department.   When you apply for                        Score=3
  ├─ When to apply for this competition                    └─ In this public offering
  └─ If the representative institutions                  If you are
      └─ In the application by the Consortium format, etc.    ├─ Become a representative organization
                                                               ├─ In the application
Therefore, the                            Score=2              └─ By Consortium format, etc.
If the representative institutions                     Please consult us.
  ├─ When to apply for this competition                    ├─ Apply Office representative
  ├─ In the application by the Consortium format, etc.       ├─ Of departments
Please consult us.                                           └─ First of all
  └─ First of all departments apply Office representative
```

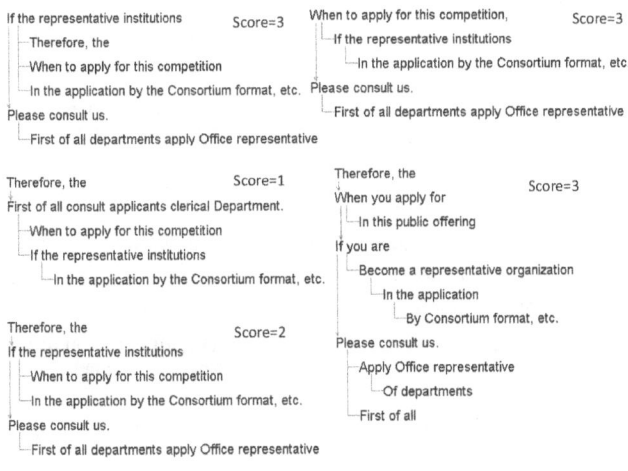

Machine translation: "When to apply for this competition, the applicant by the Consortium, etc. in national agencies if first consult to apply clerical Department."

Manual translation: "Thus, upon applying for this public invitation, in the event that the application is made in the form of consortium under the name of a representative institution, please contact the person in charge of application entry in the respective department office beforehand."

つきましては、本公募に応募する際、コンソーシアム形式等による申請で、代表機関になる場合は、まず部局の応募事務担当にご相談ください。

Figure 17. Structured sentences created by the writing task participants for sentence #8. The original Japanese sentence is shown at the bottom.

In a follow-up interview, the participants reported that the machine translation results were too poor and the structural information alone cannot make it possible to fully understand the meaning. Nevertheless, they found that the structural information provided clues in many cases, and they appreciated these clues. They also reported that they gradually learned how to "read" the machine translations and structured texts as they worked on the sentences, and were more confident about the later sentences.

CONCLUSIONS AND FUTURE WORK

We introduced a procedure for explicitly representing hierarchical sentence structure to facilitate translingual communication via imperfect machine translations. A writer adds structure to a sentence and a reader reads the translated sentence with the structure. We developed an interactive text editor for authoring structured sentences, and tested it in a small-scale user study. Writers spent an average of approximately three minutes on each sentence, which was significantly less than the time required for a professional translator to translate each sentence (approximately 10 minutes). Readers found that the structured sentences were helpful for understanding the meaning of erroneous machine translations in some cases. The result suggests that a little work by writers *without knowledge of the target language* can improve the understandability of imperfect machine translation results, which we believe is very encouraging.

This research confirmed the potential of the proposed method. In the next step, we plan to develop more practical applications by integrating the technique into various communication tools, such as e-mails, bulletin boards, and instant messages by embedding specialized text area widget for editing sentence structures. We then plan to conduct a longitudinal study of these applications in everyday work. We believe that the learning effect plays an important role in our procedure, and that such a longitudinal study would reveal its true potential.

We also plan to test other variations of the method. In this study, we assumed that the writers had no understanding of the target language, and hid the translation results from them. However, if a writer does understand the target language to some extent, it might be helpful to allow him/her to verify the appropriateness of the translation. It might also be useful to include techniques such as back translation to ensure the quality of the translation results. We also plan to experiment with a procedure in which a writer provides information to facilitate the process of turning unorganized letter sequence into word sequence, since this process can be the cause of translation errors in languages such as Japanese and Chinese (this is not a problem for languages such as English where words are delimited by spaces).

From a technical point of view, we plan to develop a customized machine translation engine that is optimized for the proposed method. We are currently using an off-the-shelf translator, which is not taking full advantage of the structure. We hope to improve the quality of machine translations by considering the structure during translation. For example, the translator may fail to leverage context information for word disambiguation in fragmented sentences. We plan to address this issue by using customized translators.

Our system might also be useful as an educational tool. Poor writers often write sentences with unclear structure, even in their native language, making it almost impossible to translate correctly, even for a human translator. Our system compels writers to be aware of sentence structure, and might train them to provide appropriate structure to a sentence.

ACKNOWLEDGEMENTS
We thank the participants for the user study for the time and discussions. We also thank the reviewers for their valuable feedback.

REFERENCES
1. Calefato, F., Lanubile, F., Minervini, P., Can Real-Time Machin Translation Overcome Language Barriers in Distributed Requirements Engineering? In *Proc. ICGSE 2010*, 257-264.

2. Fujiwara, K., Liu S. Translation Support Device and Translation Support Program, Japanese patent, P2011-18189A, 2011.

3. Conklin, J. Hypertext: An Introduction and Survey. *IEEE Computer 20*, 9, (1987), 17-41.

4. Koehn, P. 2007. *Statistical Machine Translation*. Cambridge University Press, 2007.

5. Kurohashi, S., Nagao, M. A syntactic analysis method of long Japanese sentences based on the detection of conjunctive structures. *Computational Linguistics, 20,* 4, (1994).

6. Langlais, P., Foster, G., Lapalme, G. TransType: a computer-aided translation typing system. In *Proc. the ANLP-NAACL 2000 Workshop on Embedded Machine Translation Systems*, 2000.

7. Miller, R.C., Chou, V., Bernstein, M., Little, G., Kleek, M. V., Karge, D., and schraefel, mc. Inky: A Sloppy Command Line for the Web with Rich Visual Feedback. In *Proc. UIST 2008*, 131-140.

8. Miyabe, M., Yoshino, T., Shigenobu, T. Effects of Undertaking Translation Repair using Back Translation, In *Proc. IWIC 2009*, 33-40.

9. Pool, J. Can Controlled Languages Scale to the Web? In *Proc. 5th International Workshop on Controlled Language Applications*, 2006.

10. Snover, M., Dorr, B., Schwartz, R., Micciulla, L., and Makhoul, J. A Study of Translation Edit Rate with Targeted Human Annotation, In *Proc. Association for Machine Translation in the Americas*, 2006.

11. Yamashita, N., Ishida, T. Effects of Machine Translation on Collaborative Work, In *Proc. CSCW 2006*, 515-524.

Playing the 'Silence' Card:
Email Affordances in International Inter-firm Interactions

Niki Panteli
School of Management
University of Bath,
BA2 7AY Bath,
United Kingdom
n.panteli@bath.ac.uk

Joyce Y.H. Lee
Dept of Information Management
Innovation Center for Big Data and
Digital Convergence
Yuan-Ze University
Chung-li, 32003, Taoyuan, Taiwan
yhl@saturn.yzu.edu.tw

Anne Marie Bülow
Department of International
Business Communication
Copenhagen Business School
Frederiksberg, Denmark
amb.ibc@cbs.dk

ABSTRACT
In this paper, we argue that the international business (IB) literature has given only limited attention to the technology-mediated context of language. We find, through a case study of an international inter-organizational partnership where the use of English language was the lingua franca, that email not only had a dominant role but also created several possibilities for interaction. The findings show the relevance of email affordances to inter-cultural studies. Further, the study makes a contribution by repositioning communication technology within the language stream of IB research.

Author Keywords
Email, language; lingua-franca; affordances theory

ACM Classification Keywords
K.4.3 Organizational Impacts: Computer-supported collaborative work

Do Automated Transcripts Help Non-Native Speakers Catch Up on Missed Conversation in Audio Conferences?

Ari Hautasaari
NTT Communication Science Labs
2-4 Hikaridai, Seika-cho,
Soraku-gun, Kyoto, Japan
ari.hautasaari@lab.ntt.co.jp

Naomi Yamashita
NTT Communication Science Labs
2-4 Hikaridai, Seika-cho,
Soraku-gun, Kyoto, Japan
naomiy@acm.org

ABSTRACT

Previous work has suggested that speeded up playback of recorded audio works well for native speakers (NS) to catch up on conversation they missed in real-time audio conferences. However, this might not be the case for non-native speakers (NNS) who normally have lower listening ability in their second language. In this study, we explore whether automated speech recognition (ASR) technology can aid NNS when combined with speeded up audio playback. We conducted a laboratory experiment in which 18 NS and 18 NNS listened to a pre-recorded audio conference with three English native speakers, during which they were briefly interrupted and missed parts of the ongoing conversation. They then caught up to the conversation with speeded up audio only (1.6x) and speeded up audio with ASR transcripts. Although ASR transcripts did not improve their comprehension of the conversational content when catching up, transcripts allowed NNS to shift their focus between the two modalities depending on their ability to follow second language speech in different audio speeds. The findings inform future development of ASR tools to support multilingual group communication.

Author Keywords

Automated speech recognition; real-time transcripts; multilingual communication; catching up;

ACM Classification Keywords

H.5.m. Information interfaces and presentation (e.g., HCI): Miscellaneous.

INTRODUCTION

Technological advancements continue to facilitate multimodal communication over great distances. With the

combination of cost-effectiveness and convenience, audio conferencing allows timely decision-making across borders and time zones, and has become one of the most common communication tools used by individuals, organizations and global enterprises.

While audio conferences are common platforms to hold meetings between non-collocated participants, there are numerous coordination issues involved. For some, it may not always be possible to participate in the meeting from the beginning. Others may have to attend to urgent tasks during the meeting, such as answering a phone call, and thus miss parts of the ongoing conversation [16]. Having others reconstruct these missed parts after rejoining the meeting can be disruptive for the whole group.

Technical solutions for catching up on missed parts of the audio conference without disrupting the ongoing conversation include using audio recordings and exploiting automated speech recognition (ASR) technology to present the main points of the meeting as gists [21]. Audio recordings have also been combined with ASR to provide a speeded up playback of the missed parts combined with text transcripts of the spoken dialogue to allow participants to catch up to the real-time conversation [9, 10]. For native English speakers, the speeded up audio seemed sufficient to recover from missed information [10].

However, we suspect that this would not be the case for non-native speakers (NNS). Indeed, even in normal speed, NNS face unique difficulties in audio conferences that are rarely found between native speakers (NS) [11]. Besides NNS being unable to reach the fluency level of NS in their shared language, NNS often find it challenging to follow other's speech under imperfect audio conditions [7, 24].

An increasing number of studies have focused on alleviating the difficulties that NNS face during real-time audio conferences with ASR technology (e.g., [8]). According to previous research, text transcripts may support NNS comprehension in pre-recorded meetings when the transcripts are provided with reasonable accuracy and delay [18, 19, 20, 24]. Given such positive effects of text transcripts on NNS comprehension of second language speech, we speculate that ASR technology might help NNS catch up on the missed parts of the conversation during an audio conference.

Our goal is to examine how ASR transcripts may support NNS during audio conferences. As a first step, we focused on the effects of real ASR transcripts on NNS comprehension of second language conversation. We created a catch up interface, which allows participants to briefly leave the audio conference and catch up to the missed parts of the conversation upon rejoining with speeded up audio and ASR transcripts. In the remainder of this paper we describe a laboratory study, where 18 NS and 18 NNS joined a conversation with three native English speakers as passive listeners. We manipulated the accessibility of the ASR transcripts, where the participants listened and caught up to missed parts of an audio conference with speeded up audio (1.6x) or with speeded up audio plus ASR transcripts. Lastly, we will present our results and discuss our findings in relation to previous works, and draw design implications for future development of ASR applications for multilingual audio conferencing.

BACKGROUND AND RELATED WORK

In this section, we first review previous studies on technological approaches to allow NS to catch up on missed parts of an audio conference. We then review some issues NNS normally face in audio conferencing, and discuss whether the catch up approaches are also effective for NNS. Finally, we introduce recent studies on how ASR transcripts facilitate NNS comprehension, and discuss the possibilities of ASR transcripts helping NNS catch up on missed parts of an audio conference.

Catching Up with Speeded Up Audio

Existing catch up technology allows participants in an audio conference to review any parts of the conversation they missed due to distractions, such as answering an urgent phone call. The technological development, for one, has focused on allowing users to review any missed parts of the ongoing conversation without disrupting the meeting. To achieve this, previous works have exploited audio recordings and language processing technologies to summarize the main points of the missed conversation as gists [21].

However, gisting techniques omit information from the catch up recordings, which might be important for users to fully comprehend the content of the missed conversation. Solutions that include full conversation history play back the missed parts of the audio speech in a higher speed until the point where it catches up to the ongoing conversation (e.g., [9, 10]). The speeded up audio is usually set between 1.4x [5] and 2.0x speed, which is the upper end of what NS can understand [22]. Previous studies have shown that 1.6x speed audio is a reasonable compromise between speed and understandability for NS to catch up on the missed conversation during audio conferences [9, 10].

Previous works have also experimented with using ASR transcripts to help NS catch up on missed parts of an audio

conference. However, speeded up audio seemed sufficient, and NS preferred not to view imperfect ASR transcripts while listening to the speeded up audio [9, 10]. Catching up to missed parts of a conversation with speeded up audio alone, however, may be more challenging for NNS considering the difficulties they already face during audio conferences.

NNS Difficulties in Audio Conferences with NS

Previous research has shown that NNS face unique difficulties in audio conferences. Let alone issues with language fluency [13, 23, 25], NNS are further impaired when communicating in their non-native language due to higher cognitive load, and the increased time to process NS utterances [14]. In compromised communication situations, such as audio conferencing with extraneous noise and unclear pronunciation or articulation, these processes may be even harder for NNS [15, 17].

If NS are able and willing to coordinate and adjust their speech to the NNS ability by speaking more slowly or articulating and enunciating more clearly, some of the problems faced by NNS during audio conferences might be alleviated [1, 2, 3, 4, 8]. However, especially in groups where the majority of people are native speakers, this may fall short of expectations [1], also because conversation can move forward only between NS participants (without NNS participation). In order to aid NNS minorities during audio conferences, it is important to consider supporting mechanisms that do not rely on NS ability to ameliorate the blight that NNS face.

ASR Transcripts to Support NNS

As suggested in previous research, ASR technology has potential to alleviate the difficulties NNS face in audio conferences. For example, ASR transcripts provide textual information about the spoken dialogue during audio conferences, which may complement the audio speech and improve NNS comprehension [18, 19, 20, 24]. Previous studies have demonstrated how ASR technologies can improve NNS comprehension during formal presentations and when following television programs in their second language. In a more interactive setting, where ASR transcripts are used in a live multilingual meeting, providing feedback for NS on how their speech is transcribed during real-time audio conferences may facilitate NS adaptation to the technology and improve the accuracy of the ASR transcripts [8].

Altogether, previous works suggest that NNS might benefit even from imperfect transcripts during audio conferences. We wonder whether NNS would still benefit from ASR technology in adverse situations, such as when catching up to missed parts of a conversation with speeded up audio.

CURRENT STUDY

In the current study, we analyze the effects of ASR transcripts on NNS comprehension when catching up on missed parts of a conversation during a multiparty audio conference in their second language. For our experiment tasks, we use a pre-recorded audio conference corpus in order to control for the variance between speakers.

Research Questions

Previous studies have discussed how text transcripts may improve NNS comprehension of spoken dialogue in their second language [18, 19, 20, 24]. Expanding on these previous works, our first research question asks whether *real* ASR transcripts also improve NNS comprehension during multiparty audio conferences in their second language.

RQ1: Do NNS benefit from viewing real ASR transcripts when listening to a live multiparty audio conference in their second language?

Previous studies suggest that speeded up audio is sufficient for NS to catch up on missed parts of the conversation during audio conferences [10]. However, following second language conversation at faster speed likely imposes a higher cognitive load on NNS [14, 15, 17], affecting their comprehension of the spoken dialogue negatively. Meanwhile, text transcripts seem to help NNS comprehension in their second language. Thus, it is difficult to predict how real ASR transcripts might affect NNS comprehension when combined with speeded up audio for catching up on missed conversation. Hence, our second research question asks:

RQ2: Do NNS benefit from viewing real ASR transcripts when catching up to missed parts of a conversation with speeded up audio during a multiparty audio conference in their second language?

METHOD

Overview

We conducted a laboratory experiment with a single factor (transcript accessibility: audio only vs. audio with ASR transcripts) within subjects design. 18 native English speakers and 18 Japanese non-native English speakers participated in a simulated audio conference. The audio conference was pre-recorded, and included three native English speakers discussing a solution to a survival scenario, where they deliberated on the importance of a list of items for survival [12]. The discussions were divided in to 3-minute clips that were used as individual tasks.

To simulate a brief interruption during an audio conference, the participants were asked to leave the conversation for 30 seconds during each task, causing them to miss part of the discussion. In order to catch up with the ongoing conversation, the participants reviewed the missed parts in two conditions: (1) 1.6x speed audio only, or (2) 1.6x speed

audio with ASR transcripts. In this experiment, all participants used the catch up functionality in both conditions. We chose the 1.6x speed based on previous works that considered it the best fitting compromise between speed and understandability for NS when catching up to missed conversation [9, 10].

In total, each participant engaged in 6 tasks (3 tasks in each condition). After each task, the participants answered questions about the content of the conversation. The tasks were designed as uniform, and the conditions and tasks were counterbalanced. An open-ended interview about the participants' experiences during the experiment was conducted after they finished all tasks in both conditions.

Participants

We recruited a total of 36 participants for this study. 18 participants (4 female) were native English speakers who resided in Japan at the time of the study, but grew up in English-speaking countries where they received their primary education (from the age of 6 to 18, elementary school to high school). Their mean age was 40.61 (SD = 10.08).

The other half of the participants (N=18) were bilingual native Japanese speakers (14 female) who grew up in Japan and received their primary education in Japanese. Their mean age was 37.78 (SD = 11.21). None of the Japanese participants had lived in English-speaking countries for more than 2 years (M = 0.84, SD = 0.77). We required a minimum score of 700 (M = 850.29, SD = 68.04) in the TOEIC English proficiency test (Test of English for International Communication), which indicated that they were proficient but not fluent in their second language. They did not have extensive experience in communicating in English outside a classroom (M = 2.61, SD = 1.20 on a 7-point scale ranging from 1 = never to 7 = very often).

Experiment Dataset

ASR transcript and audio recording. We hired three native English speakers (2 female) to generate a realistic audio conference recording for the purposes of this study. The contributors were told that they would be taking part in an audio conferencing experiment using ASR tools. They discussed three survival scenarios using an audio conferencing tool combined with real-time ASR transcripts of the contributors' spoken dialogue.

The ASR transcripts used in this study were generated by a speech recognition software called Dragon Naturally Speaking (DNS) [6]. DNS recognizes the speaker's speech and transcribes it into English text. According to previous research, transcripts with a word error rate (WER) below 20% and a delay no more than 2 seconds can be beneficial for NNS [20, 24].

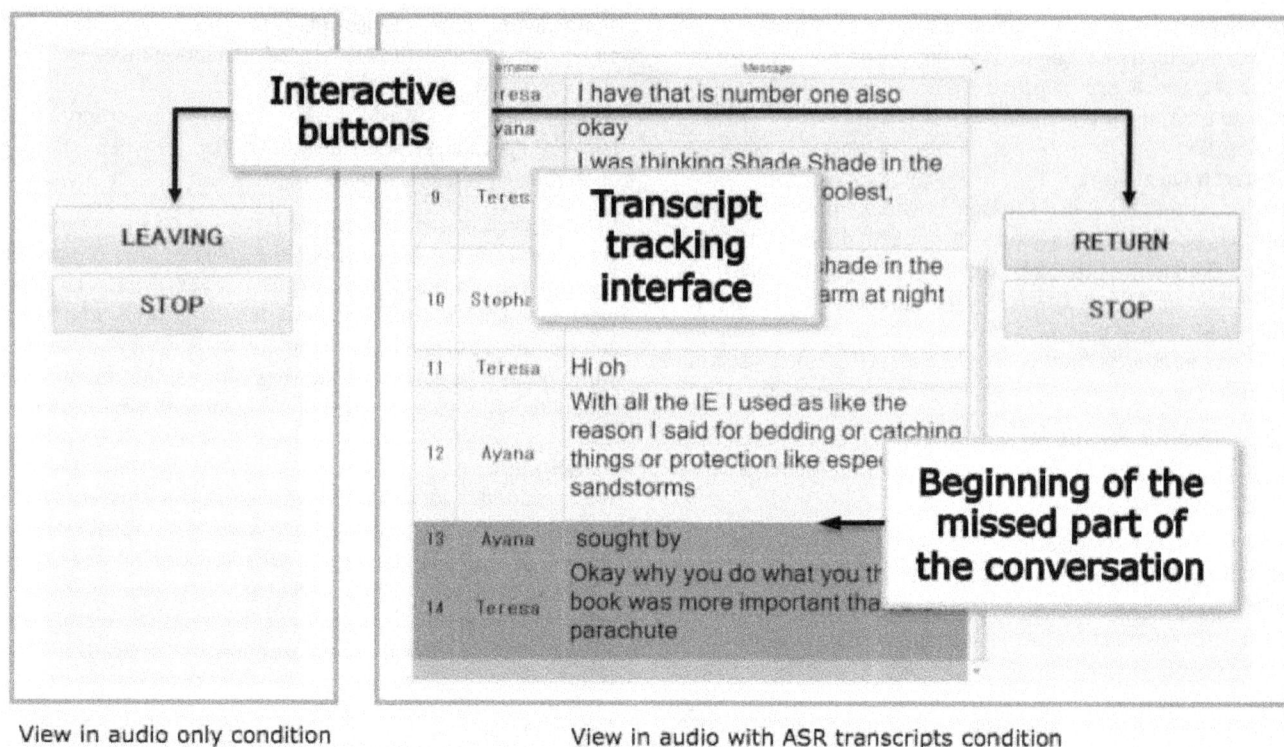

Figure 1. Catch up and real-time transcript tracking interface in audio only and audio with ASR transcripts conditions.

The contributors concluded a training session with DNS before the formal speech recognition started in order to familiarize them with the ASR software and adjust the recognition results to accommodate for their speech and articulation. WER calculated by comparing random samples of transliterated audio excerpts to ASR results was 23%, which is comparable to the reported WER in previous research with a similar setting and equipment [7].

We recorded all audio and transcripts generated during the discussions between the contributors. We then extracted 3-minute clips from each discussion, and used each clip as one task in the experiment.

Software and Equipment

Catch up interface. The catch up interface consisted of two components: interactive buttons for leaving and returning to the meeting, and a real-time transcript tracking interface. In the audio only condition, only the interactive buttons were visible to the participants (Figure 1). In the audio with ASR transcripts condition, the transcript tracking interface was shown on the left side of the screen (Figure 1, right). The transcript tracking interface displayed the ASR transcripts generated by DNS with a 1 to 3 seconds time delay as they appeared during the real-time conversation. The conversation history shows the full transcripts of the conversation. Participants could drag the scroll bar to see who said what in what order during the audio conference.

After the participants pressed the "Leaving" button on the interface, the audio was muted and the interactive button changed to display "Return" (Figure 1). When the participants pressed the "Return" button, the audio continued from the time stamp when they pressed the "Leaving" button and was played back in 1.6x speed until it caught up with the ongoing conversation. In the audio with ASR transcripts condition, the missed parts of the conversation were highlighted with a purple background in the transcript tracking interface (Figure 1, right). After the participants pressed the "Return" button, the highlighted part of the transcripts followed the speeded up audio in real time until the audio caught up with the ongoing conversation.

Tasks and Procedures

The participants were directed to a room and assigned to a laptop computer equipped with an external mouse to manipulate the catch up interface. Before the experiment began, the participants were asked to sign a consent form and fill out a demographic survey on a web browser.

After all participants finished the demographic survey, the experiment organizers explained the task instructions in English for the native speakers (NS) and in Japanese for the non-native speakers (NNS). In the experiment, the participants were asked to imagine that they are part of a multiparty audio conference as passive listeners. They were told that their task was to listen to a conversation in English and try to catch the conversational content the best they could. We allowed note-taking during this experiment.

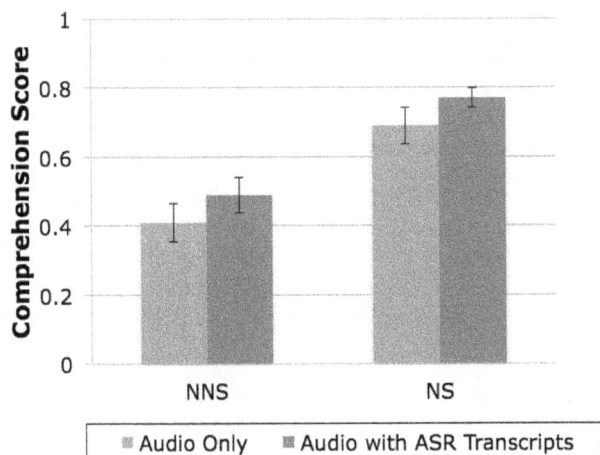

Figure 2. Mean speech comprehension score during a live audio conference in audio only and audio with ASR transcripts conditions for NNS and NS (error bars represent standard error of the mean).

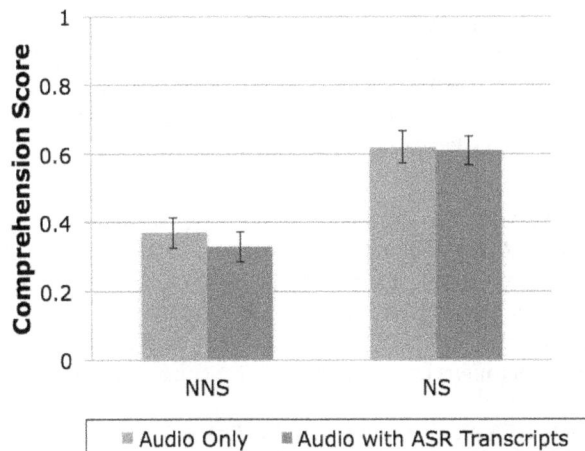

Figure 3. Mean comprehension score when catching up in audio only and audio with ASR transcripts conditions for NNS and NS (error bars represent standard error of the mean).

To simulate a short disturbance during the audio conference, such as an urgent phone call, we asked the participants to solve a short riddle. The riddles were written in English for NS participants and in Japanese for NNS participants on a piece of paper, which was turned face down on a desk next to each participants' laptop. Once the participants attended to this disturbance, they were forced to miss part of the conversation. During each of the experiment tasks, the participants attended to the disturbance (i.e., solving a riddle) once.

All together, the experiment included one practice task in each condition to familiarize the participants with the catch up and transcript tracking interface followed by three actual tasks in each condition. Each task was a 3-minute long snippet of an actual conversation between native English speakers discussing about a survival scenario. After each task, the participants answered a post-task quiz about the content of the conversation they just heard in English. Half of the questions were about the conversation they heard in live audio, and half about the missed part of the conversation they reviewed with the catch up functionality. After the entire experiment session, we conducted open-ended interviews about the participants' experiences. Interviews were conducted in each participant's native language.

Measures

We measured the participants' level of comprehension about the conversational content by administrating a post-task quiz. The participants' score (0-1) in the post-task quiz for reflected their level of comprehension.

RESULTS

Comprehension in Live Audio Conference

In order to answer our *RQ1* regarding the effects of real ASR transcripts on NNS comprehension during a live audio conference, we conducted a 2 (transcript accessibility:

audio only vs. audio with ASR transcripts) × 2 (language background: NNS vs. NS) repeated measures ANOVA (Figure 2). There was a marginal main effect for transcript accessibility ($F[1, 34] = 3.17$, $p = .085$), and a significant main effect for language background ($F[1, 34] = 29.78$, $p < .05$). The interaction effect between transcript accessibility and language background was not significant ($F[1, 34] = 1.00$, $p = n.s.$). NNS comprehension score with audio and ASR transcripts ($M = 0.49$, $SD = 0.23$) was higher than with audio only ($M = 0.41$, $SD = 0.24$). Similarly, NS comprehension score was higher with audio and ASR transcripts ($M = 0.77$, $SD = 0.12$) than with audio only ($M = 0.69$, $SD = 0.22$).

This result answers our *RQ1*, and is consistent with previous work by Pan et al. (2009, 2010) regarding the effects of ASR transcripts on NNS comprehension. Both NNS and NS comprehension marginally improved when viewing ASR transcripts during a live audio conference.

Comprehension When Catching Up

To answer our *RQ2* regarding the effects of real ASR transcripts on NNS comprehension when catching up on missed parts of an audio conference with speeded up audio, we conducted a 2 (transcript accessibility: audio only vs. audio with ASR transcripts) × 2 (language background: NNS vs. NS) repeated measures ANOVA (Figure 3). There was no significant main effect for transcript accessibility ($F[1, 34 = 0.99$, $p = n.s.$), but a significant main effect for language background ($F[1, 34] = 36.61$, $p < .05$). The interaction effect between transcript accessibility and language background was not significant ($F[1, 34] = 1.00$, $p = n.s.$). NNS comprehension score with audio and ASR transcripts ($M = 0.33$, $SD = 0.20$) was slightly lower than with audio only ($M = 0.37$, $SD = 0.19$). NS comprehension score was also slightly lower with audio and ASR transcripts ($M = 0.61$, $SD = 0.18$) than with audio only ($M = 0.62$, $SD = 0.21$).

This result answers our *RQ2*. NNS comprehension of the conversational content did not improve by viewing ASR transcripts when catching up to missed parts of a conversation during a multiparty audio conference compared to speeded up audio only.

DISCUSSION

Overall, our data suggests that NNS do not benefit from using ASR transcripts when catching up on missed parts of a conversation during a multiparty audio conference in their second language. In the next sections, we aim to illuminate our findings in more detail by reflecting on the post-experiment interviews with NS and NNS participants. [1]

Effects of ASR Transcripts on NS Behavior

In the post-experiment interviews, NS participants provided several reasons why they gained little benefit from using ASR transcripts. Firstly, NS participants often referred to the transcripts as being distracting because of the delay.

> Especially the delay of the transcripts is distracting in normal speed. [NS10]

> The transcripts are showing a different place of the discussion. [NS5]

Furthermore, some NS participants noted that the mistakes in the transcripts caused them to be less than helpful for speech comprehension. Some even referred to the mistakes in the transcripts as being entertaining.

Another reason for NS gaining little benefit from ASR transcripts seemed to stem from their familiarity in listening to fast English speech. The participants also mentioned that they would rather listen to the speeded up audio again when catching up to confirm their understanding of the conversational content rather than rely on the ASR transcripts.

> The mistakes in the transcripts are not helpful. I would rather listen to the fast sections again than read the text [if I missed some part of the conversation]. [NS12]

Meanwhile, regardless of the delay and errors in ASR transcripts, some NS participants did seem to find the ASR transcripts useful for catching up on parts of the conversation they missed.

> If I missed some parts, I checked the text transcripts to catch up with the audio. This is for the parts I didn't actually hear for some reason, [but] I was used to the fast speed because I listen to podcasts in 1.8 speed. [NS15]

Effects of ASR Transcripts on NNS Behavior

While some NNS also vocalized the detrimental effects of transcript delay and imperfect accuracy, many NNS

_____

[1] All NNS interview quotes are translated from Japanese by the Authors.

expressed the difficulties of focusing on two modalities (audio and ASR transcripts) at the same time. Interestingly, more than half of the NNS participants reported developing some sort of strategy to alleviate the burden of concentrating on the two modalities:

> In normal speed, I found it difficult to listen and read at the same time. So I tried not to look at the transcripts but concentrate on listening. When it came to fast speed, it just became impossible to understand what was said. So I started to read the transcripts. I think it helped a lot. [NNS6]

> In fast speed, I couldn't follow the conversation so I concentrated on reading the transcripts. [NNS4]

While many NNS tried to concentrate on reading the ASR transcripts when catching up to missed conversation, some NNS participants seemed to shift their focus on listening to the speeded up audio only.

> In normal speed, I looked at the transcripts when I missed some words. That was very useful. But in fast speed, I didn't have the time to check the transcripts [even when I missed some parts]. I had to move forward and concentrate on listening [to the speeded up audio only]. [NNS12]

Summary of Findings

Our results suggested that both NNS and NS might benefit from ASR transcripts even with imperfect accuracy and delay during live multiparty audio conferences. Although our results did not reach statistical significance, they indicated a trend that ASR technology might provide additional information about the conversational content for NNS and improve their understanding. Thus, our results complement previous works on the positive effects of text transcripts on NNS comprehension [18, 19, 20, 24] during multiparty audio conferences in their second language [8].

However, much like in previous works [9, 10], the NS participants in our study reported that the imperfect transcript quality combined with 1-3 second delay was distracting. Our experiment did not include interactive aspects between the NNS and NS participants during the audio conference. Thus, the behavioral adjustments that NS speakers might adopt in the presence of NNS receivers were not present in our experimental setting [1, 2, 3, 4], which may have also affected the accuracy of the ASR transcripts [8]. While few NS did find the transcripts helpful when they missed some information, our results beg the question whether the detrimental effects of current ASR technology outweigh the positive effects for NS in live audio conferences.

Our results for using speeded up audio in combination with ASR transcripts to catch up on missed parts of the conversation showed no significant difference compared to speeded up audio only for NNS or NS. This result reflects previous research, where NS reported the imperfect accuracy as a limitation for using only ASR transcripts to catch up on missed conversation [10].

However, NNS adopted an interesting strategy, where they changed their focus from audio to text depending on their ability to follow the speeded up second language speech. When the NNS were unable to adequately comprehend the audio speech in 1.6x speed, they either shifted their focus completely to the ASR transcripts ignoring the speeded up audio [NNS 4, 7] or concentrated on listening to the speeded up audio ignoring the ASR transcripts [NNS12].

This switch between modalities may explain why ASR transcripts did not improve NNS comprehension when catching up. Although some NNS preferred reading the ASR transcripts over listening to the speeded up audio, this does not mean that their reading skill level surpassed their second language listening skills. Some NNS participants were able to compensate their listening skills by reading the ASR transcripts in normal speed [NNS12], which might have helped them improve their comprehension score during the live audio conference.

We wonder whether there is a technical solution to present the ASR transcripts in a way that accommodates the NNS shift in focus between modalities when catching up on missed conversation. One way to accomplish this would be to combine automatic keyword or key phrase extraction methods with ASR technology. As audio conferences are often unstructured, include overlaps between speakers and sudden changes between topics, highlighting the keywords in the transcripts might allow NNS to focus their attention to the key points of the conversation, and better detect sudden topic changes in speeded up audio.

Future Directions
In future studies, we are interested in combining automatic keyword or key phrase extraction with ASR technology to better support NNS when catching up on missed parts of an audio conference with speeded up audio. Secondly, as our experiment did not include interactive aspects between the NNS participants and NS speakers, we are interested in exploring how ASR transcripts combined with keyword extraction might accommodate communication between NNS and NS in multiparty audio conferences. Investigating how speeded up audio and ASR transcripts might help NNS and NS catch up on longer periods of missed conversation would further inform the potential applications of the current technology for audio conferencing systems.

CONCLUSION
We presented a study, where Japanese non-native English speakers (NNS) and native English speakers (NS) participated as passive listeners in an audio conference with three native English speakers. During the audio conference, the participants were briefly distracted and missed parts of the conversation. To catch up on the conversation, the participants used speeded up audio (1.6x) and speeded up

audio with transcripts generated by automated speech recognition (ASR) software to review the missed parts of the audio conference.

Our results indicated that while ASR transcripts might improve NNS comprehension in live multiparty audio conferences, NNS did not benefit from viewing the transcripts when catching up to missed parts of the conversation with speeded up audio. However, ASR transcripts allowed the NNS to shift their focus from audio to text depending on their ability to follow the spoken dialogue in different speeds. This provided an alternative channel for NNS to catch up on the missed conversation when they were unable to follow the second language conversation in speeded up audio.

ACKNOWLEDGMENTS
We would like to extend our gratitude to the NTT development team for their technical support, and to the anonymous reviewers for their invaluable comments.

REFERENCES
1. Bradlow, A. R. and Bent, T. Perceptual adaptation to non-native speech. *Cognition 106, 2* (2008), 707-729.

2. Bradlow, A. R. and Bent, T. The clear speech effect for non-native listeners. *The Journal of the Acoustical Society of America 112* (2002), 272-284.

3. Bradlow, A. R. and Pisoni, D. B. Recognition of spoken words by native and non-native listeners: Talker-, listener-, and item-related factors. *The Journal of the Acoustical Society of America 106* (1999), 2074-2085.

4. Bradlow, A. R., Torretta, G. M. and Pisoni, D. B. Intelligibility of normal speech I: Global and fine-grained acoustic-phonetic talker characteristics. *Speech Communication 20, 3* (1996), 255-272.

5. Christel, M., Winkler, D., Taylor, R. and Smith, M. Evolving video skims into useful multimedia abstractions. In *Proc. CHI 1998,* ACM (1998), 171-178.

6. Dragon Naturally Speaking (DNS): Dragon Solutions Field Report. Full text accessible at: http://www.nuance.com/naturallyspeaking/pdf/wp_DNS _Field_Reporting.pdf.

7. Dunkel, P. Listening in the native and second/foreign language: Toward an integration of research and practice. *Tesol Quarterly 25, 3* (1991), 431-457.

8. Gao, G., Yamashita, N., Hautasaari, A., Echenique A. and Fussell, S. Effects of public vs. private automated transcripts on multiparty communication between native and non-native English speakers. In *Proc. CHI 2014,* ACM (2014), 843-852.

9. Inkpen, K., Hegde, R., Junuzovic, S., Brooks, C., Tang, J.C. and Zhang, Z. AIR Conferencing: Accelerated instant replay for in-meeting multimodal review. In *Proc. MM'10,* ACM (2010), 663-666.

10. Junuzovic, S., Inkpen, K., Hegde, R., Zhang, Z., Tang, J. and Brooks, C. What did I miss? In-meeting review using multimodal accelerated instant replay (AIR) conferencing. In *Proc. CHI 2011*, ACM (2011), 513-522.

11. Kurhila, S. Correction in talk between native and non-native speaker. *Journal of Pragmatics 33, 7* (2001), 1083- 1110.

12. Lafferty, J. C., Eady, P. M. and Elmers, J. The desert survival problem. Plymouth, Michigan. Experimental Learning Methods (1974).

13. Li, N. and Rosson, M. B. At a different tempo: What goes wrong in online cross-cultural group chat? In *Proc. GROUP 2012*, ACM (2012), 145-154.

14. Li, N. and Rosson, M. B. Instant annotation: Early design experiences in supporting cross-cultural group chat. In *Proc. SIGDOC 2012*, ACM (2012), 147-156.

15. Luisa, M., Lecumberri, G., Cooke, M. and Culter, A. Non-native speech perception in adverse conditions: A Review. *Speech Communication 52* (2010), 864-886.

16. Meetings in America V: Meeting of the minds. *An MCI® Executive White Paper*, (2003). Full text at: https://e-meetings.verizonbusiness.com/meetingsin america/pdf/MIA5.pdf (accessed: 25.6.2014).

17. Nabelek, A.K. and Donahue, A.M. Perception of consonants in reverberation by native and non-native listeners. *Journal of Acoustical Society of America 75* (1984), 632-634.

18. Pan, Y., Jiang, D., Picheny, M. and Qin, Y. Effects of real-time transcription on non-native speaker's comprehension in computer-mediated communications. In *Proc. CHI 2009*, ACM (2009), 2353-2356.

19. Pan, Y., Jiang, D., Yao, L., Picheny, M. and Qin, Y. Effects of automated transcription quality on non-native speakers' comprehension in real-time computer-mediated communication. In *Proc. CHI 2010*, ACM (2010), 1725-1734.

20. Shimogori, N., Ikeda, T. and Tsuboi, S. Automatically generated captions: Will they help non- native speakers communicate in English? In Proc. *ICIC 2010*, ACM (2010), 79-86.

21. Tucker, S., Bergam, O., Ramamoorthy, A. and Whittaker S. Catchup: A useful application of time-travel in meetings. In *Proc. CSCW 2010*, ACM (2010), 99-102.

22. Wildemuth, B., Marchionini, G., Yang, M., Geisler, G., Wilkens, T., Hughes, A. and Gruss, R. How fast is too fast? Evaluating fast forward surrogates for digital video. In *Proc. JCDL 2003*, ACM (2003), 221-230.

23. Yamashita, N., Echenique, A., Ishida, T. and Hautasaari, A. Lost in transmittance: How transmission lag enhances and deteriorates multilingual collaboration. In *Proc. CSCW 2013*, ACM (2013), 923-934.

24. Yao, L., Pan, Y. X. and Jiang, D. N. Effects of automated transcription delay on non-native speakers' comprehension in real-time computer-mediated communication. In *Proc. INTERACT 2011*, ACM (2011), 207-214.

25. Yuan, C. W., Setlock, L. D., Cosley, D. and Fussell, S. R. Understanding informal communication in multilingual contexts. In *Proc. CSCW 2013*, ACM (2013), 909-922.

Effects of Video and Text Support on Grounding in Multilingual Multiparty Audio Conferencing

Andy Echenique[1,2], Naomi Yamashita[2], Hideaki Kuzuoka[3] & Ari Hautasaari[2]

[1]University of California, Irvine
Department of Informatics
Irvine, California USA
echeniqa@uci.edu

[2]NTT Communication Science
Labs
Kyoto, JPN
naomiy@acm.org
ari.hautasaari@lab.ntt.org

[3]University of Tsukuba
Faculty of Engineering
Information and Systems
Tsukuba, Ibaraki, JPN
kuzuoka@acm.org

ABSTRACT

With computer-mediated communication (CMC) tools allowing collaborations to span the globe, teams can include multiple collaborators located in different countries. Previous research shows how audio communication supplemented by video conferencing or text transcripts improves conversation grounding between native speakers (NS) and non-native speakers (NNS) in one-on-one multi-lingual collaborations. This research investigates how supplemental cues (video or real-time text transcripts) support NNSs' participation in multiparty audio conferences. We implemented a collaborative grounding task with triad groups of NS and NNS to investigate possible effects. We found that NNSs' task accuracy dropped significantly between video+audio trials. By comparison, NNSs' ability to understand common ground increased over trials in the text transcripts+audio condition. Our results demonstrate the difficulties of common ground establishment for NNS in multiparty collaborations and how the development of supporting tools for multilingual audio conferencing can aid NNSs' communication ability.

Author Keywords: Computer-Mediated Communication; Audio Conferencing; Multilingual Communication; Non-Native Speakers

ACM Classification Keywords
H.5.3 Group and Organization Interface: Computer-supported cooperative work

INTRODUCTION
Audio conferencing is among the most frequently used communication tools in global business and social interactions. It offers a convenient and cost-effective way for multiple collaborators located in different countries and time zones to communicate and contribute to decision-making processes.

Although audio conferencing tools connect distant collaborators, non-native speakers (NNS) experience difficulties when participating in multiparty audio conferences. In particular, audio conferencing tools challenge NNSs' ability to follow the conversation and reply [25]. Imperfect audio conditions (reverberations and extraneous noise) during an audio conference also limit NNSs' ability to perceive speech [14,15]. Furthermore, when NNS try to compensate for the missed information, their ability to think about current conversational content is likely to decline, resulting in an impaired ability to respond [21]. These problems become prominent in multiparty communication with mostly native speakers (NS) because the conversation can move forward rapidly while NNS are left behind [25]. It is therefore necessary for system designers to understand and lessen the burden imposed on NNS in audio conferencing.

The aim of this paper is to investigate what supplemental cues might better support NNSs' participation in multilingual, multiparty audio conferences. Our study is motivated by two sets of previous research. One is how common ground negotiation between NS and NNS improves with the addition of video feed to an audio channel [23]. The second is the use of real-time text transcripts and audio communication and its support of NNS comprehension [17]. Although a text transcript of an audio feed may be redundant for native speakers, it may help the NNS recover from missed information and cues by allowing them to view the conversation in text format. For example, NNS in East Asian countries perform better in reading tasks compared to listening tasks, as the education systems focuses heavily on reading comprehension [21].

Previous research therefore leads us to the following research question: Does adding video or real-time text transcripts to audio conferencing assist non-native speakers negotiate common ground communication with native speakers? With previous studies already identifying how adding text transcripts and video can improve communication between native and non-native English speakers when compared to audio only, we aim to compare these two supplemental communication media. We further investigate how these added cues affect the grounding process between native and non-native speakers in a multiparty group.

We conducted a laboratory experiment investigating two communication media: audio+video and audio+real-time text transcripts. Twelve groups of NS and NNS participants (each group consisting of two NS and one NNS) participated in a tangram-matching task designed to investigate the grounding process of common references among participants.

Building off previous literature supporting the addition of supplemental communication media to audio channels in multilingual collaboration [17, 23], our results suggest that text support (real-time transcripts) in audio conferencing helps NNS retain and repair common ground between the NS and NNS during repeated referential communication. Task results while using video support exhibited a degradation of common ground during continued collaboration. Although both video and text-transcript support have been studied in previous literature, this research will identify how these technologies mediate three person groups and grounding for NNS.

We will discuss the prior research, describe our experimental design, and results. Finally, we conclude with a discussion of our findings and draw design implications for the development of tools to support multilingual audio conferencing.

RELATED WORK

NNS Communication Difficulties during CMC
Computer-mediated communication (CMC) imposes a variety of challenges for non-native speakers (NNS) [16,19,20]. Multiple parallel processes, such as speech recognition, foreign language production, recovering from missed conversational context, and intensive thinking can overwhelm NNS [15,18]. CMC, such as audio conferencing, is susceptible to extraneous noise from multiple sources, which make hearing some utterances difficult and can further impact NNSs' to follow the conversation [14]. In addition to low quality audio signals, problems with participants rapidly advancing the conversation without checking others' understanding also hinder NNS performance [25].

Previous work has attempted to improve audio conferencing for NNS [17,23]. In multiparty settings (more than two collaborators), previous research has also tried to reduce the cognitive load placed on NNS by providing him/her with additional processing time [25] or providing supplemental cues such as text transcripts [7].

Additional Communication Media to Support NNS
Previous research demonstrates how adding additional communication media to audio improves collaboration for NNS. Veinott et al. (1999) found that NNS pairs (in this instance indicating teams of English as a non-primary

language or live in and English speaking country for more than 4 years) can establish common ground more efficiently with video+audio compared to only audio [23]. This finding is further significant given that no difference was seen for NS pairs. NNS pairs also had fewer miscommunications with video+audio compared to only audio [22]. These studies support the use of video, and the non-verbal cues they provide, as assisting NNS during CMC.

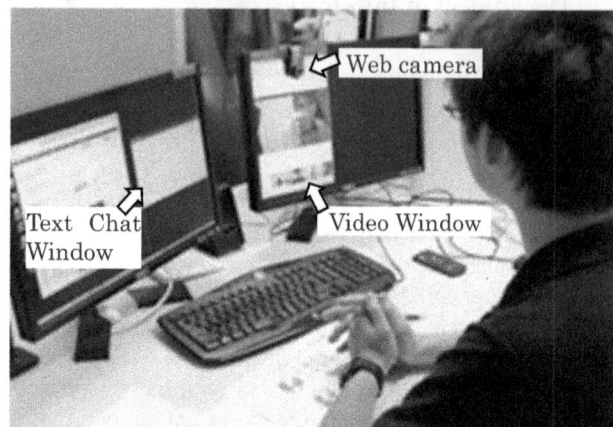

Figure 1. Dual monitor setup with video and text interface during pre-experimental introductions

Augmenting audio communication with additional text transcripts can further aid NNS during computer-mediated communication. Pan et al. (2009) studied the effects of adding text transcripts to audio and audio+video recordings to NNS in a non-interactive setting [17]. Their results show that adding transcripts improved comprehension in both conditions, although performance between audio+video+text transcripts and audio+text transcripts did not differ significantly. Extending these results into an interactive setting, Gao et. al. (2014) investigated how speech-to-text transcripts affected multiparty communication between NS and NNS [7]. Text transcripts increased the NNSs' comprehension, yet the necessity of reading lengthy transcripts with errors imposed a significant burden on NNS. Additionally, imperfect speech-to-text transcript accuracy strongly influenced the comprehension of NNSs.

In sum, prior research suggests that adding video or text transcript to multilingual audio conferencing can improve communication for NNS. Video can provide NNS with non-verbal cues that assist communication. Text transcripts can also increase comprehension, but are susceptible to poor accuracy rates and can place a cognitive load on NNS. Our research extends this previous knowledge by comparing both these supplemental media in a multiparty setting. This comparison furthers our understanding of how CMC mediates multilingual communication and improves or deteriorates NNSs' resulting collaborative capabilities.

Grounding in Computer-Mediated Communication
Grounding is the process by which conversational participants attempts to establish a common, shared

understanding [9]. One way to examine peoples' grounding processes is to examine referential communication where speakers and addressees work together to establish common ground on something in the environment [5]. Once speakers and addressees agree on the perspective included in a common referent (the thing being described), this mapping between the perspective (reference) and the object (referent) indicates that participants have established common ground.

The process of grounding illustrates how the refinement of ideas and perspectives helps collaborators decide on a common language for communication. Once these references are agreed upon, the supporting concepts used to narrow down their meaning are no longer explicitly mentioned. An example is how longer, broader descriptions used to reference an object are later shortened to simple words or phrases when referring back to it. This process is known as lexical entrainment [1]. Studies on referential communication describe how conversational participants entrain towards an expression by abbreviating their referring expressions in repetitive trials. Given the critical nature of conversation grounding in collaboration, this is our core method of evaluating common ground establishment among participants during and after group interaction.

Previous research suggests that participants develop different strategies to effectively build common ground depending on the information available in the medium they are using [26]. NNS who are not fluent in their non-native language have different communication needs than NS, and their grounding process may differ between different media conditions. To enhance multilingual collaborations, it is vital to understand entrainment on a common reference within a group across different communication media.

METHODS

Overview

We investigated how the use of either video+audio (Video condition) or text transcripts+audio (Text condition) impacts conversation grounding between native English speakers (NS) and non-native English speakers (NNS) in a multiparty (triad) collaborative setting. We used a within subjects laboratory experimental design, with each group performing both Video and Text conditions

Participants

Each group consisted of three participants: two native English speakers (NS) and one non-native English speaker (NNS). The NNS in this experiment were Japanese native speakers. None of the NNS participants lived in an English speaking country for more than 2 years. We required all NNS to have a minimum TOEIC[1] English proficiency test

---

[1] TOEIC: Test of English for International Communication (http://www.ets.org/toeic). TOEIC score of 550 is about the

score of 550. Overall, 12 groups participated (24 NS and 12 NNS) in total.

Task and Experiment Design

Tangram-matching tasks are frequently used to study common ground establishment in laboratory settings (e.g., [26]). In a tangram-matching task, participants are instructed to arrange an identical set of tangram figures (black polygon silhouettes) into matching orders. In our study, we assigned one participant the role of Leader and gave them a set of numbered figures in a predetermined order during each trial. The remaining participants, Followers, were given the same figures in random orders (i.e. each tangram was assigned a different number and serial order than that of the Leader) (Figure 2). We instructed the Leader to assist the Followers in matching the tangrams with the same numbers as are on his/her sheet.

Participants performed two tangram-matching trials during each condition to examine lexical entrainment of common references. Task sheets used between the first and second trial had an identical, but differently ordered, set of tangrams. A NS was always assigned as the Leader and a Follower (NS Follower). The NNS are always the second Follower (NNS Follower). Once assigned, roles stay consistent for the entirety of the experiment. We counterbalanced condition order across groups, with six groups performing the Video condition first and six groups completing the Text condition first. Participants would thus perform two tangram-matching trials in two conditions for a total of four tangram-matching trials performed over the course of the study.

In the Video condition, we provided a video feed showing each participant's face and upper torso to the other participants (Figure 1, only the right-side screen was used and left-side screen was turned off). Participants were not allowed to use the video feature show their task sheets or illustrations to their collaborators. In the Text condition, we provided a text chat window where participants can type direct transcripts and keywords during the task (Figure 1, right-side screen was turned off and only the left-side screen was used).

In the Text condition, we asked participants to type down the keywords or essential parts of their own utterances in a text window. Previous research demonstrates how imperfect text transcripts can increase NNS burden and impair comprehension and performance [7]. In order to maximize the positive effects of text support on NNS grounding and comprehension, we opted to use this participant-entered text input rather than imperfect transcripts, even though it may impose a burden on the NS participants. We believe that ASR and keyword extraction techniques may be used as a substitute for human-entered

---

average level of Japanese university students (TOEIC Program 2012 Data Analysis)

transcripts in the future when they reach sufficiently high accuracy. Thus, our experimental setting mimics future technological systems where speech-to-text software and conversation semantic analysis becomes highly sophisticated.

Materials and Equipment

Tangram-matching task sheets. During each trial, participants received a paper task sheet with 10 tangrams. Each sheet included the same tangrams, but in a different serial order. Only the Leader's tangram sheet contained a number above each tangram (Figure 2).

Video and Text interface. We seated each participant in front of a dual monitor setup (Figure 1) in separate rooms. The right screen displayed the video conferencing interface and the left displayed the text interface. The experiment organizers turned on only the relevant screen for each experimental condition (Video: right screen only, Text: left screen only).

We used Google Hangouts[2] to transmit audio in both conditions and video in the Video condition. We positioned the web cameras so that only participants' upper torso and face were captured. Each participant's video feed was visible on the bottom of the screen. As they talked, each participant's video feed was displayed in the large window on Google Hangouts interface.

Google Talk was used during the Text condition. The text chat window was adjusted to same size as the video window (Figure 1).

Tangram Common Reference Survey. After performing each tangram-matching task, we handed all participants a separate sheet of paper with a picture of each tangram used during the task. We asked participants to write down the common references and/or keyword used during the task. Each participant completed the Survey individually without access to any materials including notes and chat logs.

Procedure

We divided the study into three portions: self-introductions, the first condition and the second condition. At the beginning of the experiment, we turned on both displays and participants stated their name, where they are from, and typed their name into the text chat. Following the self-introductions, the experiment organizers turned off the monitor not relevant to the first condition.

In both the Video and Text conditions, participants completed an initial training trial with five tangrams to familiarize themselves with the tangram-matching task and the communication media. After the training task, the participants completed the first task of the main tangram-matching task with 10 tangrams (Trial 1). There was no time limit set for the task completion.

[2] http://www.google.com/hangouts/

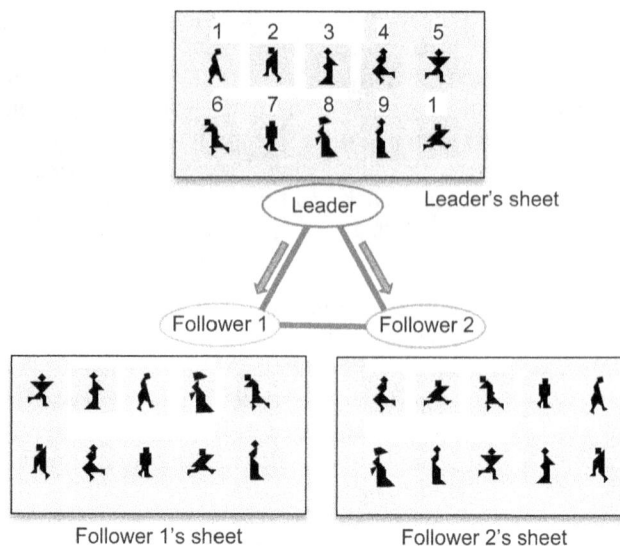

Figure 2. Diagram of experimental material setup.

After the first trial, we asked participants to complete a Tangram Common Reference Survey. After writing down the common references, the experiment organizers distributed the tangram-matching sheets for Trial 2. For trials 1 and 2, the same tangrams were used, but in a different serial position on the page and with different numbers. After completing the second trial, the participants again filled in a common reference survey.

Once two trials were finished in the first condition, the experiment organizers switched the displays and distributed the training task for the second condition. The remainder of the experiment followed the same pattern with different tangram-matching sheets (different tangrams) used for each condition. Each condition thus consists of two trials, which we label according the communication media and which trial order it is. Thus, Video is split between Video 1 and Video 2 and Text contains Text 1 and Text 2. The tangram-matching sheets assigned to each condition were counterbalanced.

Measures

The measures used will be detailed and discussed as they relate to our findings.

Task performance. We measured each Follower's task performance by how accurately they completed each tangram-matching task (i.e., the number of correctly matched tangrams according to the Leader's tangram sheet). This score acts as an indication of how successfully common ground was achieved between the Leader and Followers.

Non-verbal gestures. We videotaped the conversations with the same web camera used in the Video condition, which was placed between both screens. We analyzed the video data to understand of how participants used non-verbal gestures during the grounding process in a multilingual multiparty group. For non-verbal gestures in this study, we focused on hand gestures and body gestures directly relevant to the task and used to create common ground between participants.

NNSs' Missed References The Tangram Common Reference Survey responses indicated whether participants share a common reference (or expression/word) to identify each tangram during each trial. This is accomplished by comparing each participant's referring expressions of the same referent (tangram). As we are interested in NNSs' difficulties during the lexical entrainment process, we focused on instances where both NS used the same common reference yet the NNS did not. First, we excluded the tangrams for which NS Followers and Leaders did not have the same common reference. From this corpus, we calculated the percentages of the tangrams that the NNS did not report the same reference. This measure represents the percent of missed references the NNS failed to acknowledge, represented by a number between 0 and 1. 1 indicates 100% of the NNSs' Tangram Common Reference Survey references did not match those of the NS and 0 indicates that NNS missed no common references.

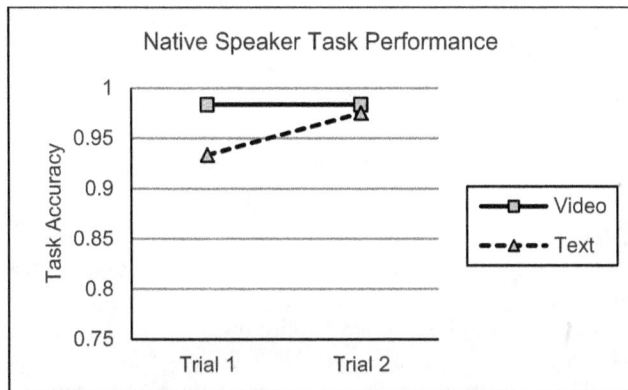

Figure 3. Native speaker task accuracy (1 indicating 100% task accuracy)

RESULTS
Our results measure how lexical entrainment and grounding between two NS (a leader and a follower) and NNS (a follower) is impacted by the two conditions: audio+video (Video) and audio+text transcripts (Text).

First, we present the task performance results, followed by an analysis of the non-verbal gestures and NNSs' Missed References, which speak to the lexical entrainment of common references. These results indicate how supplementary communication channels (Video or Text) support NNS in multiparty, multilingual communication.

Task Performance
We scored each Follower's tangram-matching sheet on how accurately participants assigned each tangram the same number as on the Leader's sheet. These scores range from 0 to 1, with 1 representing a perfect match and 0 indicating that no tangrams were assigned the same number. We used a Wilcoxon Signed Ranked test to compare our results due

to the nonparametric nature and within subject design of our study.

The results for the NS follower indicate a strong ceiling effect. As Figure 3 shows, Trial 1 performance on both the Video and Text conditions were close to perfect, with an average accuracy of 0.98 on Video 1 and 0.93 on Text 1. These averages were not statistically different (p = 0.18, Z = -1.3). Trial 2 scores also indicated a strong ceiling effect, with Video 2 performance averaging at 0.98 and 0.98 for Text 2. Differences between these scores were also not statistically significant (p=0.32, Z = -1.0).

We compared Trial 1 and Trial 2 performance to investigate the possible interaction between the continued use of a communication channel and common ground establishment. Comparisons between Video 1 and Video 2 demonstrated no statistical difference (p = 1.0, Z = 0.00). A similar trend was present between Text 1 and Text 2, with no statistical difference observed (p = 0.10, Z = -1.6). These results indicate that NS had little difficulty with the task and that the supplemental communication media had little effect on their task performance.

For the NNS, communication media did have a noticeable effect on task performance (Figure 4). Although there was no difference when comparing Video and Text trials of the same order, comparison between Trials 1 and Trials 2 did indicate one of the communication media as detrimental during continued use.

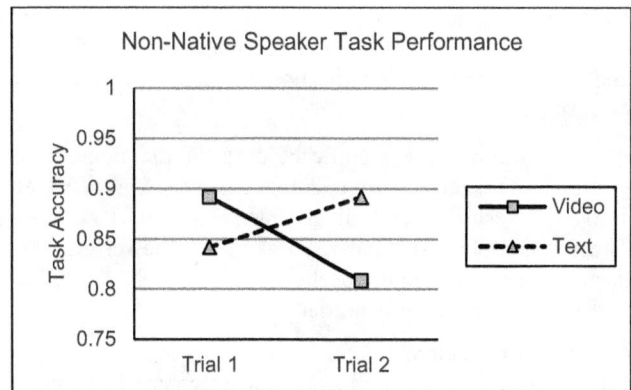

Figure 4. Non-native speaker task accuracy (1 indicating 100% task accuracy)

Comparisons between NNSs' Video and Text resulted in no statistical difference between their performances: Video 1 and Text 1 (0.89 and 0.84 respectively) show no difference in performance (p = 0.55, Z = -0.60); Video 2 and Text 2 accuracy (0.81 and 0.89 respectively) were also not statistically different (p = 0.23, Z = -1.2). However, comparisons between Trials 1 and 2 did show Video having a strong effect on performance. Video 2 indicated a statistically significant drop in performance relative to Video 1 (p = 0.04 Z = -2.4). Interestingly, this drop is only seen in the Video condition and not found in the Text condition - in fact, performance seemed to improve slightly in the Text condition although the improvement was not statistically significant (p = 0.34, Z = -0.95).

The drop in performance for the NNS in the Video condition indicates two possible difficulties for completing the Tangram task. First is that there may be less information (non-verbal gestures) provided by the leader through video channel in the second trial. Another possibility is NS Leaders may have assumed that NNS achieved common ground and removed descriptive phrases before grounding was achieved. This process will be visible through analysis of the commonality of the NS and NNSs' Survey answers. Our subsequent analysis will focus on investigating these possibilities.

Video Task Gestures

During the Video condition, the video channel was mainly used for providing supplemental non-verbal information. This information is normally provided by the Leader to clarify or provide further details on how a tangram looked or details that differentiate similar Tangrams. An example is the following excerpt:

> *Leader: Number 4, it's almost like he has a big martini glass (pretends to hold martini glass). He's relaxing, having a drink. Or maybe he's holding some 'ramen' (pretends to hold bowl of soup next to face)."*

For the NNS, such gestures seemed useful, resulting in high task performance in the first trial (Figure 4). Yet given the drop in task performance between the first and second Video conditions, a comparison was made between the number of hand and body gestures made during Video 1 and Video 2 for possible indications of its use effecting task performance.

As we speculated, a significant drop in the number of gestures was detected, from 33.4 gestures per trial in Video 1 to 19.4 gestures per trial in Video 2 (p <0.01, Z=2.8). These results show that native speakers used fewer gestures during repeated communication, affecting NNSs' task performance on subsequent trials.

Common References

We analyzed the Tangram Common Reference Surveys in order to identify how each supplemental media allowed NNS to detect the common reference after each trial. This measure indicates each participant's retention of the common reference for each tangram used during the trial. When some members during collaboration achieve a basis of communication via these references, yet others do not, it can imply misunderstandings or communication difficulties for some participants. From this data, we calculated the ratio of tangrams for which the NNS and NSs (NS leader and NS follower) did not achieve the same level of lexical entrainment. A lower number (0 being the lowest) indicates that the NNS missed fewer common references shared between the NS leader and the NS Follower, thus a lower ratio being a sign of better grounding.

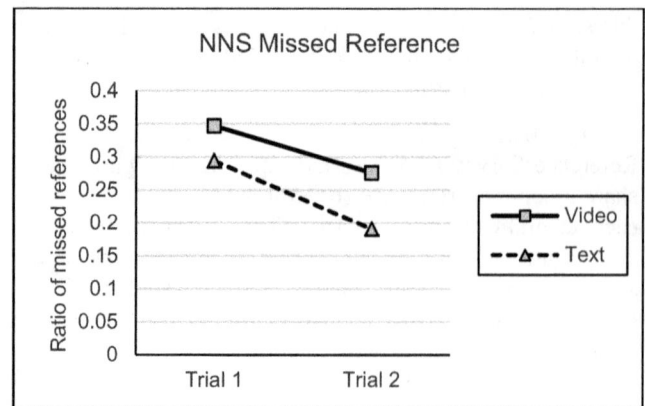

Figure 5. Non-native speaker Missed Reference (0 indicating no missed references)

While we found a consistent trend in NNS missing fewer references in the Text condition, the differences were not significant: the difference of average NNS Missed References scores between Video 1 (0.35) and Text 1 (0.29) were not significantly different (p = 0.50, Z=-0.67). We found the same between Video 2 (0.28) and Text 2 (0.19) (p = 0.20, Z = -1.3).

Trial order again had a strong effect on the survey results. While NNS Missed References in Video 1 and Video 2 showed no significant difference (p = 0.14, Z = -1.5), NNS Missed References significantly decreased from Text 1 to Text 2 (p < .05, Z = -2.7).

These findings indicate that as groups continue collaborating on a second trial, Text transcripts assist NNS in repairing misunderstood common references. For example, if both Leader and NS Follower labeled a tangram as "hawk" during Trial 1, yet NNS Follower labeled it as "owl", a misunderstanding is apparent on NNSs' part. In Trial 2, this misunderstanding is more likely repaired by the NNS when using supplemental real-time text transcripts. Thus as the groups collaborate, Text transcripts are more effective at repairing common ground misunderstandings.

DISCUSSION

Our results present three findings:

1. Non-native English speaker's (NNS) ability to match referents with common references (ground) diminished between Video 1 and Video 2.

2. Native speaker leader (NS Leader) reduced the amount of non-verbal gestures provided between Video 1 and Video 2.

3. NNSs' number of Missed References decreased between Text 1 and Text 2 (ability to detect common references increased).

These findings suggest two factors affecting communication for NNS. The first is the differences between NS and NNS in establishing and retaining common ground through repeated communication (trials 1 and 2) as seen through task performance. The second is how computer-mediation mitigates these differences in common ground establishment.

Differences in Common Ground Establishment between NS and NNS

Our findings highlight the differences between NS and NNS in establishing common ground, especially during repeated, multiparty collaboration. As demonstrated in Figure 3, NS had little trouble completing the tasks accurately with either supplemental communication medium throughout the experiment. Our results supports previous findings [19], demonstrating NSs' comprehension during audio conferencing as not changing significantly with the addition of supplemental communication media. Between the NS leader and NS Follower, common ground was established easily and confidently within the first trial.

The ease with which both NS established common ground likely influenced Leader's to reduce non-verbal gestures during repeated Video trials (Video 2), as seen in our results. Communication between NS became more efficient and less supporting information was provided. In some cases, NS Followers even notified Leaders that they don't need clarification, and dissuaded them from doing so:

> Leader: John, you're fine?
>
> NS Follower: Yeah, I'm good. If I have a question, I'll let you know.

This process was not specific to our study, as lexical entrainment and refining of established phrases or references during collaboration is a common behavior associated with establishing common ground [16,26]. Even with this reduction of non-verbal information, NS Followers' task performance was still consistent.

NNSs' results demonstrate that common ground is not as easily attained for them. The reduction in tangram-matching task performance seen in our study reflects a weak common ground understanding for NNS. The reduction of Leader's non-verbal gestures likely had a large effect on NNSs' Video 2 task performance results, with NS not acknowledging the status of the NNS Follower's understanding and the value of non-verbal gestures for NNS. NS Leaders may also have overestimated NNSs' level of understanding, and expected verbal feedback when common ground was not reached. Thus, just as the NS follower's silence indicated understanding, the same may not have been the same for NNS. The combined effect of NS Leader's lack of awareness of NNSs' imperfect understanding as well as the positive reinforcement for streamlined communication from the NS Follower demonstrate how multiparty settings further tax NNS in multilingual communications.

Communication Media and Common Ground Establishment for NNS

Communication media also had a strong effect on common ground establishment, as seen in our analysis of the Video and Text condition results. During repeated trials, continued use of Video as a supplemental communication media resulted in a reduction in common ground establishment. By comparison, the ratio of NNSs' missed references improved between Text 1 and Text 2. These results illustrates that even when common ground is not perfectly attained in the first trial (i.e. succeed in identifying the same tangram but having different references), Text transcripts may help NNS achieve common ground in subsequent trials by repeatedly and visually showing the key referring expressions. By doing so, NNS repair their references to the same reference shared among other NS members. Text may thus be a more robust supplemental communication media compared to Video during repeated collaboration.

Design Implications

The findings and discussion from our study support the implementation of instant messaging and text transcriptions for NNS collaborating with two or more NS. Especially if the collaboration is intended to extend beyond a single interaction among collaborators, Text is expected to provide continued benefits to the group. Given our use of a grounding task, our findings also demonstrate how negotiating common ground is affected by the use of these supplemental communication media. This understanding of how common ground is achieved, maintained, or deteriorated through Text or Video has significant implications for their efficiency and use in communication.

A technological implementation that would extend this work would be to automate text chat creation. During our study, in order to ensure accuracy, we asked NS to write down keywords. Automating this process may reduce the cognitive load on NS during the task. Allowing NS to edit and correct erroneously transcripts produced by ASR technology may also further the accuracy of this type of implementation.

Our research also hints at the beneficial aspects of combining Video and Text transcripts. During Video 1, task accuracy was similar to those of Text, indicating that the non-verbal gestures provided through video channel were useful for NNS. As the drop in NNS task performance in Video 2 coincided with a reduction of gestures, combining the additional cues Video provided in a persistent and reviewable manner would likely help NNS. This can be implemented by allowing the recording of gestures over video as they are performed. Recorded video gestures can then be tagged with a keyword (much like our Text condition). This allows for easier reference in the future and allows the supplemental visual information to be completely preserved.

CONCLUSION AND FUTURE WORK

Our research extends previous research in computer-mediated multilingual collaboration by providing a comparison of supplemental real-time transcripts or video conferencing when used alongside audio communication in a multiparty context. This study describes some of the methods in which each of these communication media mitigate common ground establishment for NNS. Video conferencing, though initially effective at negotiating common ground, is suspect to a decrease in task performance during repeated trials. Real-time text transcripts, conversely, are better at assisting NNS in repairing common references as displayed through common reference analysis during a second trial. Thus, Text and Video may affect NNS differently, yet Text seems to be a better supplemental communication media over repeated collaborations.

Our results thus pose two considerations for computer-mediation in multilingual, multiparty collaboration. The first is that NS and NNS do not build, repair, or attend to common ground in the same way. As seen in previous research, NNS are frequently faced with considerable difficulties in distance communication. When collaborating in larger groups, NNS' communication abilities are further taxed and their necessity for repair may go unnoticed.

The second consideration is how communication media mitigate communication difficulties, such as a lack of common ground. Repeated collaboration relies heavily on a firm foundation of common terms to ease communication. Video conferencing, due to an observed reduction in the necessary support information NNS need, significantly affects NNSs' communicative capabilities. By comparison, text transcripts are a more recognizable and comprehensible supplemental communication medium for NNS, and assist in keeping performance consistent and even promote common ground repair over time.

Future work should elaborate on how much detail Text should contain in order to be effective for the NNS during the collaboration. Given that the text chat in our study did not provide a detailed transcription of the audio, understanding how varying levels of detail in the text chat affects collaboration would give further insight to its use. In addition, text chat in our study was sourced from participants. Future work may compare text selected by the collaborators or by an automated process (such as transcripts and keywords automatically generated and extracted by the system). We believe that these results highlight non-native speakers' difficulties in multiparty CMC and how communication media can aid and advance collaboration.

ACKNOWLEDGMENTS

The authors would like to thank the support and assistance from all the members of the NTT Communication Science Laboratory, who have been tremendous partners over the course of the project. We would also like to thank the anonymous reviewers for their feedback and time.

REFERENCES

1. Brennan, S.E. Lexical entrainment in spontaneous dialogue. In *Proc. International Symposium on Spoken Dialogue* 1996, Acoustical Society of Japan (1996), 41-44.

2. Broadbent, D. Perception and communication. Oxford: Pergamon (1958).

3. Cho, H., Ishida, T., Yamashita, N., Koda, T. and Takasaki, T. Human detection of cultural differences in pictogram interpretations. In *Proc. IWIC 2009*, ACM (2009), 165–174.

4. Clark, H.H. and Marshall, C.E. Definite reference and mutual knowledge. In *Joshi, A.K., Webber, B.L and I. A. Sag, L.A. (eds.) Elements of discourse understanding*, Cambridge University Press (1981), 10-63.

5. Clark, H.H. and Wilkes-Gibbs, D. Referring as a collaborative process. *Cognition 22* (1986), 1-39.

6. Diamant, E.I., Fussell, S.R. and Lo,F.-L. Collaborating across cultural and technological boundaries: Team culture and information use in a map navigation task. In *Proc. IWIC 2009*, ACM (2009), 175–184.

7. Gao, G., Yamashita, N., Hautasaari, A., Echenique, A., and Fussell, S., Effects of public vs. private automated transcripts on multiparty communication between native and non-native English speakers. In *Proc. CHI '14*, ACM (2014).

8. Hirai, A. The relationship between listening and reading rates of Japanese EFL learners. *The Modern Language Journal 83, 3* (1999), 367-384.

9. Isaacs, E. and Clark, H.H. References in conversation between experts and novices. *Experimental Psychology, 16, 1* (1987), 26-37.

10. Jensen, C., Farnham, S.D., Drucker, S.M. and Kollock, P. The effect of communication modality on cooperation in online environments. In *Proc. CHI 2000*, ACM (2000), 470–477.

11. Koschmann, T., and LeBaron, C.D. Reconsidering common ground: Examining Clark's contribution theory in the OR. In *Proc. ECSCW 2003*, Kluwer Academic Publishing (2003), 81-98.

12. Krauss, R.M. and Weinheimer, S. Changes in reference phases as a function of frequency of usage in social interaction: A preliminary study. *Psychonomic Science 1* (1964), 113-114.

13. Li, Y., Li, H., Mädche, A. and Rau, P-L. P. Are you a trustworthy partner in a cross-cultural virtual environment?: Behavioral cultural intelligence and receptivity-based trust in virtual collaboration. In *Proc. ICIC 2012*, ACM (2012), 87–96.

14. Luisa, M., Lecumberri, G., Cooke, M. and Culter, A. Non-native speech perception in adverse conditions: A Review. *Speech Communication, 52* (2010), 864-886.

15. Nabelek, A.K. and Donahue, A.M. Perception of consonants in reverberation by native and non-native listeners. *Journal of Acoustical Society of America, 75* (1984), 632-634.

16. Olson, G.M. and Olson, J.S. Distance matters. *Human-Computer Interaction 15* (2000), 139-179.

17. Pan, Y., Jiang, D., Picheny, M. and Qin, Y. Effects of real-time transcription on non-native speaker's comprehension in computer-mediated communications. In *Proc. CHI 2009*, ACM (2009), 2353–2356.

18. Rogers, C., Lister, J., Febo, D., Besing, J. and Abrams, H. Effects of bilingualism, noise and reverberation on speech perception by listeners with normal hearing. *Applied Psycholinguistics, 27* (2006), 465-485.

19. Setlock, L.D., Fussell, S.R. and Neuwirth, C. Taking it out of context: Collaborating within and across cultures in face-to-face settings and via instant messaging. In *Proc. CSCW 2004*, ACM (2004), 604-613.

20. Setlock, L.D., Fussell, S.R., Ji, E. and Culver, M. Sorry to interrupt: Asian media preferences in cross-cultural collaborations. In *Proc. IWIC 2009*, ACM (2009), 309–312.

21. Takano, Y. & Noda, A. A temporary decline of thinking ability during foreign language processing. *Journal of Cross-Cultural Psychology, 24* (1993), 445-462.

22. Veinott, E.S., Olson, J.S., Olson, G.M. and Fu, X. Video matters!: When communication ability is stressed, video helps. In *Proc. CHI EA 1997*, ACM (1997), 315–316.

23. Veinott, E.S., Olson, J., Olson, G.M. and Fu, X. Video helps remote work: Speakers who need to negotiate common ground benefit from seeing each other. In *Proc. CHI 1999*, ACM (1999), 302–309.

24. Wang, H-C. and Fussell, S.R. Cultural adaptation of conversational style in intercultural computer-mediated group brainstorming. In *Proc. IWIC 2009*, ACM (2009), 317–320.

25. Yamashita, N., Echenique, A., Ishida, T. and Hautasaari, A. Lost in transmittance: How transmission lag enhances and deteriorates multilingual collaboration. In *Proc. CSCW 2013*, ACM (2013), 923-934.

26. Yamashita, N., Inaba, R., Kuzuoka, H. and Ishida, T. Difficulties in establishing common ground in multiparty groups using machine translation. In *Proc. CHI 2009*, ACM (2009), 679–688.

Promoting Intercultural Awareness through Native-to-Foreign Speech Accent Conversion

Takeshi Nishida

Graduate School of Intercultural
Studies, Kobe University
1-2-1 Tsurukabuto, Nada-ku
Kobe, Hyogo, JAPAN
tnishida@people.kobe-u.ac.jp

Abstract

Large difference in pronunciation between languages
often causes technical and mental difficulty in listening
comprehension as well as in speech production. In
spite of the rationale provided for native speakers to
support non-native speakers in international contexts,
negative reactions to foreign accents are common. To
promote intercultural awareness in communication, we
implemented a prototype system to convert native
speech to have a foreign accent by combining speech
recognition and text-to-speech engines.

Author Keywords

Intercultural awareness, accent conversion.

Introduction

Japanese people tend to be described as having serious
trouble in English conversation, and difference in
pronunciation has been considered to be one of the
major obstacles in acquiring conversation skills.
Listening to and imitating native speech has been a
longtime custom in language learning; however, this is
questioned by researchers, reporting that only a small
minority acquires accent comparable to native-speakers,
and others just lose motivation to language learning [2].

Usage Scenarios 1:
Listening support for NNS

N2F accent conversion can be
used to support NNS in
conversation with NS. As
well as making it technically
easier to comprehend what
natives are saying, sharing
the same accent can take off
embarrassment and pressure
to speak in a foreign accent.

We expect the following two
styles for this application: the
press-to-talk style and the
hearing-aid style. Hearing-aid
style would be more difficult
to implement, since utterance
detection and accent
conversion has to work
accurately in real-time.

N2F accent conversion is also
appropriate for foreign
language learning just as the
training wheels for bicycles.
For this purpose, we should
consider ways to support
taking the training wheels off
later, for example by features
to gradually reduce the level
of accent conversion.

Usage Scenarios 2:
Cultural shock experience for NS

N2F accent conversion can provide NS the opportunity to compare international communication with their own accent and with an accent similar to the person he/she is communicating with. Through this shocking experience of accented speech comprehended better than the original speech, people can feel and learn that "natural English" is not necessarily the only best language, and hopefully improve their attitude toward intercultural communication.

N2F conversion can also be used for listening practice of foreign-accented English. Expecting NS to understand accented speech should be a more realistic goal than to expect NNS to speak in native-level accent.

While on the other hand, more people worldwide come to speak English with various accents, which is referred to as "World English." We believe that this provides a strong rationale for "natives" to show willingness to compromise on accented speech and share more burden in communication. Quite a few native speakers actually show willingness to compromise on foreign accents; however, negative reactions to foreign accents are common and deep-rooted [1, 4].

To fill this cultural gap between native speakers (NS) and non-native speakers (NNS) and promote intercultural awareness in communication, we propose to convert native speech to foreign accented speech. This native-to-foreign (N2F) speech accent conversion can make NNS concentrate better on expressing their thoughts during conversation, since it is often easier for them to comprehend utterances similar to their own accent [2]. Moreover, NNS may feel easier to speak if same accent is shared within the group. It can also help NS get rid of their preconceived notions about "natural speech" and enhance their tolerance to accented speech, through experiences where accented speech is comprehended better than their own speech.

Prototype Implementation

We implemented a prototype to explore the possibilities of N2F accent conversion. It works similarly to voice translation applications; users press a button before start talking, and after the user finishes a phrase, the system plays accent converted speech.

Conversion Methods

Speech recognition (SR) and text-to-speech (TTS) are used to convert native speech to foreign accented

speech[1]. Converted speech will be played immediately after the input using an ordinary Windows laptop.

We implemented two conversion modes which combine the two engines in a different way. In the first mode (Figure 1), speech accent is converted by having Japanese TTS read out the recognized English text. Resulting speech sounds like a novice English speaking Japanese person pronouncing the phrase word-by-word. We expect that converting to other foreign accents is also possible by using TTS of other languages.

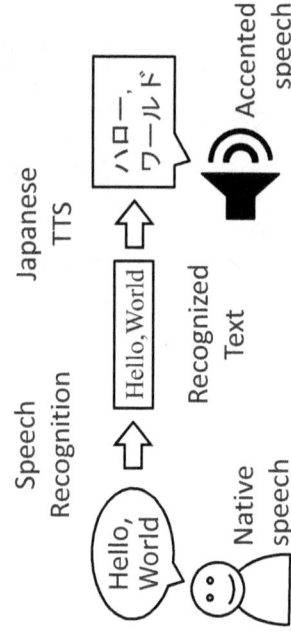

Figure 1. (N2F conversion mode 1) Accent converted by English speech recognition + Japanese TTS.

However, some words will not be pronounced correctly (not like Japanese nor English-native), probably due to the dictionary used to read non-Japanese word with the Japanese TTS.

Conversion mode 2 uses the recognized phonetic symbols instead of text. In this mode, accent is converted by applying string replacement rules to the

---

[1] We used SR and TTS engine for Microsoft Windows.

Usage Scenarios 3: Contribution balancing in large group meeting

Even for people with sufficient language skills in one-to-one or small group setting, multiparty communication is difficult, where prompt response is required for taking turns among NS. This often results in imbalanced contribution between NS/NNS [6].

N2F converted accent at group meetings can help balance the contributions; because effort to comprehend others' speech will be balanced, and sharing the accent can make NNS feel free from worries regarding their own accents.

Real-time speech detection is not strictly required for this setting because we can expect per-participant microphones with a push-to-talk button. However, accent conversion has to work in nearly real-time to be used in meetings, otherwise it will slow down the meeting too severely.

(conversion mode 1). Speed of the output speech can be configured in two different ways: the speech speed slider control and the word-by-word checkbox.

recognized phonetic symbols and reading out the phonetic symbols using TTS. SR may still have unknown words problems but the conversion works reasonably well for phonetically close guesses.

The second mode allows more precise control on the conversion; for example, "replace R with L" rule can be emitted for people capable of discriminating those two consonants. In addition, the second mode allows the use of English or even TTS of any other languages for accent conversion. For example, speech converted using English TTS sounds like an English native person trying to imitate the pronunciation of a novice English speaking Japanese. We expect that converting to other accents is possible similarly.

One of the major problem of the both modes is that they also convert the voice. We believe that this can be solved by using voice conversion methods.

User Interface

Figure 2 shows the screenshot of the application we implemented to support various type of experiments and real situations. The window consists of conversion parameter setting (upper-left), input selection (lower-left), and recognition history list (right). The prototype supports both real-time input from microphone and input from recorded audio file.

The prototype can handle different input accents of English such as British or American and languages other than English by selecting an appropriate SR engine. Conversion mode 2 is used when "Japanizer" is checked, then TTS engine of any available language can be used for conversion. Japanese TTS has to be selected for conversion without the Japanizer

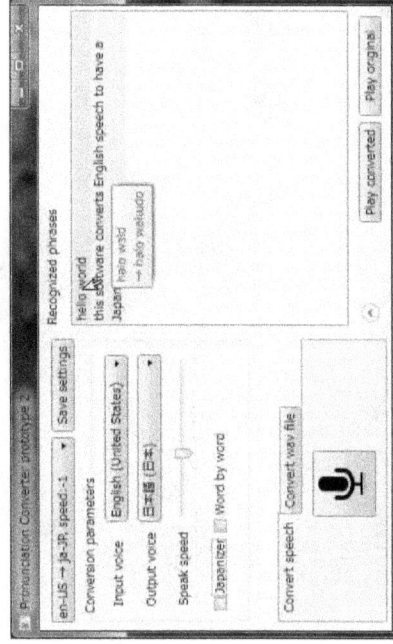

Figure 2. Screenshot of the prototype application.

SR results in text will be displayed on the right side. Users can check the phonetic symbols before and after conversion in the popup. Clicking an item will replay the accent-converted speech. This enables us to easily compare resulting speech by different conversion parameter, and to compare N2F conversion with other supportive methods, for example showing recognized text of what is being said.

Related Work

Previous work has examined multilingual collaboration mediated by a text-chat system equipped with machine translation [7, 8]. Variety of voice translation apps are ready for end-users, where users can speak in their mother tongue to generate translated speech. However, difficulty of multilingual communication remains since even the most accurate systems not infrequently make

Early User Feedback

We collected early feedback from users of various backgrounds, after playing with the prototype: Japanese university students, a native English speaker teaching English conversation at a Japanese university, and Chinese student studying as foreign students in Japan.

All users commented that the accent-converted speech by the first conversion mode simply using Japanese TTS, definitely sounds like a novice English speaking Japanese person. Users also agreed that the speech converted by the second mode was Japanese accented as well, but more difficult to comprehend.

The native English teacher suggested the use of accent conversion software in her English conversation class as an ice-breaker tool.

translation errors. Errors are inherent in N2F accent conversion as well; however, accent conversion errors can be infrequent and less fatal than translation errors. It can produce a phonetically close speech even if the speech recognition fails.

Audio processing technologies has been used to support second language learning mainly by voice conversion, based on the knowledge that imitating speech of their own voice with native accent helps to improve speaking and listening skills [3]. Not as much work has been done on speech accent conversion, and all of them were attempts to generate native-like speech [3].

Simply slowing down the speech or showing recognized text can largely support NNS. In addition, using systems such as Speech Repair [5] to correct speech recognition errors by hand, can resolve the difficulty of using error-prone systems. Yamashita et al. proposed to add artificial lags of 0.2-0.4 seconds only to the channels between NS, to make extra time for NNS to cut into multiparty discussion [6]. N2F conversion also puts extra obstacle to NS, but in a more noticeable way, to bring out gentleness from NS.

Future Directions

Experiments on both NS and NNS are required to examine in detail the effects of N2F accent conversion in listening comprehension and in communication. We would also like to explore N2F accent conversion by direct audio processing, to achieve better accuracy, to convert in real-time, and to maintain voice identity. Based on the work, we will conduct studies on practical systems to support non-native of speakers of English in international communication, and provide cultural shocking experience to native English speakers.

Acknowledgements

This work was supported by JSPS KAKENHI Grant Number 26870362.

References

1. Derwing, T. M. and Munro, M. J. Accent, intelligibility, and comprehensibility: evidence from four L1s. *Studies in second language acquisition*, 19(01):1-16, 1997.

2. Derwing, T. M. and Munro, M. J. Second Language Accent and Pronunciation Teaching: A Research-Based Approach. *TESOL Quarterly*, 39(3):379-397, 2005.

3. Felps, D., Bortfeld, H., and Gutierrez-Osuna, R. Foreign accent conversion in computer assisted pronunciation training. *Speech Communication*, 51(10):920-932, 2009.

4. Munro, M. J. A Primer on Accent Discrimination in the Canadian Context. *TESL Canada Journal*, 20(2):38-51, 2003.

5. Ogata, J. and Goto, M. Speech Repair: Quick Error Correction Just by Using Selection Operation for Speech Input Interface. In *Proc. Eurospeech '05*, pp. 133-136, 2005.

6. Yamashita, N., Echenique, A., Ishida, T., and Hautasaari, A. Lost in transmittance: how transmission lag enhances and deteriorates multilingual collaboration. In *Proc. CSCW '13*, 923-934. ACM, 2013.

7. Yamashita, N., Inaba, R., Kuzuoka, H., and Ishida, T. Difficulties in establishing common ground in multiparty groups using machine translation. In *Proc. CHI '09*, 679-688. ACM, 2009.

8. Yamashita, N., and Ishida, T. Effects of machine translation on collaborative work. In *Proc. CSCW '06*, 515-524. ACM, 2006.

Comparison on Negative Attitude toward Robots and Related Factors between Japan and the UK

Tatsuya Nomura

Department of Media Informatics,
Ryukoku University

1-5, Yokotani, Seta-ohe-cho,
Otsu, Shiga 520-2194, Japan

nomura@rins.ryukoku.ac.jp

Abstract

As one of further researches on cross-cultural comparison on attitudes toward robots, an online survey was conducted in Japan and the UK, using the Negative Attitudes toward Robots Scale and items on perceptions of the relation to the family and commitment to religions. The results found some differences on the attitudes between the nations and age groups, and correlations between the attitudes, perceptions of the relation to the family, and commitment to religions only in specific nation and age groups.

Author Keywords

Attitudes toward robots; perceptions of the relation to the family; commitment to religions; age

ACM Classification Keywords

H.1.2 [User/Machine Systems]: Human factors

Introduction

Negative Attitudes toward Robots Scale (NARS) is a psychological scale to measure humans' attitudes toward robots, that is, psychological states reflecting opinions that people ordinarily have about robots [3]. Since the development of this scale, some research works have found influences of negative attitudes into human perception and behaviors toward robots, and factors affecting these attitudes [2,4,7,9].

Moreover, some studies used this scale to explore cultural differences on attitudes toward robots. Bartneck, et al., [1] suggested cultural differences on the NARS scores through an international comparative survey among seven different countries. Wang, et al., [8] found in their experiment of human-robot interaction that Chinese participants had more negative attitudes toward robots than did the USA, and relied less on the robot's advice.

As one of further researches on cross-cultural comparison on attitudes toward robots, an online survey using the NARS was conducted in Japan and the UK. The survey aimed at verifying differences on attitudes toward robots between these nations and exploring factors influencing these attitudes. As factors to be explored, the survey firstly focused on age. In the survey conducted in Japan about ten years ago, our research group found that 40's persons had positive opinions of robots in comparison with other generations [5]. Thus, the survey aimed at comparison between 50's and 20's to clarify age differences. Moreover, perceptions of the relation to the family and commitment to religions have been adopted as indices reflecting differences between societies in different nations [6]. The survey included these two factors.

Method

Date and Participants

The survey was conducted from January to February, 2014. 100 Japanese and 100 UK respondents were recruited by a survey company at which about one million and six hundred thousand Japanese and one

million and one hundred thousand UK persons have registered. Respondents in each nation were limited to people who were born and had been living only in the corresponding nation. The respondents consisted of fifty persons in 20's (male: 25, female: 25) and fifty persons in 50's (male: 25, female: 25) in each of the nations.

The homepage of the online survey had been open for these participants during the above period.

Survey Design

The questionnaire of the online survey was conducted with the native language for the respondents in each of the nations. It did not instruct the definition of robots, or include any photo and image of robots. The questionnaire consisted of the following items.

PERCEPTIONS OF THE RELATION TO THE FAMILY AND COMMITMENT TO RELIGIONS

The following two items, which were used in the comparison survey between Japan and the Northern Europe by Otsuka et al. [6], were presented on the face sheet:

Do you think you relate to your family members?
(five-graded answer from "1. I completely agree" to "5. I completely disagree")

Does such notion as "I have nothing to do with religion or faith" apply to you?
(five-graded answer from "1. It strongly applies to me" to "5. It does not apply to me at all.")

NEGATIVE ATTITUDES TOWARD ROBOTS SCALE (NARS)

The scale consists of 14 items classified into three subscales. The first subscale (S1, six items) measures negative attitude toward interaction with robots (e.g., "I would feel paranoid talking with a robot."). The second subscale (S2, 5 items) measures negative attitude toward the social influence of robots (e.g.,

"Something bad might happen if robots developed into living beings."). The third subscale (S3, 3 items) measures negative attitude toward emotional interaction with robots (e.g., "I feel comforted being with robots that have emotions."). Each item is scored on a five-point scale: 1) strongly disagree; 2) disagree; 3) undecided; 4) agree; and 5) strongly agree, and an individual's score on each subscale is calculated by adding the scores of all items included in the subscale, with some items reverse coded.

Results

NARS Scores, Nations, and Age Groups

Cronbach's α-coefficients of the NARS subscales were .854, .779, and .842 on S1, S2, and S3, respectively. These values showed the sufficient internal consistencies of these subscales.

ANOVAs with nations (Japan v.s. the UK) x age groups (20's v.s. 50's) found statistically significant levels of the main effect of nations on negative attitude toward interaction with robots ($F(1, 196) = 4.073, p = .045, \eta^2 = .020$), and interaction effect on negative attitude toward emotional interaction with robots ($F(1, 196) =$

4.743, $p = .031, \eta^2 = .023$). Figure 1 shows the means and standard deviations of these subscale scores. The UK respondents had more negative attitude toward interaction with robots than did the Japanese respondents. A simple main effect test with Bonferroni's method revealed that the UK respondents in 20's had less negative attitude toward emotional interaction with robots in comparison with the UK respondents in 50's and the Japanese respondents in 20's.

Perceptions of the relation to the family and commitment to religions

Table 1 shows Pearson's correlation coefficients between the NARS subscale scores and item scores of perceptions of the relation to the family and commitment to religions based on the nations and age groups. Tests of equality on correlation coefficients found a statistically significant difference between the four respondents groups on the correlation between negative attitude toward interaction with robots and perception of the relation to the family ($\chi^2(3) = 8.824, p = .032$), differences at statistically significant trend levels on correlations between negative attitude toward social influences of robots and perception of the relation

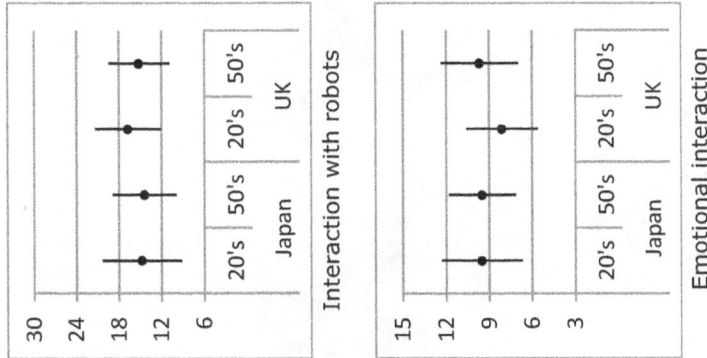

Figure 1. Means and Standard Deviations of the NARS Subscale Scores

			Religion commitment	Interaction	Social influences	Emotional interaction
Perception of the relation with the family	Japan	20's	.254	-.061	-.130	.240
		50's	.012	.374**	.218	-.017
	UK	20's	.043	-.048	-.079	-.056
		50's	-.040	.348*	.311*	.289*
Commitment to religions	Japan	20's		-.052	-.096	.000
		50's		-.014	.298*	.068
	UK	20's		-.042	-.196	.218
		50's		.115	.107	.047

Table 1. Correlation Coefficients between the NARS Subscales, Perception of the Relation with the Family, and Commitment to Religions (*$p < .05$, **$p < .01$)

to the family ($\chi^2(3) = 6.962, p = .073$), and between negative attitude social influences of robots and commitment to religions ($\chi^2(3) = 7.101, p = .069$).

Discussion

There was a trend, which was not found in the previous study [1], that the UK people had more negative attitudes toward interaction with robots than did the Japanese people. Moreover, the elder people perceiving weaker relation to their family members had more negative attitude toward interaction with robots in both the nations. The elder UK people perceiving weaker relation to their family members also had more negative attitude toward social influences of robots, and the elder Japanese people having stronger commitment to religions had more negative attitude toward social influences. These results suggest that factors influencing negative attitudes toward robots may differ dependent on cultures and age.

The survey reported here was at a preliminary level, and did not take into account concrete attitudes toward the relation to the family and commitment to religions. Moreover, the survey did not adopt any image stimulus of robots in order to avoid influences of images of specific types of robots. Future surveys should include more sophisticated items while exploring dominant images of robots in the corresponding nations.

References

[1] Bartneck, C., Suzuki, T., Kanda, T., and Nomura, T. The Influence of People's Culture and Prior Experiences with Aibo on their Attitude towards Robots. *AI & Society, 21,* 1-2 (2007), 217-230.

[2] Cramer, H., Kemper, N., Amin, A., Wielinga, B., and Evers, V. 'Give me a hug': the effects of touch and autonomy on people's responses to embodied social agents. *Computer Animation and Virtual Worlds, 20* (2009), 437-445.

[3] Nomura, T., Suzuki, T., Kanda, T., and Kato, K. Measurement of Negative Attitudes toward Robots. *Interaction Studies, 7,* 3 (2006), 437-454.

[4] Nomura, T., Suzuki, T., Kanda, T., Yamada, S., and Kato, K. Attitudes toward Robots and Factors Influencing Them. *New Frontiers in Human-Robot Interaction,* John Benjamins Publishing (2011), 73-88.

[5] Nomura, T., Tasaki, T., Kanda, T., Shiomi, M., Ishiguro, H., and Hagita, N. Questionnaire-Based Social Research on Opinions of Japanese Visitors for Communication Robots at an Exhibition. *AI & Society, 21,* 1-2 (2007), 167-183.

[6] Otsuka, M., Akiyama, M., Mori, K., and Hoshino, H. Comparative Study of Values, Work Ethics, and Lifestyles in Japan and Sweden: An Initial Report. *Bulletin of Human Science, 33* (2011), 105-119. (in Japanese).

[7] Riek, L.D., Rabinowitch, T-C., Bremner, P., Pipe, A.G., Fraser, M., and Robinson, P. Cooperative gestures: effective signaling for humanoid robots. *Proc. 5th ACM/IEEE Int. Conf. Human-Robot Interaction* (2010), 61-68.

[8] Wang, L., Rau, P-L.P., Evers, V., Robinson, B.K., and Hinds, P. When in Rome: the role of culture & context in adherence to robot recommendations. *Proc. 5th ACM/IEEE Int. Conf. Human-Robot Interaction* (2010), 359-366.

[9] Weiss, A., Bernhaupt, R., Tscheligi, M., and Yoshida, E. Addressing user experience and societal impact in a user study with a humanoid robot. *Proc. 1st Symposium on New Frontiers in Human-Robot Interaction* (2009), 150-157.

Unintentional Intercultural Collaboration in the 17th Century: German "Ballen", Japanese "Balen" and Portuguese Missionaries

Mami Hild

Kyoto College of Arts and Crafts, Professor

1-1 Nihonmatsu, Sonobe, Nantan City, Kyoto Prefecture 622-0041

JAPAN

hild-m@kyobi.ac.jp

Abstract

Baren or *balen* is a well-known rubbing pad used in Japan for printing woodblocks. *Balens* had been in widespread use during the Edo period (17th – mid-19th century) for sophisticated multicolored woodblock prints, including *ukiyo-e*. The general belief is that *balen* is a word of Japanese origin. However, through documents and interviews with professionals in hand-printing, I investigated the possibility that the word *balen* is a German loanword, and that this tool is actually a product of unintentional intercultural collaboration.

CABS'14, Aug 21-22 2014, Kyoto, Japan
ACM 978-1-4503-2557-8/14/08.
http://dx.doi.org/10.1145/2631488.2634060

Author Keywords

Ballen (in German); *balen* (in Japanese); Johannes Gutenberg's printing press; Jesuit missionaries; *ukiyo-e* woodblock prints

ACM Classification Keywords

H.1.2 [Models and Principles]: User/Machine Systems - Human factors;

Introduction

Baren or *balen* (Figure 1) is a well-known pressing and rubbing pad used for printing woodblocks in Japan. (Japanese does not have a phonetic distinction between "l" and "r." The spelling of *balen* is used in this article, as the author finds that the sound *ba-len* is closer to Japanese pronunciation than *ba-ren*.) The rubbing pad called *balen* had been in widespread use during the Edo period (17th – mid-19th century) for sophisticated multicolored woodblock prints, including *ukiyo-e*. In an *ukiyo-e* print by Kitagawa Utamaro (1753 – 1806), titled "Edo Meibutsu Nishiki-e Kosaku" (Figure 2)[1], female figures printing *ukiyo-e* with *balen* are precisely depicted. The shape of the rubbing pads in the print looks almost identical to the *balen* now seen in Japan. The accepted belief is that *balen* is a word of Japanese origin, as it denotes a traditional Japanese tool for traditional Japanese art. However, based on documents and interviews with "rubbing" professionals, I examined the possibility that this word appeared in Japan during the 17th century, when Jesuit missionaries were printing their documents in Japan, and that the word derives from the German word "Ballen" indicating a printing pad for the printing press invented by Johannes Gutenberg in Germany.

Figure 1 (left) "Balen" sold in Japan

Figure 2 "Edo Meibutsu Nishiki-e Kosaku" by Kitagawa Utamaro. Two women are holding a balen. [1] Detail drawings (right)

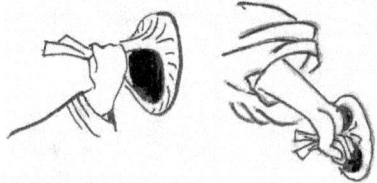

RUBBING TOOLS FROM CHINA AND KOREA

Newly invented tools, ideas and culture had been introduced to Japan from China and Korea in the course of history. Woodblock prints and printing techniques were not exceptions. In the year 971 during the Northern Song dynasty in China, a project to print the *Complete Collection of Buddhist Texts* began. The Korean (Koryo) version of the *Complete Collection of Buddhist Texts* was printed in 1010. In the 12th century many scrolls of printed Buddhist texts were brought to Japan, and printed texts became common in Japan.

Figure 5 Korean horse-hair rubbing tool

The Chinese traditional rubbing tool tool was "a bunch of fibers of hemp-palm, coiled around a piece of wood.""(Figure3)[2] In "A Study of the Techniques of Woodblock Color Prints" a small rubbing tool on the printing desk is depicted, with the caption "hemp-palm skin rubber".(Figure 4)[3] On the other hand, Korean rubbing tools were made of horsehair, bound with strings and shaped with yellow wax (Figure 5). It was termed "horsehair". Together with the printing techniques, rubbing tools must have been introduced to Japan from China and Korea, but their shapes, materials, and names are totally different from the disk-shaped *balen* in Japan, which was wrapped in a bamboo sheath and used much later, since the 17th century.

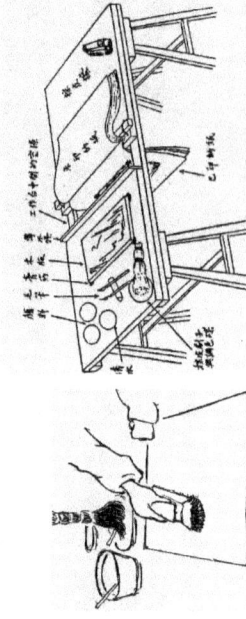

Figure 3 (left) Chinese hemp-palm-skin rubbing tool
Figure 4 (right) Printing desk and a hemp-palm rubber

BALEN AS A PLANT AND A BRUSH IN JAPAN

The Latin-Portuguese-Japanese dictionary (*Dictionarium Latino Lusitanicum, ac Iaponicum*), compiled in 1592, and the Japanese-Portuguese Dictionary (*Vocabulário da Língua do Japão com a declaração em Portugues.*), compiled in 1603 by Jesuit missionaries, introduce approximately 30,000 Japanese words (The Latin-Portuguese-Japanese) and 32,000 words (Portuguese-Japanese), which almost thoroughly reflect life in Japan in those days. These dictionaries include

balen as follows: "A small plant that is similar to an iris. This word also refers to a small brush made from the roots of this plant. This brush is used to clean iron kettles for the tea ceremony." From this information, I infer as follows: When printing techniques were introduced from China and Korea, Japanese used an ordinary brush made of plant roots as a replacement for the hemp-palm rubbing tool from China or the horsehair rubbing tool from Korea. At this stage *balen* did not indicate a special rubbing tool, but an ordinary plant and an ordinary brush made of that plant.

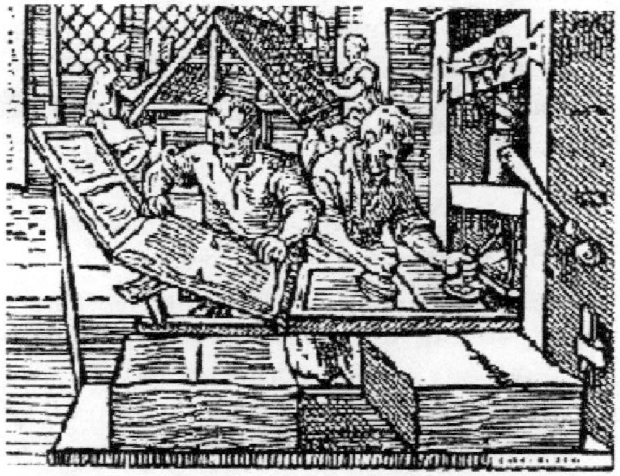

Figure 6 The man on the right is holding inking Ballen.

JESUIT MISSIONARIES AND GUTENBERG'S PRINTING PRESS

Alessandro Valignano, a Jesuit missionary in Japan, organized a Japanese Delegation in 1582 to visit several European cities. One of the purposes of the delegation was to acquire a printing machine, which had been invented by Johannes Gutenberg in Germany. The Gutenberg printing machine consisted of the printing press, the movable type system, and some peripheral tools including "Ballen"s (capital "B" and double "l" in German). As can be observed in the illustration (Figure 6) by Jost Amman (1539 –1591), a printing craftsman is holding round tools to put ink on the page in a frame. These are inking *Ballens*. Another type of *Ballen* was used as a rubbing tool to rub on the back of paper on woodblocks of illustrations. Both types of *Ballens* were stuffed with wool and covered with dog's leather. The pronunciation of the German word, *Ballen,* is almost the same as that of Japanese *balen*. Not like Chinese and Korean rubbing tools, the shape and the make of this German rubbing tool are much closer to the Japanese *balen.*

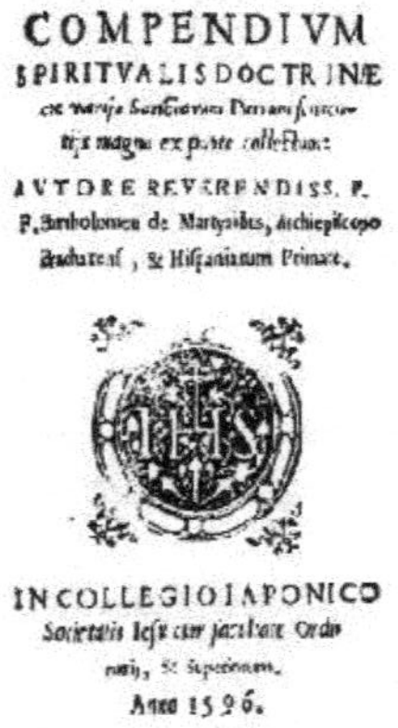

COMPENDIVM

SPIRITVALIS DOCTRINÆ

IN COLLEGIO IAPONICO

Anno 1596.

Figure 7 Christian document printed in Japan

GERMAN "BALLEN" IN JAPAN

Between the periods of harsh religious repression, Christian missionaries continued to propagate their faith in Japan. Antonio Harada, a Japanese Christian, opened the Harada Antonio Printing Office in Kyoto around the year 1610 and printed Jesuit documents, using movable printing types. One of the extant Christian text, "De Imitatione Christi Contemptus Mundi" printed in Kyoto, has been proved that it was printed with wooden type-pieces and a rubbing pad.[2] Curious Kyoto citizens, who had enjoyed adopting foreign words into Japanese, had plenty of opportunities to observe this eye-catching round rubbing tool wrapped with dog leather and to hear the foreign name, *Ballen*, which was easy to pronounce for Japanese tongues.

CONCLUSION

A number of factors were necessary for the invention of the current disk-type *balen*. The major factor is the availability of woodblocks with a perfectly level surface, which was fulfilled between the late 16th and early 17th century through the availability of modern carpentry tools including hand planes.

In order to meet the demand for the mass production of sophisticated woodblock prints including *ukiyo-e*, and thanks to the availability of woodblocks of ideal quality, unknown Japanese artists, who were in charge of rubbing in the printing business, managed to invent the ideal shape for a rubbing pad some time during the 17th century. Unlike the Chinese and Korean rubbing tools, the new rubbing pad was round and wrapped in bamboo slivers. When this round rubbing tool was invented in Japan, the German round rubbing tool was also being used by Christian missionaries in Japan. As there was a big boom to adopt foreign names into

Japanese in those days, it was quite natural that the Japanese began to use the German name *"Ballen"* for the newly invented model of rubbing pads. In response to the popularity of *ukiyo-e* multicolored woodblock prints, this new disk-shaped rubbing tool along with its adopted name *balen* spread throughout Japan. It is an example of unintentional intercultural collaboration in the 17th century between Japanese artists, German craftsmen, and Portuguese missionaries.

Acknowledgements

I would like to express my gratitude to Mr. Toshiyuki Yano of Baiyo Shoin Printing House, who kindly showed me the original printing woodblocks of the Edo period, and explained the traditional woodblock printing techniques to me. I also would like to thank Mr. W. Becker of the Gutenberg Museum in Mainz, Germany, who showed me the "Ballen" and explained its usage.

References

1. Kitagawa Utamaro. Edo Meibutsu Nishiki-e Kosaku, *Nihon Bijutsushi Jiten*. Heibonsha Ltd. (1987) 58.
2. Nakane, Masaru. *Nihon Insatsu Gijutsu-shi*, Yagi Publishing Inc.(1999) 5, 141, 192.
3. Li Hue. A Study of the Techniques of Woodblock Color Prints. Quoted by Kurosaki, Akira. *Hanga-shi Kaibo*. Abe Publishing Ltd. (2002) 112.

Cross-Cultural Communication Protocol Analysis

Kenji TERUI
Graduate School of Creative
Science and Engineering
Waseda University
Okubo 3-4-1
Sinjuku-ku, Tokyo, 169–8555
Japan
terken-06@ruri.waseda.jp

Reiko HISHIYAMA
Graduate School of Creative
Science and Engineering
Waseda University
Okubo 3-4-1
Sinjuku-ku, Tokyo, 169–8555
Japan
reiko@waseda.jp

Abstract

Miscommunication problems are often caused by not only language barriers but also cultural ones. To avoid this, it is effective to know in advance about intercultural differences, such as differences in behavior, attitudes, and ways of thinking. We propose a methodology for cross-cultural understanding by exploring and looking at analytical thought process variation. Through the participatory case study experiments, we found that we could extract differences of protocol patterns among the participants groups: American, South Korean, and Japanese.

Author Keywords

multicultural communication; diversity; multicultural understanding.

ACM Classification Keywords

H.5.m [Information interfaces and presentation (e.g., HCI)]: Miscellaneous.

Introduction

Due to globalization, non-native language (common language of participants) communication and lack of cross-cultural understanding need to be overcome to accomplish mutual understanding among people who have different languages and cultures. Anything to do with language and culture is difficult to represent by words. If something differs in the tellers culture, not only the spoken contents but also the way it is said differ [1]. It is important to know different patterns of thinking and differences in perception or sense [1]. Moreover, no culture is understood and inherited unless its contents are explained. In fact, it is necessary in global human resource education to understand and experience cross-cultural communication.

Method

In this study, we explain how material containing cross-cultural factors can be effectively used for communication protocol analysis and create a sharable environment using high quality case material containing cross-cultural factors for people with various languages and cultures [2]. We conduct cross-cultural communication protocol analysis by using discussion data obtained from participants who communicate in this environment.

Procedure of experimentation

First, each participant logs in, selects their native language, and reads the case materials shown on the Web. The selected case is described in their native language. Next, they choose a sentence in the case contents and note it with a line number and case passage by using analysis notes for organizing information. Participants discuss the problems in the case using multilingual chat. After the case discussion, we conducted a questionnaire about impressions of each nationality, mistranslations, this system, and this case method. We conduct cross-cultural analysis by using discussion data. We apply discussion data which are recoded dynamically on the process of interactive communication between the participants to analysis of thinking processes and behavior.

Protocol analysis

We show how to analyze the discussion log. We apply analysis of discussion data to protocol analysis to reveal the process of communication for all participating nationalities.

We classify utterances into six types in Table 1 as chat logs by the method of Wang et al. [4] for discussion logs. Moreover, we make a state transition diagram by using the method of Torii et al. [3] by dividing discussion logs into minimum discussion topics. We also analyze behavioral tendencies of each participating nationalities.

Table 1: Utterance types.

Type	Definition
Opinion	Own opinion about case material
Agree/Disagree	Agreement/disagreement with other participants
Question	Utterance asking for feedback
Explanation	Supplemental explanation about own opinion
Procedure	Mainly facilitators utterance
Other	Unclassifiable utterance

Results and Discussion

We conducted our experiment with American, South Korean, and Japanese university students on one-on-one basis. We analyzed discussion logs (JPN:KOR=139 utterances:110 utterances, JPN:USA=31 utterances:56 utterances), obtained in nine experiments (JPN-KOR: 6 experiments, JPN-USA: 3 experiments).

Analysis of discussion data

The data obtained in the multilingual chat discussion are analyzed below. In the analysis of the chat discussion logs, we divided chat discussion logs into two threads: source and translated. [2].

After the pre-analysis, we divide discussion data into short topics and give them utterance tags on the basis of utterance types (Table 1) to each utterance. We observe the condition of each participant by tag information and extract some states. We similarly extract utterance types that move from their current state to the next state. After that, we tally up data described above.

Figure 1 shows a state transition diagram from discussion logs obtained in the experiment.

The obtained process of state transition is as follows. Participants transit to A: Information arrangement, in which a participant gives his/her own opinion at the facilitators direction. If a participant cannot understand the meaning of a facilitators direction or the other participants utterance (because of mistranslation), the participant requests an explanation and transits to C: Waiting for explanation. When a participant wants to know the other participants opinion, he/she transits to B: Waiting for other opinion by asking a question.

We found four patterns opinion-making behavior: (1) opinions stated after a facilitators direction, (2) opinions that agree/disagree with anothers stated opinion, and (3) opinions that answer a question. The above three behavior patterns reveal ones own opinion. On the other hand, we also find the last pattern: (4) opinions that explain or additionally supplement ones own opinion.

Moreover, the flow of discussion begins to be disrupted after references are passed to each other. Then, participants scent discussion get stacked up and transit to D: Waiting for facilitators direction. If a facilitator finds a

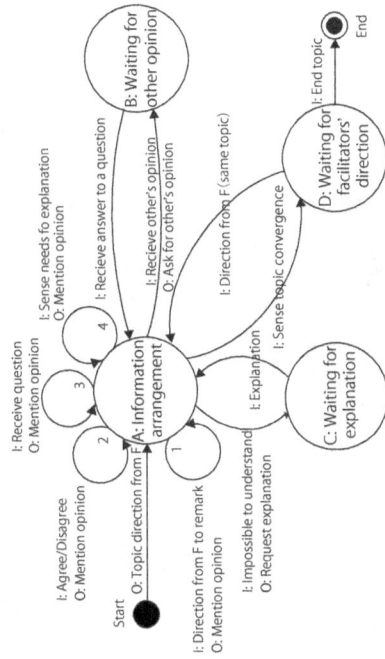

Figure 1: Ratio of behavior for every nationally.

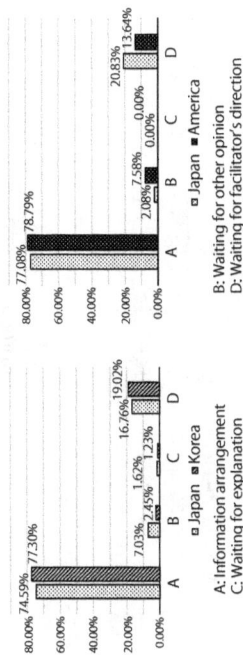

Figure 2: Ratio of state for every nationally.

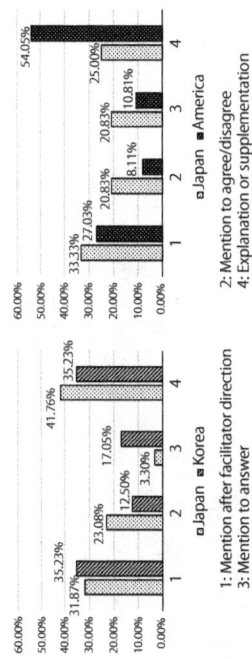

Figure 3: Ratio of mention type for every nationally.

point of discussion that needs to be advanced and tells the participants to do so, they transit to Information arrangement again and discuss the point. If not, the topic is closed and a new topic is introduced by the facilitator.

Figure 2 shows the ratio of states (A–D in Figure 1). Figure 3 shows the ratio of transition patterns from Information arrangement (1-4 in Figure 1). In the state graph, state A is the highest of all states for every nationality, followed by D, B, and C. Thus, we found no noted difference. Therefore, conceivably no cultural difference exists in the ratio of these states.

On the other hand, we found differences in the number of transition patterns. First, in relation to (1), South Koreans stated their opinions more. Thus, South Koreans were most likely to state opinions at ones own initiative or at others direction. Next, in (2), Japanese students stated agreement/disagreement more. It can be said that the Japanese were most likely to agree or disagree openly after listening carefully to other participants. In (4), Americans are most likely to give explanations and explore their own opinion, but the other two nationalities often do this too.

Discussion
We found some differences and similarities in the results of protocol analysis. Japanese had a high propensity for listening carefully to other participants' points of view. Moreover, Japanese responded to others' opinions and respected other's points of view. On the other hand, South Koreans tended to push their opinions more strongly to convince other participants. Americans tended to argue strongly for their own opinions. However, they considered other opinions but tended to disagree with them.

Conclusion

We conducted cross-cultural communication protocol analysis by providing a realistic cross-cultural experience from native language communication activity. We conducted congregative analysis of cross-cultural differences by dealing in linguistic communication and cultural difference discussion logs obtained by this system. In the results, we distilled the utterance behavior model in chat discussion into a one state transit diagram and identified the cultural differences as action patterns.

Acknowledgements

This work was supported by JST/RISTEX, and by a Grant-in-Aid for Scientific Research (S) (24220002, 2012-2016) from JSPS.

References

[1] Omi, J. *Japanese post-secondary ESL students' perspectives on communicative competence in the cultural contexts of the United States.* University of San Francisco, 2003.

[2] Terui, K., and Hishiyama, R. Multilingual case method system for cross-cultural analysis. In *International Conference on Culture and Computing* (2013), 117–122.

[3] Torii, D., Ishida, T., Bonneaud, S., and Drogoul, A. Layering social interaction scenarios on environmental simulation. In *Multi-Agent and Multi-Agent-Based Simulation*, P. Davidsson, B. Logan, and K. Takadama, Eds., vol. 3415 of *Lecture Notes in Computer Science*. Springer, 2005, 78–88.

[4] Wang, H.-C., Fussell, S. F., and Setlock, L. D. Cultural difference and adaptation of communication styles in computer-mediated group brainstorming. In *Proceedings of the SIGCHI Conference on Human Factors in Computing Systems*, CHI '09 (2009), 669–678.

Enhancing Machine Translation with Crowdsourced Keyword Highlighting

Mei-Hua Pan

College of Electrical Engineering and
Computer Science
National Tsing Hua University, Taiwan
s9960125@m99.nthu.edu.tw

Hao-Chuan Wang

Department of Computer Science
Institute of Information Systems and
Applications
National Tsing Hua University, Taiwan
haochuan@cs.nthu.edu.tw

CABS'14, August 21-22, 2014, Kyoto, Japan
ACM 978-1-4503-2557-8/14/08.
http://dx.doi.org/10.1145/2631488.2634062

Abstract

Machine translation (MT) has the potential to bridge the
language barrier in multilingual community, but its
utility to support cross-lingual communication is often
limited by its quality. Recent studies have shown the
supporting effect of keyword highlighting on translation
comprehension. What's missing is a way to identify and
highlight keywords in translations efficiently and
reliably. In this paper, we investigate crowdsourcing
strategies for keyword highlighting. We compare three
methods that involve human workers to highlight
keywords in English-to-Chinese translations: *English-
only* for adding keyword highlights on the original
English sentences, *Chinese-only* for adding keyword
highlights on the translated sentences, and *Bilingual*
that allows people to choose keywords in either the
original or the translated sentences. Results show that
adding highlights to translated sentences (*Chinese-only*)
is the fastest but doesn't improve the comprehensibility
of translation. Highlighting both sentences (*Bilingual*)
helps improve the understandability of hard-to-
understand translations.

Author Keywords

Machine translation; cross-lingual communication;
crowdsourcing; highlighting interface

ACM Classification Keywords

H.1.2. User/Machine Systems: Human information processing

Introduction

There's increasing opportunity to encounter cross-lingual information in everyday life and work with the prevalence of Internet and social network these days. On social networking sites like Facebook and Twitter, users often choose to use a lingua franca (usually English) to communicate with one another. However, it may be uneasy for non-native speakers to express themselves properly. New designs start to employ machine translation (MT) to mediate this sort of cross-lingual communication. However, machine-translated messages with messy word order and improper word choice may disrupt comprehension. Studies have shown that using MT to communicate within groups is less efficient than using a common language [2].

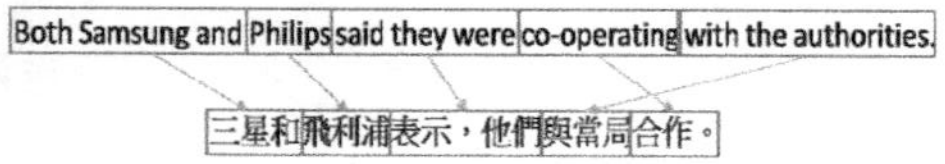

To enhance MT-mediated cross-lingual communication, improving the performance of the underlying natural language processing algorithms is just one direction. Alternatively, it's potentially useful to consider integrating human processing and machine translation for better overall communication outcomes. For example, simple modification of how MT presents the translations to users can be helpful. Simply highlighting the keywords in a translation can enhance its understandability [1].

We consider keyword highlighting a lightweight solution worth of further work of technology development. What's required is a way to generate quality highlights on any translations. The paper investigates the utility of phrase pairing provided by Google Translate to identify the smallest units of highlighting for the original English and the translated Chinese sentences.

expert workers. To understand how to achieve fast and reliable crowdsourced keyword highlighting, we conducted a study to compare three different crowdsourcing strategies by varying the locus of language processing, either asking the workers to add highlights to the original sentences, the translated sentences or both at the same time. In an experimental study, we compared the comprehensibility of highlighted sentences generated by different strategies.

Data Collection

We collected highlight annotations on the sentences in three different interface conditions (English-only, Chinese-only and bilingual) using a within-subject experimental design.

Participants

Eighteen undergraduate students (12 male and 6 female) from a university in Taiwan participated in this part of the study. All had lived in Taiwan for more than 15 years, spoke Mandarin Chinese as their native language, and learned English as their second language for more than 5 years with TOEIC scored higher than 750. Their mean age was 21.01 years (SD = 0.94).

Materials

Nine English sentences were randomly picked from BBC news. All the sentences were translated into Mandarin Chinese using Google Translate. We define *phrase pair* as the smallest translation unit defined by the MT engine. Figure 1 shows an example of how the original and translated sentences are decomposed and matched with phrase pairs. We leverage the information of phrase pairing provided by Google Translate to identify the smallest units of highlighting for the original English and the translated Chinese sentences.

Figure 1. Phrase pairs in a sentence.

Evaluation

To evaluate how well keyword highlights obtained from each condition support translation comprehension, thirty raters were recruited to rate the understandability of highlighted translations.

Participants

Thirty undergraduate students (14 males and 16 females) from a university in Taiwan participated in this part of experiment. All had lived in Taiwan for more than 15 years and spoke Mandarin as their native language. Their mean age was 21.63 years (SD=1.47).

Materials and Procedure

In the previous phase of highlight collection, each of the nine sentences was annotated by six workers in each of the three conditions, resulting in a total of 162 highlighted sentences (54 per condition). By using the phrase pair information provided by Google Translate, we could show Chinese translations with highlights collected from all conditions, including the English-only condition. For the purpose of comparison, two new highlighting conditions: random highlighting and no highlighting were created and included, resulting in a dataset consisting of 270 translated sentences. We randomly divided all the 270 sentences into 30 groups, each consisting of nine distinct sentences presenting in a random order.

Each rater was given a form showing a randomly selected group of sentences. Raters were asked to rate the comprehensibility of each sentence in a 1-5 scale, where 1 means that the sentence is extremely confusing and 5 means that the sentence is extremely easy to understand.

Highlighting tool

We developed a small mobile application for Android phones. The interface allows the participants to add highlight annotations on the original and/or the translated sentences, according to the experimental design. In all conditions, when participants tap on a word, that word would be highlighted yellow. In the English-only condition, only the original English sentence is displayed and available for highlighting. Similarly, in the Chinese-only condition, only the machine translated Chinese sentence is displayed and available. In the bilingual condition, both the original and translated sentences are displayed and available for highlighting (see Figure 2). Once a phrase in either the original or the translated sentence is tapped, the corresponding paired phrase will also be highlighted.

Procedure

We asked the 18 participants to use the highlighting tool running on a 4.7-inch Android phone to annotate keywords in sentences displayed to them. In order to eliminate the order effect of this within-subject experiment, the order of three highlighting conditions (English-only, Chinese-only and bilingual) was counterbalanced and the sentences displayed each time were randomly selected. Each participant has to highlight three sentences in each condition, thus nine sentences in total and the sentences would not appear more than once to the participant.

Measure of highlighting latency

Behavioral logs were collected when workers start working on a sentence, tap on a word, or finish a sentence. We could obtain the latency of highlighting from the logged data, which is the elapsed time that each participant spends on highlighting each sentence.

Dozens of flights have been cancelled, hitting travellers at Berlin Tegel, Copenhagen and smaller airports.

航班幾十已被取消，擊中旅客在柏林泰格爾，哥本哈根和較小的機場。

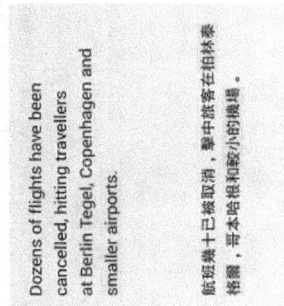

Figure 2. The highlight tool. In the bilingual condition, a phrase in one sentence is highlighted, the corresponding phrase in another sentence will also be highlighted.

Results

Time latency of highlighting

As shown in Figure 3, highlighting on translated Chinese sentences is faster in time than the other two conditions ($F[2, 161] = 4.31, p<.05$). Although the bilingual condition sentences appeared later naturally require less time to highlight, during the study we have counterbalanced the order of condition, and have also randomized sentence selection. Thus the result is reliable and noteworthy.

Comprehensibility rating

Although the overall comprehensibility of highlighted translations in the bilingual condition is slightly better than the other conditions, the difference was not significant ($F[4, 269] = 0.88, n.s.$). However, we noted that individual sentence has a strong effect on rating ($F[8, 269] = 18.44, p <.0001$). This suggests that some sentences are harder to understand than the others, and so that these sentences may benefit the most from keyword highlights. Thus, we selected a sample of difficult sentences with mean rating lower than 2 according to ratings from the non-highlighting condition, resulting in a subset of three difficult sentences. As Figure 4 shows, for these difficult sentences the comprehensibility rating in the bilingual condition is significantly higher than other conditions ($F[4, 89] = 16.908, p < 0.05$).

Discussion

In summary, adding keyword highlights to the translated sentences is the fastest in time, but doesn't lead to better quality than others. This may not be surprising as Chinese is the native language to the workers. However, the lack of improvement on the comprehensibility of translation also suggests that

choosing keywords in machine-translated sentences remains a difficult task even to native speakers.

On the other side, highlighting on both the original and translated sentences (i.e., the bilingual condition) clearly improves the understandability of difficult sentences. There're two possible reasons behind. One is that with bilingual information the workers can better recognize translation errors, and thus know where to emphasize. Another possibility is that the workers can access more contextual information to figure out what the original sentences mean and thus they could make better decisions, while in other conditions they don't have access to this big picture.

In this study, we show that crowdsourcing keyword highlighting with bilingual information is a potentially useful strategy for supporting the comprehension of machine translations. There're still several limitations of this approach, such as the reliance on bilingual skills of the worker, and the long latency of highlighting (15-25 seconds per sentence), requiring future work.

Acknowledgements

This research was supported in part by Ministry of Science and Technology, Taiwan under NSC 102-2815-C-007-045-E and 102-2221-E-007-073-MY3.

References

[1] Gao, G. Wang, H.C., Cosley, D., Fussell, S.R. (2013). Same translation but different experience: the effects of highlighting on machine-translated conversations. *Proc. CHI 2013*, 449-458.

[2] Yamashita, N., & Ishida, T. (2006). Effects of machine translation on collaborative work. *Proc. CSCW 2006*, 515-523.

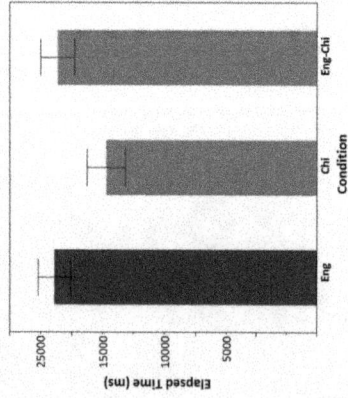

Figure 3. Mean elapsed time by condition.

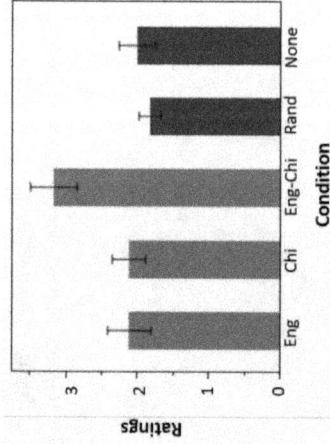

Figure 4. Mean rating of comprehensibility by condition for difficult sentences.

Social Media Use in Higher Educational Organizations: A Comparison of the US and Singapore

Mary Beth Watson-Manheim
Department of Information and Decision Sciences (IDS)
University of Illinois at Chicago
Chicago, IL 60607 USA
mbwm@uic.edu

Steve Jones
Department of Communication
University of Illinois at Chicago
Chicago, IL 60607 USA
sjones@uic.edu

Jodie Eason
Department of IDS
University of Illinois at Chicago
Chicago, IL 60607 USA
Jeason3@uic.edu

Chei Sian Lee
Wee Kim Wee School of
Communication and Information
Nanyang Technological University
Singapore 639798
leecs@ntu.edu.sg

Eric W. Welch
Department of Public Administration
University of Illinois at Chicago
Chicago, IL 60607 USA
ewwelch@uic.edu

CABS 2014, August 20-22, 2014, Kyoto, Japan.
ACM 978-1-4503-2557-8/14/08.
http://dx.doi.org/10.1145/2631488.2634063

Abstract

In this research, we aim to explore the adoption of social media initiatives in the increasingly global higher education market. We collect survey data from individuals in different administrative positions at large public universities in Singapore and the United States. We are particularly interested in the consequences for information flows in the organization, as well as the potential impact on traditional coordination, control, and accountability mechanisms. We expect that these consequences may take different forms and have different implications in the two national contexts. Preliminary survey results from the US are briefly discussed.

Author Keywords

Social Media; Higher Education; Cross-cultural Communication

ACM Classification Keywords

H.5.m. Information interfaces and presentation (e.g., HCI): Miscellaneous. H.5.3 Group and Organization Interfaces (Web-based interactions)

Introduction

Widespread access to the Internet and inexpensive computing devices, as well as the rapid development of social software applications, e.g., Twitter, Facebook, YouTube, Instagram and WhatsApp, is facilitating open collaboration and information sharing. However, use of these technologies highlights a fundamental tension between openness of communication and information flows and traditional coordination, control, and accountability mechanisms at multiple levels of organizations. We aim to explore this tension in a specific type of organization, higher educational institutions, which are increasingly adopting social media initiatives. As well, these organizations operate in a global marketplace, often collaborating and competing across national borders for faculty and students. We will compare the adoption of social media tools and resulting consequences in two national cultures, Singapore and the United States. We expect that organizational and individual consequences may take different forms and have different implications in the two national contexts.

Specifically we are examining higher education administration professional use of social media. Social media usage is increasing across all industries and youth adoption rates (18-29 years old) are over 90%. Universities target youth, and for universities to effectively reach this demographic they must adopt new media channels. We seek to compare professional administrative staff usage as a contrast to personal usage to better understand the impact of institutional policy on higher education social media implementation. We are particularly interested in the consequences for information flows in the organization, as well as the potential impact on coordination, control,

and accountability mechanisms. We are limiting the scope of this study to organizational activities such as brand management, current and prospective student engagement, and alumni relations. Activities related to teaching and research are out of scope, and deliberately excluded.

Cross-cultural Comparison

The higher education systems in the United States and Singapore are comparable and both adhere to traditional Western-style education methodology. To gain a richer understanding of institutional affects on social media usage in higher education, we seek to examine institutions that reflect an individualistic orientation (the United States) as well as a collectivist orientation (Singapore).

We expect that organizational use of social media is accompanied by internal changes in structure and process [1]. Our second proposition is that these relational changes may take different forms and have different consequences in different cultures. Tsui, Nifadkar, Ou [5] review a wide range of studies investigating organizational behavior where national culture was a major explanatory variable. They find significant evidence that different cultures have different influences on interpersonal, or relationship-oriented work-related outcomes, such as negotiation, trust and cooperation, and team behavior and processes. For example, Tinsley and Brett [4] compare conflict resolution strategies used by Hong Kong and US managers. The authors found that US managers were more like to discuss and resolve issues while Hong Kong managers were more likely to show concern for authority and send issues to higher management.

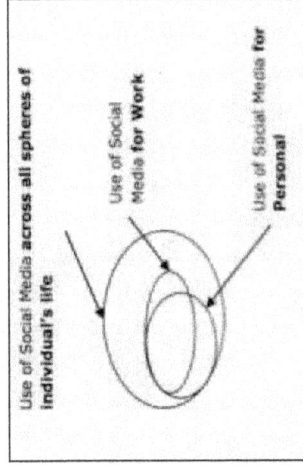

Figure 1: Conceptual Overview of Research

Both Singapore and the US have high social media usage across all age groups. It is estimated that over 90% of Internet users in Singapore use social media [2]. Similarly, according to a 2013 Pew Internet Project report, 73% of all Internet users in the US use social networking sites. (http://www.pewinternet.org/fact-sheets/social-networking-fact-sheet/).

Method

We will collect quantitative survey data from individuals in different administrative positions at universities in each country about the use of social media technology in the workplace both for work and non-work purposes. The primary objectives are to understand: 1) the extent of social media use in the organization and the purpose of this use, 2) how employees use the tools to manage and integrate or separate work and non-work activities, 3) how social media networks coincide (or not) with an individual's work network 4) what implications there are for collaboration and other work-related outcomes.

As shown in Figure 1, the orienting framework for our research recognizes that individuals utilize social media applications in many different social contexts. Our aim is to understand how the use of social media might be influencing work related outcomes such as access to information and network ties, as well as the impact on boundaries between professional and personal life.

The study survey consists of four major sections: work, professional social network, technology use, and outcomes. The following sections provide a high level description of questions in each section of the current survey.

Survey Section - Work

The survey first seeks to understand the individual respondent's work. What are the specific tasks and broader focus of the individual's professional activities? Respondents are asked to characterize their work in terms of common university administrative activities, e.g., student support, budget management, and procurement. Further, the instrument seeks to understand the complexity of the work and draws upon Morgeson & Humphrey (6) to assess complexity, information processing, problem solving, etc.

Survey Section – Professional Social Network

A key survey goal is to characterize the network of individuals that each respondent collaborates with and the characteristics of collaborators. For example, are network connections within the same or different college, organization, and/or profession? How does the respondent utilize social media to maintain or expand their professional and social networks?

Survey Section – Technology Usage

Of primal importance is the respondent usage of technology, specifically social media applications, as well as other collaboration technologies such as Google Docs. The survey queries participants on both personal and professional usage. Additionally, we assess where usage occurs, home or work, with whom, and for what purpose, e.g., arranging meetings, or report writing.

Survey Section – Outcomes

The survey measures a variety of job satisfaction indicators. We use several established protocols, including but not limited to Spector, P.E. (7).

Status

The survey has been distributed to administrative staff at one educational institution, a large public university in the Midwestern United States. Data scrubbing and analysis is currently underway but preliminary results indicate considerable use social media for work purposes (40% of respondents) and, more so, for personal reasons (73%). Among people that use social media for work, there is significant use of Facebook (63%), with somewhat less use of Twitter (37%) and Google Plus (17%). A response rate of 24% implies a strong interest in this research topic and initial results indicate that those that utilize social media at work use a variety of collaboration applications.

We plan to distribute the survey to administrative staff at a large university in Singapore in 2014. The survey questions will be modified to fit the Singaporean context.

Acknowledgement

The authors gratefully acknowledge the support of Creative and Collaborative Information Technology Laboratory (CCIT), University of Illinois at Chicago.

References

[1] Alfaro, I., Watson-Manheim, M.B. (2014). A Technology that Needs No Support from IT ... Yet: Organizational Use of Social Media. Journal of Computer Information Systems (forthcoming)

[2] IDA (2012) Info-communications Development Authority of Singapore. Social media. In IDA Infocomm Technology Roadmap 2012. http://www.ida.gov.sg/~/media/Files/Infocomm Landscape/Technology/TechnologyRoadmap/SocialMedi a.pdf

[3] Ministry of Education. (2014). Opening Address by Mr Heng Swee Keat, Minister for Education, at the International Conference of Teaching and Learning with Technology (iCTLT). http://www.moe.gov.sg/media/speeches/2014/04/09/o pening-address-by-mr-heng-swee-keat-at-the-international-conference-of-teaching-and-learning-with-technology.php

[4] Tinsley, C. H., & Brett, J. M. (2001). Managing workplace conflict in the United States and Hong Kong. Organizational Behavior and Human Decision Processes, 85(2), 360-381.

[5] Tsui, A. S., Nifadkar, S. S., & Ou, A. Y. (2007). Cross-national, cross-cultural organizational behavior research: Advances, gaps, and recommendations. Journal of Management, 33(3), 426-478

[6] Morgeson, F.P., & Humphrey, S. E. (2006). The Work Design Questionnaire (WDQ): developing and validating a comprehensive measure for assessing job design and the nature of work. Journal of Applied Psychology, 91(6), 1321.

[7] Spector, P. E. (1985). Measurement of human service staff satisfaction: Development of the Job Satisfaction Survey. American Journal of Community Psychology, 13(6), 693-713.

Catching Up in Audio Conferences: Highlighting Keywords in ASR Transcripts for Non-Native Speakers

Ari Hautasaari

NTT Communication Science Labs
2-4 Hikaridai, Seika-cho,
Soraku-gun, Kyoto, Japan
ari.hautasaari@lab.ntt.co.jp

Naomi Yamashita

NTT Communication Science Labs
2-4 Hikaridai, Seika-cho,
Soraku-gun, Kyoto, Japan
naomiy@acm.org

CABS'14, Aug 21-22 2014, Kyoto, Japan
ACM 978-1-4503-2557-8/14/08.
http://dx.doi.org/10.1145/2631488.2634064

Abstract

Previous works suggest that non-native speakers (NNS)
may benefit from viewing textual transcripts of spoken
dialogue generated by automated speech recognition
(ASR) technology during audio conferences. However,
viewing ASR transcripts while listening to the ongoing
conversation may impose a higher cognitive load on
NNS, especially in adverse audio conditions. We
examined how automatically highlighted keywords in
real-time ASR transcripts might benefit NNS when
catching up on missed parts of an audio conference by
reviewing a speeded up (1.6x) audio playback of the
missed conversation.

Author Keywords

Automated speech recognition; real-time transcripts;
keyword detection; multilingual communication

ACM Classification Keywords

H.5.m. Information interfaces and presentation (e.g.,
HCI): Miscellaneous.

Introduction

Audio conferencing is among the most common
communication tools used by individuals and
organizations on a global scale. Multilingual teams often

rely on English as a common language to communicate between non-collocated team members. However, as non-native speakers (NNS) rarely reach the fluency level of native English speakers (NS) they may often experience difficulties when following second language conversations in audio conferences [7].

Besides challenges related to language diversity, there are numerous coordination issues involved in holding audio conferences between non-collocated team members. For example, some participants may have to attend to urgent tasks during a meeting, such as answering a phone call, causing them to miss parts of the conversation. Technical solutions for catching up on these missed parts without disrupting the ongoing conversation include using audio recordings and textual transcripts of the conversation generated by automated speech recognition (ASR) technology [2, 3, 6]. In this paper, we examine how automatic keyword highlighting in real-time ASR transcripts might benefit NNS when catching up on missed parts of a multiparty audio conference by reviewing a speeded up audio playback.

Current Study

Previous studies suggest that speeded up audio is sufficient for NS to catch up on missed parts of the conversation during an audio conference [3]. Textual transcripts, on the other hand, may improve NNS comprehension of spoken dialogue in their non-native language [5]. However, following textual transcripts and second language conversation at a faster speed likely increases NNS's cognitive load [1, 4, 7], which may in turn have a negative impact on their comprehension of the spoken dialogue. Drawing from these previous works, we ask:

RQ: Do NNS benefit from viewing highlighted keywords in real-time ASR transcripts when catching up on missed parts of a conversation with speeded up audio during a multiparty audio conference in their non-native language?

Method

We conducted a laboratory experiment, where 18 native English speakers and 18 Japanese non-native English speakers participated in a simulated audio conference as passive listeners. During the audio conference, they were briefly distracted and missed parts of the ongoing conversation. They then had to catch up on the missed conversation using speeded up (1.6x) audio playback and real-time ASR transcripts. We manipulated the accessibility of automatically highlighted keywords when catching up on these missed parts (audio and ASR transcripts vs. audio and ASR transcripts with highlighted keywords).

The participants listened to three 3-minute conversation clips between three native English speakers (2 female) discussing a solution to a survival scenario in both conditions. The ASR transcripts of these conversations were generated by a speech recognition software called Dragon Naturally Speaking[1]. The word error rate (WER) was comparable to the reported WER in previous research with a similar setting and equipment at 23% [1]. Keywords in the ASR transcripts were automatically extracted using a keyword extraction software called GENSEN-Web[2]. Each extracted keyword was highlighted with a red font in a

---

[1]http://www.nuance.com/naturallyspeaking/pdf/wp_DNS_ Field_Reporting.pdf.

[2]http://gensen.dl.itc.u-tokyo.ac.jp/gensenweb_eng.html

real-time transcript tracking interface displayed on a laptop computer assigned to each participant (see [2] for details).

Measures

We measured the participants' level of comprehension about the conversational content regarding the parts they missed and had to review with the catch up functionality by administrating a post-task quiz. The participants' score (0-1) in the post-task quiz reflected their level of comprehension.

The participants' perception of the utility of ASR transcripts when catching up on missed conversation with speeded up audio was measured using three 7-point Likert scales ("real-time transcripts/highlighted keywords helped me organize my thoughts", "real-time transcripts/highlighted keywords helped me recover from missed information in the conversation", and "real-time transcripts/highlighted keywords helped me follow the flow of the conversation", 1 = strongly disagree, 7 = strongly agree). The questions formed a reliable scale (Cronbach's α = .95) and were averaged to create a measure of utility.

Results

In order to answer our *RQ*, we conducted 2 (keyword accessibility: audio and ASR transcripts *vs.* audio and ASR transcripts with highlighted keywords) × 2 (language background: NNS *vs.* NS) repeated measures ANOVAs on the effects of highlighted keywords in real-time ASR transcripts on NNS comprehension and perceived utility when catching up on missed parts of an audio conference.

There was no significant main effect for keyword accessibility (F[1, 34]=0.30, p=*n.s.*), but a significant main effect for language background (F[1, 34]=38.63, p<.05) on the level of comprehension about the speeded up audio content (Figure 1). The interaction effect between keyword accessibility and language background was not significant (F[1, 34]=0.65, p=*n.s.*).

Secondly, there was no significant main effect for keyword accessibility (F[1, 34]=0.03, p=*n.s.*), but a significant main effect for language background (F[1, 34]=17.53, p<.05) on the perceived utility of ASR transcripts when catching up with speeded up audio (Figure 2). The interaction effect between keyword accessibility and language background was not significant (F[1, 34]=0.06, p=*n.s.*).

These results partly answered our *RQ*. While NNS level of comprehension did not improve significantly when automatically highlighted keywords were available in ASR transcripts, they perceived the utility of ASR transcripts and highlighted keywords higher than NS for catching up on missed parts of an audio conference with speeded up audio.

Discussion

In this section we discuss our results in more detail by reflecting on the post-experiment interviews with NS and NNS participants. [3]

NS participants, despite the ASR transcripts including errors, found the ASR transcripts and highlighted keywords including errors, found the

[3] All NNS interview quotes are translated from Japanese by the Authors.

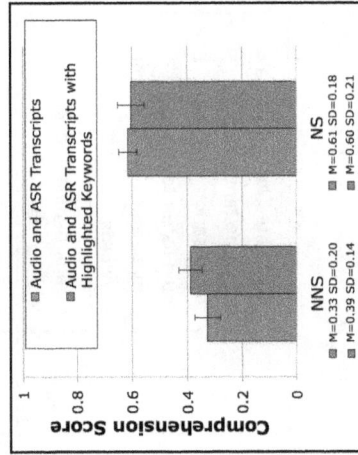

Figure 1. Mean speech comprehension score by keyword accessibility condition when catching up on missed conversation for NNS and NS (error bars represent standard error of the mean).

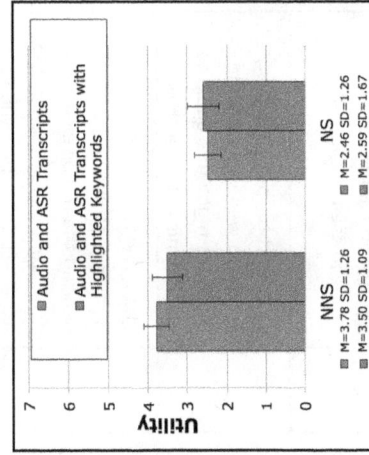

Figure 2. Perceived utility of ASR transcripts by keyword accessibility condition when catching up on missed conversation for NNS and NS (error bars represent standard error of the mean).

reminders of the conversational content, and as an additional supporting channel for keeping up, especially, with speeded up review of an audio conversation.

keywords useful for checking if they missed any information when using the catch up functionality (Table 1: NS6, NS13). Further, the highlighted keywords worked as visual reminders of the audio content for some NS participants (Table 1: NS5).

NNS were also able to make use of the keywords to confirm their understanding of the ongoing conversation. Moreover, the highlighted keywords offered the NNS a supporting channel to follow the second language conversation when they could not keep up with the speeded up audio alone (Table 2: NNS9). Similarly to NS participants, NNS also vocalized the value of highlighted keywords as visual reminders of the audio content (Table 2: NNS4). However, due to errors in ASR transcripts and automatic highlighting, some NNS participants may have found them distracting (Table 2: NNS16).

While we found no significant increase in NNS comprehension of speeded up audio content when catching up, our results suggest that enriching real-time ASR transcripts with automatically highlighted keywords may benefit both NNS and NS during multiparty audio conferences.

Conclusion

We presented a study, where 18 native English speakers and 18 Japanese non-native English speakers caught up to missed parts of an audio conference with speeded up audio and real-time ASR transcripts. Our results showed that automatically highlighted keywords in the ASR transcripts did not significantly improve NNS comprehension of the conversational content in speeded up audio. However, NNS may benefit from highlighted keywords in ASR transcripts as visual

References

[1] Gao, G., Yamashita, N., Hautasaari, A., Echenique A. and Fussell, S. Effects of public vs. private automated transcripts on multiparty communication between native and non-native English speakers. In *Proc. CHI 2014*, ACM (2014), 843-852.

[2] Hautasaari, A. and Yamashita, N. Do automated transcripts help non-native speakers catch up on missed conversation in audio conferences? In *Proc. CABS 2014*, ACM (2014), to appear.

[3] Junuzovic, S., Inkpen, K., Hegde, R., Zhang, Z., Tang, J. and Brooks, C. What did I miss? In-meeting review using multimodal accelerated instant replay (AIR) conferencing. In *Proc. CHI 2011*, ACM (2011), 513-522.

[4] Luisa, M., Lecumberri, G., Cooke, M. and Culter, A. Non-native speech perception in adverse conditions: A Review. *Speech Communication 52* (2010), 864-886.

[5] Pan, Y., Jiang, D., Yao, L., Picheny, M. and Qin, Y. Effects of automated transcription quality on non-native speakers' comprehension in real-time computer-mediated communication. In *Proc. CHI 2010*, ACM (2010), 1725-1734.

[6] Tucker, S., Bergam, O., Ramamoorthy, A. and Whittaker S. Catchup: A useful application of time-travel in meetings. In *Proc. CSCW 2010*, ACM (2010), 99-102.

[7] Yamashita, N., Echenique, A., Ishida, T. and Hautasaari, A. Lost in transmittance: How transmission lag enhances and deteriorates multilingual collaboration. In *Proc. CSCW 2013*, ACM (2013), 923-934.

NS6	Keywords help find information in the transcripts that I missed in the fast sections.
NS13	I listened to the audio first, and then went through the text with highlights again to see if I missed something.
NS5	The keywords helped me remember them without hearing them. For example, I didn't remember hearing the word 'scissors', but when I filled out the questionnaire, I remembered seeing it as a keyword. I forgot to read the transcripts, so keywords helped me more.

Table 1. NS interview quotes.

NNS9	Highlighted keywords gave me some hint what the conversation was about. I could listen to the conversation based on these keywords.
NNS4	I think highlighted words tend to stay in my mind.
NNS16	Highlighted keywords caught my attention, but I didn't think they were particularly useful or important keywords.

Table 2. NNS interview quotes.

Come_IN@Palestine: Adapting a German Computer Club Concept to a Palestinian Refugee Camp

Konstantin Aal[1], George Yerousis[2], Kai Schubert[1], Dominik Hornung[1], Oliver Stickel[1], Volker Wulf[1]

[1]University of Siegen,
57068 Siegen, Germany
[konstantin.aal, kai.schubert,
dominik.hornung, oliver.stickel,
volker.wulf]@uni-siegen.de

[2]Birzeit University
PO Box 14, Birzeit
West Bank, Palestine
gyerousis@birzeit.edu

ABSTRACT

Come_IN computer clubs are a well-established approach to foster learning, social networks and integration in German neighborhoods with a high percentage of migrant population. We have transferred this concept to a different part of the world: a Palestinian refugee camp. Similar to the German neighborhoods we deal with, refugee camps are also the result of migration moves; however, in this case - an enforced one. This paper describes the come_IN approach and investigates its adaptation to a Palestinian refugee camp. Obviously it exhibits fundamental cultural, social, and political dissimilarities from the German setting. Refugees living in camps have to deal with a number of local living and subsistence challenges, as well as having to tackle mounting critical issues related to their refugee status. Here we describe the first three years of activities and experiences.

Author Keywords

Computer Club; children; integration; communities; international collaboration.

ACM Classification Keywords

H.5.m. Information interfaces and presentation (e.g., HCI): Miscellaneous.

INTRODUCTION

The intercultural computer clubs, called *come_IN*, offer a place to share practices among children and adults of diverse ethnical backgrounds. Once a week the participants gather voluntarily in the computer club to work on joint projects, study, play, or realize individual ideas supported by the use of information and communication technology (ICT). The participants create personal meaningful artifacts together in order to express themselves. The establishment of these practices is apt to develop an effect both on an individual as well as at community level. Engaging in computer supported project work, the club participants can extend their social networks and learn from other participants – often across cultural boundaries [19,21]

Like other western societies, Germany is facing migration from countries with distinctly dissimilar socio-cultural backgrounds. The lack of social as well as cultural integration seems to lead to unequal opportunities and lower levels of education. For instance, the German Turkish community which has existed for over forty years in Germany still finds itself confronted with these issues.

Since 2003 we have built a network of come_IN computer clubs in Germany [17,19]. They are located in socially and culturally diverse neighborhoods. Most of them are based in elementary schools, being part of their afternoon activities. Each weekly session brings children and adults of diverse migration backgrounds together. The projects carried out in these clubs are typically linked to issues relevant to the particular neighborhood, e.g. the creation of animation films using stories from the neighborhood [18].

In this paper, we investigate the establishment of a first computer club in a Palestinian refugee camp. Through the use and appropriation of ICT, these marginalized Palestinian refugee communities may be supported to positively engage in their own society and in the Palestinian-Israeli conflict-to-peace transformation process. Another major objective in transferring our approach is to network Palestinians among themselves - especially women and children - across different sites, even countries, at the same time promoting their integration into the local societies and finally enabling them to access the information society.

The paper is structured as follows: a review of the literature discusses the underlying concepts and the Palestinian context. The next chapter describes Jalazone, a refugee camp where we started our first computer club in Palestine. It is followed by a description of our basic approach, the research methods, and our empirical findings. The paper ends with a discussion of the findings.

STATE OF THE ART

The concept of the come_IN computer clubs follows the tradition of computer clubhouses in the US which later evolved into a global network, now with over 100 computer clubhouses (two of which are in Palestine). The first of these computer clubhouses was established for underprivileged youngsters in Boston in the year 1993; the principles of situated, collaborative learning and constructionist thinking offered them opportunities to express themselves with the use of ICT and new media [5]. The pedagogical concept behind the clubhouses is an extension of the constructivist-learning paradigm. Constructivism describes the learning process as constructing individual cognitive structures. Papert extended this idea; he stated that these cognitive structures have to be put in practice by constructing artifacts. This is now known as *constructionism* [13]. Hence, in the computer club sessions the participants have the opportunity to work on their own ideas, but also to work together in a team, which "emerges" informally over time, coalescing around a common interest [14]. Resnick [15] mentioned that communities are flexible and dynamic, "evolving to meet the need of the projects and interests of the participants." To support the young people, adult staff and volunteer mentors offered intellectual, technical, and very often emotional support [9].

One of the tools which the participants use to create virtual artifacts such as video games, animations, images and sound, is Scratch. It is an End User Development [8] environment based on a building-block metaphor, in which pieces of code are put together to create scripts and manipulate the figures on the screen [9].

The come_IN approach developed this concept further, applying it to issues of inter-generational learning and the integration of migrant communities in Germany. The computer club was erected at schools, which serve a central point of exchange among the people of the city district. The computer club provides opportunities for children in elementary school, their parents and tutors to engage in group-oriented project work [19]. Once a week, they gather in one of the six clubs, work on joint projects or realize their individual ideas on the computer with the support of the tutors. They can also explore and practice their skills in ICT and multimedia. Most of the projects last for several months and can contain different multi-media artifacts. During this time, the learning situations are more intensive for the parents and their children based on the active participation by dealing with the chosen topics of their projects and by evaluating how to solve any emerging problems. Several volunteers support the participants and teach them how to use the different tools [19].

There are relatively few studies dealing with computer supported learning and community building under the specific conditions of Palestinian refugee camps. Khalili [7] has investigated the 'cyberculture' of Palestinian refugee camps in Lebanon and how the internet "distributes modes of nationalist understanding, using images and leaflets, across borders" (p.127). Wahbeh [20] analyzed a number of cases that involve students and teachers in public, private and United Nation Relief and Work Agency (UNRWA) schools in the West Bank, where institutions like the Intel Club performed training courses for young people. The studied computer labs were not connected to the internet due to budgetary reasons, so the pupils had to rely on the clubs and internet cafés to use the computers and access the internet for doing their homework. While the percentage of internet users has grown strongly during the last decade (57.7 % of the population in Palestine in mid-2012 according to [23]), the digital divide between the students in a camp and those outside is still obvious. The term "digital divide" was defined by Mehra [11] as "the troubling gap between those who use computers and the internet and those who do not." To narrow this divide and to empower students in a refugee camp, Sawhney [16] hosted storytelling workshops over a period of three years. The young people in refugee camps have stories to tell and reflect a lot on "their identity, heritage, environment, and life experience." Storytelling can also be used to work through intractable conflicts; this enables people with traumatic social experiences to digest these experiences and learn to live with the events. Working with a Palestinian-Israeli group, Bar-On [12] demonstrated in a similar manner that storytelling often helps to cope with painful events.

The potential benefits that computer clubs provide to the community have not yet been academically investigated in the Palestinian context. However, Wulf et al. [22] describe how an early attempt of such an investigation led to a study on political activists in a Palestinian village in the West Bank. In the context of exploring the potentials of computer clubhouses, the authors describe how the activists made use of email and social media to articulate their protest against the Israeli expropriation of their land and how they stay in touch with an international network of supporters.

JALAZONE: A PALESTINIAN REFUGEE CAMP IN THE WEST BANK

Jalazone is a Palestinian refugee camp in the West Bank, situated approximately 7 km north of Ramallah and 3 km east of Birzeit University. Ramallah has developed into a bustling political and economic center on the West Bank. The Palestinian political administration, called the Palestinian National Authority (PNA), is located there.

Like most other refugee camps, Jalazone was established in 1949, built on plots of land leased by the UNRWA from the Hashemite Kingdom of Jordan. Individuals living in a neighboring village named Jifna owned the plots of lands privately. The inhabitants of the camp were expelled or fled from their homes in nowadays Israel, specifically the area around Ramleh and Lydd, during the Arab-Israeli War in 1948. The actual number of inhabitants of the camp is unclear. While there are various official statistics or estimations, the camp services popular committee – an in-camp elected committee – estimates the population of Jalazone between 10,000 and 15,000. A high population density as well as crowded and precarious living conditions characterizes the camp. The unemployment rate is much higher than in the neighboring urban region (40% in Jalazone according to the camp administration).

The existence of the refugee camps more than 60 years after their establishment is politically a highly sensitive issue, since they symbolize the need and desire of the Palestinian people to return to their land which was lost to Israel in 1948. The positioning of the refugee camps' population within the Palestinian society is a complex one. While their continued existence is seen to be a political necessity ("right to return"), the in-camp population is looked upon in a demeaning manner and they are often regarded as second-class citizens. They are generally considered to be poorly dressed, behave aggressively, and use street language. People expect negative interaction with them due to perceived differences in morals, values, and attitudes. In general, members of the Palestinian middle class would typically prefer not to enter any of the refugee camps and very rarely do so. There are also severe economic and social obstacles to be overcome by refugee camp inhabitants who want to move out. So there is little social esteem and exchange with regard to the inhabitants of a refugee camp.

The camp is run by an administrative council of 21 members who appoint a management board. M. is the head of the camp's services popular committee – he is a member of the Fatah movement. A female Palestinian politician, H., an alumni of Birzeit University, represents the camp in the Fatah movements. She was instrumental in establishing the contact which led to the development of the computer club. Upon the request of Birzeit University, the camp's administration set up an association specifically to run the computer club.

As with all 59 recognized refugee camps in Jordan, Lebanon, Syria, the West Bank and the Gaza Strip, the United Nations Relief and Works Agency (UNRWA) offers rudimentary medical, educational, and solid waste collection services to the population of Jalazone. Within the framework of these services, UNRWA runs two schools, one for boys and one for girls, which are located at the main entrance to the camp. These schools have rather large class sizes of 40 to 50 children and follow Palestinian national curricula combined with a rather teaching-by-instructions pattern [20]. The population of Jalazone receives additional aid from USAID, the PNA, the Fatah movement, and a variety of other donors.

The Jalazone's camp services popular committee estimates that about 60% of the in-camp families have access to the internet at home. The actual usage is unclear since the majority of the adults are often not adept at using computers. There are also several Internet cafés in the camp, which have opened in recent years. However these places have a bad reputation among the parents since they are rarely supervised properly by adults and it is suspected that they are used for computer games, gambling, and watching pornography.

RESEARCH METHODS

The main methodological framing for our research comes from Participatory Action Research (PAR) by Kemmis & McTaggert [6,10]: Our work is attached to real world problems as laid out in the previous sections and given the lack of infrastructure as well as the relatively volatile and difficult setting, mere immersion in the field is not enough. We actually had and have to engage in action and intervention (from founding the club through specific projects and political justifications to camp-political issues, explained in more detail below). This approach is similar to that employed by other researchers in difficult settings, e.g. Braa and Manya [3] who worked towards a decentralized, bottom-up health ICT in Africa. The action research phases *in situ* by researchers from our home university – usually a few days up to a few weeks in the field several times a year - are alternated with more reflective phases. The analysis of our findings, notes and documentation were realized by a qualitative content analysis, entailing the controlled analysis of texts within their context of communication. This was conducted not only among our research group but also with colleagues not immersed in the field, as well as internationally together with our local partner university. We also take care to send multiple and alternating researchers and students into the field, ensuring a broader perspective and actively working against possible bias stemming from a high degree of participation and action. Hence data gathering as well as analysis is dispersed over a large group of researchers, local as well as at home, including both those who are and who are not immersed in the field. This leads to a high degree of explication of tacit understandings and thicker descriptions. The contrasting cases of Germany / Palestine as club locations also reflect on the principles of Grounded Theory.

Throughout our researchers' fieldwork, qualitative research methods were used to observe the field in as much detail as possible. The authors conducted the research presented in this paper over a period of 46 months, from May 2010 to March 2014. While the local coordinator (and first author) visited the computer club once a week and on a regular basis, the other authors visited the computer clubs at least every six months, seven visits by March 2014 with a total stay of 16 weeks. During these visits, our researchers attended, observed and took part in the weekly club sessions.

The visits were documented via field notes and photos. Every evening, extensive documentation was written pertaining to the respective day. Since the non-Palestinian researchers do not speak Arabic, the local coordinator translated for them. Moreover, the German researchers were accompanied by a translator on three of the visits. It was therefore possible for the researchers who do not speak Arabic themselves to conduct workshops and interviews with the volunteers, children and inhabitants of the refugee camp in their native language. During a stay in August and September 2012, 7 semi-structured interviews (each with a duration between 30 minutes and 3 hours) were conducted as well as more than ten informal interviews, almost all of which were audio recorded. For her Master thesis, a native speaker carried out 13 semi-structured interviews with children from the refugee camps about the computer clubhouses. Additionally, protocols and feedback sheets from the weekly computer club sessions written by the tutors and other materials were collected and were included in the analysis.

For privacy and security reasons, we have substituted names with abbreviations in this.

RESEARCH SETTING
Building a computer club in this context is a challenge, not only regarding the scientific methods employed: As seen above, there are considerable political constraints. Finding and building a trustworthy relationship to local partners willing to implement the come_IN approach was another big issue.

In May 2010 the first author went to the West Bank to explore opportunities for research and academic cooperation. He was specifically interested in exploring whether computer clubhouses, which were conceptualized for and implemented in German neighborhoods, could be transferred to the context of the West Bank. In April 2011, two authors went to Jalazone to meet the administration staff from the Camp Services and Administration Council. The administration staff had already realized a project with Birzeit University in the past and was willing to cooperate again with the University. They promised to look for a location and a local NGO to act as cooperation partner. At the end of 2011, the German Federal Foreign Office approved a project proposal for setting up a first come_IN computer club within a Palestinian refugee camp.

Establishing and successfully running a community-based computer club in a refugee camp environment proved to be a daunting task. Hence there was a need for the local project manager from Birzeit University to visit existing computer clubs in Germany. After a potential location for the computer club had been selected, the local project manager visited the come_IN team in Germany to learn more about the project. In different workshops combined with visits to the computer clubs, he came to understand the come_IN approach better. In discussions with the come_IN team about the concept, some necessary adaptions became obvious. To fit in with the context of the refugee camps, the technical infrastructure had to be adjusted, as had the mentoring of the children (more on that in the Findings).

Following several months of preparation, the computer club was opened in May 2012. The popular committee of the camp as well as representatives of the PNA and Birzeit University were present at the opening ceremony. The technical infrastructure with 13 thin-clients and two host computers was installed; the only problem was the non-existent internet connection, which was supposed to be available some days later. First, under the authors' guidance, a workshop with all the volunteers took place in the computer club to prepare the volunteers for working with children and to understand the concept. One week later, the first computer club session started with more than 20 children and five tutors. During the next four months the participants met on Saturdays to work together on different projects.

During the summer semester, Birzeit University organizes an annual 3-week-long summer enrichment program for school children. Arrangements were made with Jalazone's popular committee along with the children's parents to hold the weekly club sessions on the University campus – on a daily basis – and as part of the summer camp. For a period of three weeks, a bus would transport the 20 participating children from Jalazone camp to the campus of Birzeit University. Ameeneh, a university student volunteer, accompanied the children on the 10-minute bus journey. The summer camp focused on 2 major themes: programming with Scratch and building robotic prototypes utilizing Lego Mindstorm kits. In addition to experiencing Birzeit's college life, Jalazone children were able to meet other children from middle schools around Ramallah who were participating in the summer camp.

During Ramadan, the computer club took a time out. This was a good opportunity to reflect together with the participants, volunteers and other people involved. During a workshop, the authors and student volunteers exchanged and compared their experiences. In the course of additional personal interviews, more intimate conversations were initiated and these often disclosed problems. Some participants were interviewed in order to gain another view on the computer club sessions. A further goal of this visit was to keep the club running which necessitated preparations being made. With the help of the local coordinator, the search was started both for new volunteers as well as for further locations for additional computer clubs.

In 2013, we were able to open a second computer club in the Al Am'ari camp – a Palestinian refugee camp located 2 km south of Ramallah in the central West Bank. This paper will however focus on our experiences with the Jalazone camp alone.

EMPIRICAL FINDINGS
This chapter presents the findings and results related to different dimensions and aspects of our work during the last two years.

Location

In Germany, the computer clubs are usually hosted in elementary schools. The UNRWA administrates schools in Palestinian refugee camps. However, setting up a new project like a computer club means overcoming a lot of bureaucratic barriers of centralized UN sub-organizations. Another option was to choose a local NGO to cooperate with as they can act more freely. Negotiations regarding the conditions of the cooperation then ensued. With the help of H., a female Fatah politician, we got in touch with the head of *Dima* – Association of Creativity. This newly formed organization was quickly registered as an NGO, just in time to host and run the computer club. It is physically located inside the building which is home to the camp services' popular committee.

While the installation of the technical infrastructure and the introduction of weekly activities of the computer club were relatively quickly established, other issues appeared. The building is also used for other activities, e.g. as a gym, and was therefore very often crowded and busy, which often disturbed club sessions.

Volunteering Students

The weekly sessions of the German computer clubs are tutored by a schoolteacher and a university student. Although some of the students already have experience in working together with children, all of them receive practical training during their first months. At Birzeit University in Palestine, undergraduate students are mandated to complete 120 hours of community service during their studies as a pre-requisite for graduation. This community service has to be performed in a socially important environment such as in a health or community center. After receiving approval from the Student Affairs Office at Birzeit University, the local coordinator announced – via the University's online bulletin board - the availability of community service work in the form of tutoring children at Jalazone refugee camp.

In the first round, 20 female students from diverse study backgrounds registered to serve as volunteer computer club tutors one month later; most of them were living in the refugee camp. In the first round, not one single male student was interested in working as a tutor. However, over time the reputation of the project grew among the Birzeit students. The number of students wanting to volunteer has currently risen to some 40 students. Moreover, the gender ratio has relaxed slightly over time. Currently, some 30% of the volunteers are male. One of the female volunteers commented on the continuing over-representation of female students as follows: '*Most of the male students prefer volunteer hours which are not too demanding and easy to carry out, such as organizing exhibitions on campus*'.

By holding interviews, the local project coordinator tries to figure out which applicants suit the project and he selects some 5 – 7 volunteers for each of the two clubs. He commented that it sometimes takes time to distinguish between those whose sole interest is to have the hours accredited and those who really want to get involved.

The student volunteers accepted to work with the camp children are then added as members to the Facebook (FB) group that was set up by the coordinator at the beginning of the project (note: Organization, even of official / job related matters via FB, is very common here). The FB group contains brief descriptions of each clubhouse session along with photos of the sessions and screen shots of the children's work on the computers. The new volunteers can browse through the feed of past postings inside the group to get a feeling of how the sessions have been run in the past. In addition, the FB group is used as an interactive space for student volunteers to participate in an exchange of ideas related to their clubhouse tutoring work. For example, volunteers can suggest, vote for, and comment on new ways to make the work with the children more fun and engaging. The coordinator uses the FB group to post important alerts and announcements.

In contrast to our second computer clubhouse in Al Amari, the volunteers who finally decide to work in Jalazone are mostly - but not completely – based in the camp itself. There are a couple of reasons for this. First, Jalazone borders on Beit El, an Israeli settlement and a military outpost. Similar to most Israeli settlements, and for security reasons, Beit El is built on top of a steep hill and is protected by a 12-meter-high wire fence, equipped with high-tech security and surveillance equipment. It is approximately 500 meters away from the camp and is separated from it by a road which Palestinians use to access the camp. Israeli settlers use a special road on the other side of the settlement. Due to the close proximity of the settlement to the camp, there are frequent clashes between young people in the camp and Israeli settlers and soldiers. During the last nine months, three unarmed youngsters (aged 14 – 21) were shot and killed by Israeli soldiers, while many others have been seriously injured by rubber bullets. Residents of the camp have told us that on more than one occasion, IDF (Israel Defense Forces) soldiers from Beit El's army outpost have utilized the Jalazone camp as a training field. We were told that training exercises are carried out at night by Israeli soldiers in full combat gear. These involve random house raids and mock arrests, sparking clashes with the civilian in-camp residents and panic among children and the elderly.

Consequently, the Jalazone camp is usually perceived to be more dangerous than other refugee camps in the region. Secondly, Jalazone is more difficult to reach by public transport from the university campus.

Compared with other volunteer options, the students found working as a tutor to be very time-consuming, labor-intensive and emotionally engaging. Although most volunteers have lived in the camp all their lives, they appreciated having the chance to carry out meaningful work for the community within the camp. They valued the opportunity of working with young children as well as making friends with each other. Moreover, the work in the computer club gave visibility to them inside the camp community. For instance, M, the head of the camp administration, expressed his surprise that so many of the camp's residents attended Birzeit University. This fact was not in line with his assumptions about the educational trajectories of young people inside the camp.

Most of the volunteers did not have any experience in working with children and only a few of them were studying computer science or computer systems engineering. Due to this, they initially expressed concerns that their computer skills were not profound enough. We also learnt that other Birzeit students from the camp did not want to volunteer in their own camp. One female student told us that she feels ashamed to live in a refugee camp and doesn't want to be associated with it. Volunteering in the computer club project would only stress her situation.

Ever since volunteering at the beginning of the project, three females, all from the camp, have decided to continue working in the clubhouse. This engagement is over and above the hours for which they are accredited. One of the students even extended her engagement after finishing her studies, despite being hired by a foreign telecommunications company. These three students have developed into lead volunteers who play an important role in helping the new volunteers understand both the local conditions and their tasks.

Participants

Since most of the computer club participants are elementary school children, the average age of participants in Germany is between 6 and 10 years old. While most of the schools in Germany are co-educative, mono-education is common in Palestine. This also applies to the Jalazone refugee camp. In the first workshop with the female tutors and the head of Dima organization, the authors discussed the possibility of drawing boys and girls together in the computer club. On one hand, the tutors deemed it difficult to have mixed-gender sessions and recommended two different sessions, one for the boys and another for the girls. This is because they envisaged that the parental preference would be single-gender sessions which conforms to what they have been accustomed to in the camp's schools. They also assumed that only mothers would participate with their children as the fathers had to work all day long and would be too tired in the afternoon. On the other hand, the head of *Dima* promised to get girls and boys to attend the computer club at the same time. During the first two sessions, and in contrast to the schools, both genders – boys and girls – attended the computer club together at the same time, in the same room. However, 'un-forced' gender segregation was clearly seen in the room as the girls sat next to each other while the boys sat at the opposite ends in a U-shaped seating configuration. When asked to work in groups, the participants almost always formed single-sex teams.

Consequently, and also due to the high number of attendees, the tutors decided to hold 2 sessions per week – one for each gender. As time progressed, the number of boys attending sessions decreased and the tutors then decided to revert back to mixed-gender sessions: '*We have mostly boys and not so many girls. I wish more girls would attend the sessions. I'm ashamed, when I'm alone*' (Bissan, female, 11-years old).

To advertise the computer club, the tutors created posters during the first session and distributed them within the refugee camp in places like shops and cafés. After this campaign, the head of the NGO insisted on taking responsibility for the advertising. As a result, the rather large weekly fluctuation in the number of participants made it difficult for the tutors to follow-up the children's projects. Also the age gap of eight to 15-year old participants wasn't easy to deal with, since the older ones didn't want to work together with the younger participants due to different interests.

Club Sessions

Usually, the weekly German club sessions are timed to have round-table discussions at the beginning and end. This means that the principle of informal learning without a fixed curriculum is being followed. There is also an explicit leisure time slot for the children to play games and suchlike. We tried to establish a similar sequence in Jalazone and explained both the principle and our experiences to the student volunteers. Since the very first sessions tended to be a little disorganized, the local project coordinator outlined a curriculum together with the student volunteers. For the following year, the participants were taught a different component of Scratch every session. Besides their self-created curriculum, they used different, more extensive educational material. Due to the great demand, the group of 25-30 participants was split into two smaller groups. However, the idea of having two club sessions one after the other on the same day didn't fully work out: '*The tutors told me to leave after the session. But I stayed, I want to learn something*' (Ahmed, 14-years old). Instead of leaving the club after their session, children from the first group stayed behind and tried hard to join the second group. This resulted in tutors still having to look after a lot of children at the same time (see Figure 1). Over the following months, the number of participating children fluctuated depending on schoolwork, weather conditions, and other reasons such as sports events and the soccer games that occasionally took place at the same time as clubhouse sessions. The computer club therefore began to run one or two sessions per week depending on demand. As in the German computer clubs, the weekly club sessions in Jalazone camp lasted for an hour and half each.

As a consequence of their abject living conditions due to overcrowding, Palestinians living in refugee camps are subject to mental health issues and stress [2]. While working with the children in the clubhouse sessions, we observed that many had conduct issues such as lacking a sense of responsibility, aggressivity and fighting with other children, and unwillingness to work within a team. The project coordinator had to assign 3 - 4 mentors to be present at each of the sessions to work alongside the children in order for the session to proceed according to plan.

Figure 1. Computer club participants in Jalazone

Projects

After an introduction to Scratch, the participants engaged in their first projects. Most of them created animations or games, but a group of three children wanted to prepare a presentation about the history of the camp and the hardship endured by people living there. As Chahd told us: '*We can develop ideas. And create programs to tell stories with pictures*' *(Chahd, female, 12 years old)*.

They collected personal pictures from their parents and grandparents and wrote down the stories their relatives told them. With the help of the tutors, they articulated everything together in a single presentation. In this project, they had to deal with the conflict and the forced displacement of their families. A lot of these activities and projects can be compared to those in the German computer clubs, where Scratch is also very popular and has been used for many years, mainly to create animations and games. The use of Scratch and presentation software can be seen as tools used in "digital storytelling" [4,18] in both the Palestinian as well as in the German computer clubs. In one of the German computer clubs, the children – supported by their parents – created a brochure about the neighborhood where they lived and this was very similar to the Palestinian family stories. For the Palestinian children, Scratch also serves as a tool for expressing their feelings and emotions in regard to their poor socio-economic living conditions: Bet El, an Israeli settlement, is situated very close to Jalazone; therefore incidents such as violent demonstrations, shootings and struggles between settlers and refugees take place very often. For example, a 14-year old boy was shot dead by Israeli soldiers in late 2013. In the following weeks some of the participants created several Scratch projects relating to this incident (see Figure 2). '*My friends and I programmed a story in which we passed the settlement and helped youngsters to throw stones at the settlement*' *(Salsabil, 13-years old)*.

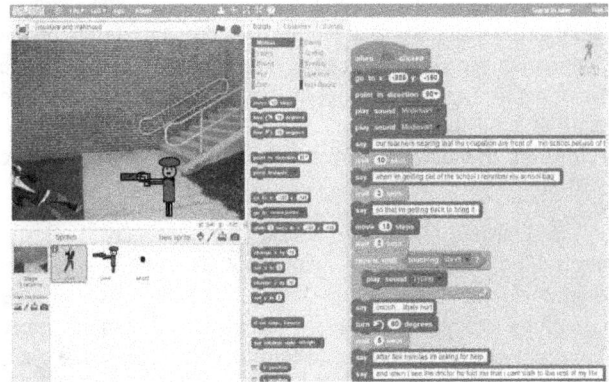

Figure 2. Scratch project regarding an incident in which a boy from the refugee camp was shot dead by Israeli soldiers.

Technical infrastructure

M. was very eager to have the computer hardware set up as quickly as possible. At first, M. insisted that a minimum of 20 desktop computers were needed, as he expected a high number of participants. After careful planning, a system of 13 thin-client networked computers along with 2 host (server) computers was deployed. This system was cheaper, easier to administrate and not as theft-prone as normal personal computers, but also came with some disadvantages. Creating Scratch projects with sound became very difficult without USB, microphone and speaker plug-in. The computers were connected to the internet despite the fact that the connection wasn't always reliable. Occasional electricity outages, common within the camp, are even more critical. As in Germany, the computer clubs were also provided with a B/W laser printer, a scanner and a projector. After almost two years' use, the system and the other hardware is still operational and in use. M. looks after it and has even updated the whole system with a new version of the operating system without any professional help. This unfortunately led to compatibility issues. Generally speaking, the lack of both professional maintenance and IT skills has led to virus issues, configuration issues, system slowdowns and similar sys-admin problems.

Exclusion Mechanisms

In September 2012, we conducted informal interviews with young people in Jalazone's commercial internet cafés as well as on the street in front of one of these cafés. The goal was to find out why they were not attending the clubhouse sessions. All of the youngsters we talked to were boys who did not know about the existence of the come_IN computer club which had opened some four months previously.

A shop owner whose business is located in the vicinity of the come_IN computer club expressed the opinion that the people in charge of organizing the come_IN computer club did not make enough effort in terms of announcing the existence of the computer club to the refugee camp's inhabitants. This led to a situation where the computer club is – according to his perception – only visited and used by youngsters who are either family members or friends of the team which manages the camp. As time progressed, more in-camp families learned about the clubhouse sessions and began to send their children. At some point in time, we had 2 children attend who were residents of the nearby village of Jifna.

In the German computer clubs, we also saw specific patterns of participation. Typically, the existence of the computer clubs is rather well communicated in the elementary schools. However, participation is much more likely among the children and families who are in the class of the teacher responsible for running the clubs. Still, the phenomenon in Germany is less one of family relationship and exclusion but is rather related to the fact that families in Germany try to use the computer club to build relationships with the teacher responsible for their children's class.

DISCUSSION

In Palestine, interacting with computers seems to be just as much an attractor as it is in Germany. There is a huge amount of interest among the children in Palestinian refugee camps in working with modern technology. However, it turned out that the socio-cultural and institutional framing of the clubs is more of a challenge.

Cooperating with an established local organization is a crucial factor for being noticed and supported by the camp's rather closed society. Since the schools in Palestinian refugee camps are run by UNRWA who do not have the capacity to support such extracurricular activities, the camp's popular committee or other local NGOs should be taken into consideration as potential cooperation partners for establishing and running computer clubs. These organizations not only have the resources in terms of buildings or rooms which can be used for the club sessions but are also very well-connected and respected within the camp's society. While in Germany computer clubhouses almost always benefit from schools' staff and housing, this cannot be provided in the case of Palestinian refugee camps. We hope to foster more collaboration between the computer clubs and the UNWRA schools in the future. However, such attempts prove to be quite a challenge.

The technical infrastructure is a major point regarding a proper and trouble-free implementation of the sessions. Decisions for a traditional desktop or a thin-client solution should be grounded in local security concerns, the projected needs and demands as well as IT skills on hand locally. In the Jalazone case, the thin-client architecture works but faces issues regarding long-term stability and maintenance. Those problems could be alleviated by the incorporation of local computer experts into the project. However, hardware-related issues - such as sound problems - are due to the system architecture and directly influence the projects.

The use of Facebook (FB) as a means of coordination is very well accepted and established in Palestine. Even in University settings, FB groups serve as a platform for the tutors and the local coordinator not only to share past experiences in terms of pictures and reports but also to coordinate sessions, discuss further actions, and quickly rearrange dates in case of unexpected events. Even most of the children are very active in FB, so the communication between tutors and children outside the sessions can be conducted via group chats.

Of course, privacy is an issue in Palestine too, so no information regarding the children should be publicly accessible. The projects worked on by attendees cover similar topics to the children's projects in Germany. They are mainly interested in presenting their home, their background and their own interests. The difference being that the Palestinian children are more used to existential issues, such as violence and death and thus integrate these themes into their project work. Letting them choose the project topics by themselves has worked very well so far and should be continued in the same way in future to ensure a high intrinsic motivation.

Committed voluntary tutors are a major factor in ensuring reasonable and reliable club sessions. In our case, the mandatory social service program of BZU was a perfect match for the club's needs and on the whole, the student volunteers are greatly committed to their work in the clubs. In the case of Jalazone, it was extremely valuable to acquire a large number of volunteers who themselves live in the camp as this alleviated the widespread suspicions of the refugees towards strangers. These insiders can serve as a connecting link, spanning boundaries towards the local population as well serving as positive role models for the children in terms of educational opportunities. At the beginning of the project, external female tutors felt the need to be driven directly in front of the club doors. Even after four months of working there, they still felt they were in a strange and potentially dangerous environment. No similar problems pertaining to tutors' perceived safety have been experienced in any of the neighborhoods we work in in Germany. As time progressed, the coordinator and tutors became more habituated to the camp's environment. One year after their first visit to the camp they had developed a greater and stronger feeling of safety and security although not to the point at which they felt completely invulnerable. This can be regarded as an indication of the benefits arising from the socio-cultural integration and also transcends the clubs. Strong connections between the volunteers and the children which have formed over time and have also motivated volunteers to keep working in the clubs for extended periods of time emphasize this point.

Compared to the participation pattern of children with a migrant-background in Germany, we see more fluctuation and less regularity among the participants in the Palestinian computer clubs as well as more attendees who are related to the people involved in the organization of the clubs. A better and more constant advertisement of club activities among the camp's families and local schools would be likely to attract a more diverse range of participants and lead to a higher commitment. More regular attendance could be achieved by creating better awareness and producing recurrent reminders for the families. The attendance of mainly family members of the club's officials can be put to good advantage in the first months of a new club opening as these children can spread the word informally about the existence of club sessions, thus attracting more children who are not related to the club officials. However, care and persistence are necessary to really spread the word and to avoid perception of the club as an elite institution for the administration's families.

Furthermore, the camp administration is responsible for channeling resources to the camp's population, thus assigning them a very strong position. The computer clubhouse, from the administrations point of view, can be understood as one of these resources. This viewpoint reflected negatively on how the club was perceived, as well as on the pattern of club participation. Tutors coming in from outside felt threatened by certain practices prevalent in the masculine culture of the camp's leadership, and while these structures and practices had a problematic impact on the flourishing of the computer club, it would have been difficult to circumvent this institutional given. Despite this, we continue to see masculine practices throughout the club being influenced, e.g. through the growing acceptance of female tutors as well as mixed gender club session which benefit inclusion.

Relying on the camp administration may mean that the clubs become a part of the resources which stabilize the existing power structures inside the camp. At some point, such a position might pose a threat to some of the overarching goals of the clubs, specifically the better inclusion of people living in the camps with those in the rest of Palestinian society [19]. The camp administration's raison d'être is the very existence of the camp. Complete integration in the rest of the West Bank society would threaten their position and – in the local perception – the Palestinian people's right to return to their pre-1948 lands, i.e. it is the intention of the camp *not* to be fully integrated in West Bank society." These conditions mean that care must be taken to position the club houses 'politically correctly'. In contrast, in Germany there is a certain consensus in the political mainstream that the integration of migrants is politically desirable. In all likelihood, this massive constraint will continue to be an issue for the Palestinian computer clubs.

To sum up some of the focal points in the manner of a primer for other attempts at building similar bottom-up structures in refugee camps (although this should not be viewed as a universal checklist – every camp is different and situated research is *always* necessary):

- Careful research into local practices and basic values is crucial – goals such as "immigrants should be included in mainstream society" might be far from universal; and even if the (action) researcher believes them to be true, outside intervention should be well considered.
- Partnering up with a local university is very helpful since they provide not only insight into local practices and values but can also help with much needed structure as well as volunteers.
- Persistence and multiple angles of approach regarding research and PR are important – both help overcome issues like exclusion and dissemination practices (e.g. the focus on relatives as members for the computer club in the beginning).
- Bottom-up training and exchange are valuable, in the sense that they bring local coordinators and volunteers to already established clubs.
- Technical infrastructure should be lean and agile; however, long-term support regarding the IT administration should be provided.
- Entanglement in (camp) micro politics is unavoidable, however, a careful analysis is crucial to avoid being utilized as a resource in unforeseen and possibly unwanted political or social ways.

CONCLUSION

While the come_IN approach itself was inspired by Resnick's [14] work, it was yet another stretch to transfer this approach to Palestine. Germany and Palestine are very distinct in many cultural as well as socio-economic dimensions. Specifically, the living conditions of refugees in the West Bank camps are distinct from the various migrant communities in German neighborhoods. Along with the rest of Palestinian society, the camp population has been living for an even longer period of time in a complex relationship along than have the migrant communities in German neighborhoods. While being economically disadvantaged and considered outsiders, the status of the Palestinian camp inhabitants offers a number of benefits and resources mostly channeled through UNWRA and the camp administration.

The challenge of our research endeavor was to share insights gained in Germany while adapting the socio-technical concept to the different context. We assumed that our publications and written materials would only provide limited insight into the experience we gained during almost ten years of project work in Germany. We therefore organized an exchange of expertise among the partners at different points in time [1]. Various members of the German project team spent substantial amounts of time in understanding the local context and preparing for the opening of the club. Moreover, we invited the Palestinian project manager to Germany for a week to let him see the German clubs in action. Such a bottom-up approach to mutual learning is distinct from Intel's way of spreading their version of computer clubhouses around the world [24].

Our model entails a partnership between a university and a computer club, one in which the university supports the club activities through student mentors, coordination, obtaining funds, and expertise sharing. Many aspects of this model were transferred across different contexts from Germany to Palestine, albeit in interesting ways. In Palestine, we decided to work with a local university, Birzeit, to build the club, adding a second university player to the support structure. Even though they coordinate the local activities and engage undergraduate students to tutor the club, their social recognition in the camp is quite diverse.

Over time, as part of a long-term plan for sustainability, it is our hope that most if not all of the local university roles can be taken over by Birzeit.

ACKNOWLEDGMENTS

We thank Batya Friedman, University of Washington, for kind comments on an earlier draft of this paper.

REFERENCES

1. Ackerman, M.S., Pipek, V., and Wulf, V. *Sharing expertise: Beyond knowledge management*. MIT press, 2003.

2. Baker, A.M. Psychological Response of Palestinian Children to Environmental Stress Associated With Military Occupation. *Journal of Refugee Studies 4*, 3 (1991), 237–247.

3. Braa, J. and Manya, A. Developing decentralised health information systems in developing countries. *The Journal of Community Informatics 9*, 2 (2013).

4. Burke, Q. and Kafai, Y.B. Programming & storytelling: opportunities for learning about coding & composition. *Proc. IDC '10*, ACM Press (2010), 348.

5. Kafai, Y.B., Peppler, K.A., and Chapman, R.N., eds. *The Computer Clubhouse: constructionism and creativity in youth communities*. Teachers College Press, New York, 2009.

6. Kemmis, S. and McTaggart, R. Communicative action and the public sphere. *Denzin, NK & Lincoln, YS (red.), The Sage handbook of qualitative research 3*, (2005), 559–603.

7. Khalili, L. Virtual nation: Palestinian cyberculture in Lebanese camps. *Palestine, Israel, and the Politics of Popular Culture*, (2005).

8. Lieberman, H., Paternò, F., and Wulf, V., eds. *End User Development*. Springer Netherlands, Dordrecht, 2006.

9. Maloney, J., Burd, L., Kafai, Y., Rusk, N., Silverman, B., and Resnick, M. Scratch: a sneak preview. IEEE (2004), 104–109.

10. McTaggart, R. and Kemmis, S. *The action research planner*. Deakin university, 1988.

11. Mehra, B., Merkel, C., and Bishop, A.P. The internet for empowerment of minority and marginalized users. *New Media & Society 6*, 6 (2004), 781–802.

12. Bar-On, D. and Kassem, F. Storytelling as a Way to Work Through Intractable Conflicts: The German-Jewish Experience and Its Relevance to the Palestinian-Israeli Context. *Journal of Social Issues 60*, 2 (2004), 289–306.

13. Papert, S. *Mindstorms: children, computers, and powerful ideas*. Basic Books, Inc., 1980.

14. Resnick, M. and Rusk, N. The computer clubhouse: helping youth develop fluency with new media. *Proceedings of the 1996 international conference on Learning sciences*, International Society of the Learning Sciences (1996), 285–291.

15. Resnick, M. Towards a practice of constructional design. *Innovations in learning: New environments for education*, (1996), 161–174.

16. Sawhney, N. Voices beyond walls: the role of digital storytelling for empowering marginalized youth in refugee camps. *Proc. IDC '09*, ACM Press (2009), 302.

17. Schubert, K., Weibert, A., and Wulf, V. Locating computer clubs in multicultural neighborhoods: How collaborative project work fosters integration processes. *International Journal of Human-Computer Studies 69*, 10 (2011), 669–678.

18. Schubert, K. and Weibert, A. How the social structure of intercultural 'come_IN' computer clubs fosters interactive storytelling. *International Journal of Arts and Technology 7*, 1 (2014), 78.

19. Stevens, G., Veith, M., and Wulf, V. Bridging among ethnic communities by cross-cultural communities of practice. In *Communities and Technologies 2005*. Springer, 2005, 377–396.

20. Wahbeh, N. ICT and Education in Palestine: Social and Educational Inequalities in Access to ICT. Qattan Center for Educational Research and Development(2006).

21. Weibert, A. and Wulf, V. "All of a sudden we had this dialogue...": intercultural computer clubs' contribution to sustainable integration. *Proc. ICIC '10*, ACM Press (2010), 93.

22. Wulf, V., Aal, K., Abu Kteish, I., et al. Fighting against the wall: social media use by political activists in a Palestinian village. *Proc. CHI '13*, ACM Press (2013), 1979.

23. Internet World Stats: Internet Usage in the Middle East. http://internetworldstats.com/stats5.htm.

24. Intel Computer Clubhouse Network. http://www.computerclubhouse.org/locations.

Cultural Differences in how an Engagement-Seeking Robot should Approach a Group of People

Michiel Joosse
Human Media
Interaction
University of Twente
Enschede, the
Netherlands
m.p.joosse@utwente.nl

Ronald Poppe
Information and
Computing Sciences
University of Utrecht
Utrecht, the
Netherlands
r.w.poppe@uu.nl

Manja Lohse
Human Media
Interaction
University of Twente
Enschede, the
Netherlands
m.lohse@utwente.nl

Vanessa Evers
Human Media
Interaction
University of Twente
Enschede, the
Netherlands
v.evers@utwente.nl

ABSTRACT

In our daily life everything and everyone occupies an amount of space, simply by "being there". Edward Hall coined the term proxemics for the studies of man's use of this space. This paper presents a study on proxemics in Human-Robot Interaction and particularly on robot's approaching groups of people. As social psychology research found proxemics to be culturally dependent, we focus on the question of the appropriateness of the robot's approach behavior in different cultures. We present an online survey (N=181) that was distributed in three countries; China, the U.S. and Argentina. Our results show that participants prefer a robot that stays out of people's intimate space zone just like a human would be expected to do. With respect to cultural differences, Chinese participants showed high-contact responses and believed closer approaches were appropriate compared to their U.S. counterparts. Argentinian participants more closely resembled the ratings of the U.S. participants.

Author Keywords

human-robot interaction, cross-cultural survey, proximity, social robotics, social interaction, online survey.

ACM Classification Keywords

J.4 [**Computer Applications**]: Social and Behavioral Sciences

INTRODUCTION

In our daily life everything and everyone occupies an amount of space, simply by "being there". When moving through around, people keep a certain distance between each other, and this distance depends on factors like culture, familiarity and personality, as well as the context of the situation.

In 1966 Hall coined the term proxemics to describe this phenomenon. According to Hall [5], one's body is surrounded by ellipse-shaped bubbles. Each of these bubbles is appropriate for different social interactions. One of these zones, the personal space zone, acts as a virtual buffer zone around our body. Hall describes it as *"a small protective sphere or bubble that an organism maintains between itself and others"*. When this buffer zone is invaded, people compensate for this intimate contact, by non-verbal or verbal compensation behaviors such as stepping away, or limiting eye contact [14]. While every human adheres to others' personal space, what individuals regard as appropriate distances in certain social situations depends on culture [e.g., [19], [7], [17]).

Individual people keep certain distances towards each other, but small groups of people also organize themselves spatially in patterns; such as circles or lines. When such a pattern is stable, it is called a formation. Kendon [10] introduced the term *F*-formation to refer to a specific formation which occurs *"whenever two or more people sustain a spatial and orientational relationship in which the space between them is one to which they have equal, direct and exclusive access"*.

Our work focuses on the spatial organization of small groups in Human-Robot Interaction (HRI). Previous research has provided support for the Media Equation theory, which holds that people treat computers and other media as if they were either real people or real places [15]. A most relevant example is a study by Hüttenrauch et al. [8], which found that most people place themselves in Hall's personal zone (between 0.45 and 1.2 meters distance) when interacting with a robot.

While research in HRI has focused to some extent on the concept of proxemics, this research has been limited in that it has mostly studied robots approaching single persons – usually from Western countries - in controlled lab settings. We intend to extend this state of the art by looking at small groups of people from different cultures. Specifically, we try to identify optimal approach and placement position for a robot which is seeking to gain the attention of a small group of people. As social robots are envisioned to operate in contexts in which they have to interact with people having different cultural backgrounds (such as airports and fairs), we are particularly interested in finding out if a robot requires different spatial behavior depending upon the cultural background of its users. To do so, we have conducted an online survey which we distributed to three different cultural regions in the world through a crowdsourcing platform. In this paper we report on the methodology we used and we provide first results.

RELATED WORK

This section reviews the two major themes of our work: cross-cultural proxemics and group formations. We will conclude this section with our hypotheses, which provide the basis for the experimental method.

Proxemics and culture

In his book, *The Hidden Dimension*, Hall [5] defined four interpersonal distance zones. These zones are called the *intimate, personal, social* and *public* space zones (Table 1).

As stated in the introduction, research has found that the proxemics zones depend on multiple factors, among which culture. Based upon observations, Hall noted that people from low-contact cultures maintain a larger personal space compared with their counterparts from high-contact cultures. Northern European cultures are considered being low-contact, whereas Southern European, Southern American and Arab [4, 5, 19] cultures on the other hand are considered high-contact cultures.

Little [12] used the placement of dolls to infer at which distance people from either the U.S., Sweden, Scotland, Italy and Greece would place people in 19 different social situations. He found that people from North European cultures placed dolls significantly further apart compared with their Mediterranean counterparts. This could be explained by Hall's explanation of high contact- and low contact cultures.

Sussman & Rosenfeld [19] conducted a study in which 105 students from three different countries (Japan, U.S. and Venezuela) had a five-minute conversation with a same sex, same-nationality confederate. They found that, when they were speaking English, participants from the low-contact culture (Japan) sat further apart from each other compared to participants from a high-contact culture (Venezuelan). Within their respective cultural groups, male participants sat further apart than female participants.

Zone	Range	Situation
Intimate	0-0.45m	Lover or close friend
Personal	0.45-1.2m	Conversation between friends
Social	1.2-3.6m	Conversation
Public	3.6m+	Public speech

Table 1: Proxemics zones as defined by Hall [5].

Furthermore, when speaking in their native language, participants from high-contact culture sat closer together than when speaking English. This research implies that human personal spaces zones are dependent on peoples' cultural background.

Also in the field of Human-Robot Interaction (HRI) some studies have been conducted in the area of proxemic zones. Research on proxemics found that people appear to "respect" a robot's personal space zone [8, 23] and maintain a distance from a robot that would be considered respectful when approaching a fellow human. When a robot approaches a person, the comfortable approach distance has been found to be roughly 57 cm [22], which is comparable with distances between people when they have a conversation (see Table 1). Furthermore, similar to human encounters behaviors such as a robot's gaze can influence the distance people chose [21]. If the robot is gazing at people, they tend to stay further away. Work on proxemics in HRI also found that people show similar compensating behavior as they would do when a person invades their personal space [18]. While these findings provide important insights for robot behavior design, HRI research has not yet taken the impact of users' culture into account for proxemics research. As culture is an important factor in human spatial interaction, our work centers around this factor.

F-formations

People organize themselves spatially not only by interpersonal distance, but also in terms of their spatial arrangement when being part of small groups. Kendon [10] introduced the concept of *F*-Formations to capture this phenomenon. According to Kendon, activity is always located in a space. This space can be called the 'transaction segment'.

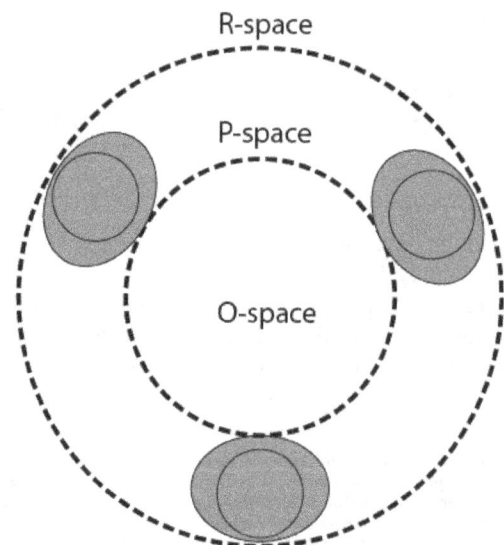

Figure 1 circular *F*-formation around an O-space.

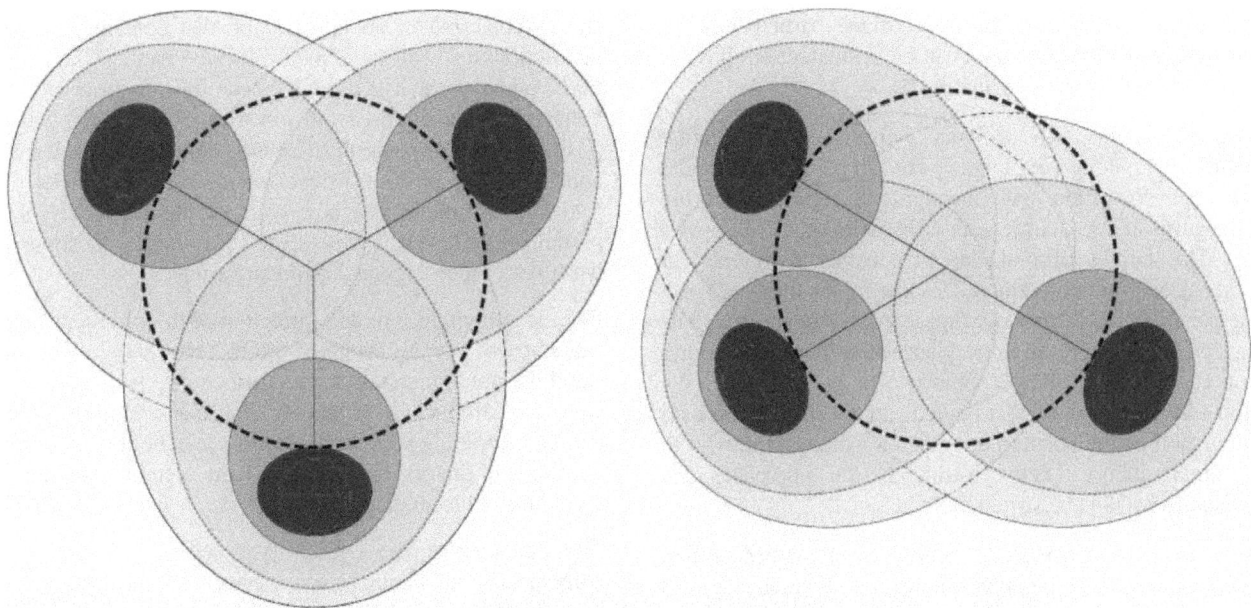

Figure 2: Circular *F*-Formation with congruent (left) and incongruent (right) angles.

When two or more people form a group, they arrange the spatial formation of the group in such a way that the individual transaction segments overlap; thus creating a joint transactional space, also called the o-space (Figure 1). Whenever two or more people establish an o-space, an *F*-formation exists. The o-space is enclosed by the p-space, in which the persons making up the formation are located. The r-space is the space located beyond the p-space. Kendon [10] describes this latter space as *"under the influence of the F-formation [...]"*, and provides as example that when multiple *F*-formations occur in a space without physical barriers, these formations tend to be spread out over the space.

F-formations can assume different spatial arrangements. For instance, a circle such as in Figure 2 but also other formations such as a side-by-side or vis-à-vis arrangement. The type of arrangement depends on a number of factors, for instance the number of participants and the context in which the arrangement occurs [10].

Rehm et al. [16] report the "six most occurring formations", and divide these six in open and closed formations. People in open formations are said to allow others to join the conversation; while this is not the case with closed formations. In an experiment with virtual characters, Rehm et al. [16] found that participants were more likely to join an open formation (84% of the trials) than a closed formation. All participants positioned themselves at a social distance, half in the close-social, and half in the far-social distance. However, the authors found that two Arabic participants positioned themselves in the close-social space, which is consistent with findings in cross-cultural research in that Arabic people generally stand closer to each other.

The role different people take on in the *F*-formation could be related to their spatial position. For instance, Kendon [9] observed that speaking rights are reflected in the formation.

In a circular formation, rights tend to be equal, in other formations such as a rectangular formation the one in the spatially differentiated position (i.e. the one person sitting opposite others) has the right to speak more compared with others [9].

The arrangement of an *F*-formation can change depending on numerous factors. According to Kendon [10, pg. 221] an L-shape arrangement can for instance become a side-by-side arrangement when the participants focus their attention at an event in the vicinity instead of each other. A participant joining or leaving the specific *F*-formation can also result in a change as the group maneuvers' to maintain the *F*-formation. Thus: *F*-formations can be highly dynamic.

In the field of HRI, research has been conducted investigating the use of *F*-formations in modelling a robot's position. Yamaoka et al. [25] developed a model in which the o-space was established between a robot, listener and an object. The position based upon the developed model was preferred over positions in which the robot was placed either close to the object or to the listener. Kuzuoka et al. [11] investigated the capability of an information-providing robot to change the *F*-formation of a group of listeners. The underlying premise is that a robot which can change the *F*-formation can thereby direct the attention of its listeners. It was found that a robot could achieve this most effectively by rotating it's whole body. While these results are really important for robot design, in HRI, the role of culture with respect to a robot's most optimal position within the *F*-formation has not yet been taken into account.

Personal space and *F*-formations in HRI - Hypotheses
Work on personal space zones has mostly focused on the personal space of single people, and while numerous works call these zones "elliptical", only one distance is reported,

which is the distance to the front of the participant. The diameter of the different zones can be estimated, but has not been researched extensively up till now.

Figure 2 contains two different *F*-formations: a circular formation with congruent angles between participants, and a more open formation with incongruent angles. There are three figures along a circle with a diameter of 122 cm (or 4 feet). The circles around the participants represent our hypothesized proxemics zones, these being the intimate zone, close personal and far personal space zone, respectively. The initial position where an actor places him-/herself to join a group can be found more appropriate or inappropriate. We would like to introduce this optimal approach position as a combination of the position an actor chooses with respect to the group members in between which he/she approaches, and the distance he/she takes from those actors.

Based upon the proxemics theory, we hypothesize that participants will find the approach of a robot which stays out of their intimate zone more appropriate. Our first hypothesis is therefore:

> H1: Participants will rate an approach by a robot as more appropriate when the robot stays out of every group member's intimate space zone.

We often have preferences to join a group at a particular position where there is a person we know, or that seems otherwise appropriate. We are interested in small groups such as families (father, mother and child). It may for instance, be seen as more appropriate to approach a group in between the mother and father as compared to in between the child and one of the parents, essentially cutting off a child from one of the parents. This leads us to the second hypothesis.

> H2: Participants will rate a robot approach as less appropriate when a robot approaches in between a child and parent, as compared with approaching in between both parents.

Given that different cultures exist, and that research by Rehm et al. [16] found that participants from high-contact cultures stand closer to a group of people compared with people from low-contact cultures, we hypothesize a similar cultural dependent preference will exist when a robot approaches.

> H3: Participants from a high-contact culture (China, Argentina) are more comfortable with a closer approach by a robot than participants from a low-contact culture (U.S.).

METHODOLOGY

We conducted a 3 (nationality) x 3 (position in the group) x 6 (distance from the group) online study. A survey-based questionnaire was distributed through a crowdsourcing platform (crowdflower.com) to a targeted population. Participants were shown images of small families of 3D people and a robot (see Figure 3). These groups were composed of three people: a man, a woman and a child. The survey consisted of an introduction that contained detailed instructions as well as a picture of the family (Figure 4). Participants were asked to indicate how appropriate they believed the position of the robot was, imagining that the position was the position after the robot had completed its approach. The position of the robot was manipulated two-fold within-subjects (see next section), the nationality of the participants was a between-subjects variable. A questionnaire was used to measure the dependent variables.

For the groups, a circular formation with congruent angles was chosen. We are aware of the fact that people will often stand in non-congruent angle formations, however, if we were to introduce a formation with non-congruent angles and/or people spaced differently we would introduce a multitude of factors that would be hard to control for and that would make the study overly complex.

The diameter of the o-space was set to 122 cm, which corresponds to Hall's social space. The height of the participants was based upon average international height[1]. The male was scaled to 178 cm, the female to 152 cm, and the child to 140 cm. The height of the robot was scaled to 140 cm, as can been seen in Figure 4.

Figure 3 Example top-down still as shown to participants

Figure 4 The fictional family was scaled to average international dimensions based on [1]

[1] http://dined.nl//ergonomics/

Independent variables

Two variables were manipulated within-subjects: approach position (the position between which family members the robot approached, Figure 5), and the approach distance of the robot. We refer to the combinations of position and angle as scenes.

For each of the three different approach positions, the robot was placed at six different distances, measured from the center of the circle. These distances were 20, 40, 60, 80, 100 and 120 centimeter. As a control method, participants were exposed to each scene **twice**. Thus: participants were asked to rate (2 (ratings) *3 (approach directions) *6 (distances)) = **36 scenes**.

Circles 1 and 2 (20 and 40 cm) are within participants' intimate zone, circles 3 and 4 (60 and 80 cm) in the personal zone, and circles 5 and 6 (100 and 120 cm) lie in the social zone.

Dependent variables

The dependent variables were measured using a 112-item online questionnaire, measuring a total of 6 constructs. The questionnaire was divided into three consecutive blocks: appropriateness rating of the robot-group scenes, questions regarding participants' cultural background and personality, and general demographic questions.

In the first block, participants were asked to rate the 36 'robot approaches a family' scenes that have been described in the previous section. To avoid order-effects, the order of all scenes was randomized. Participants were provided with the instruction: *"The robot approached the family and has come to a halt between particular family members at a particular distance. Now it will interact with them"*, and asked to indicate on a 7-point Likert scale how appropriate the position of the robot was. Another four items were included in this block to measure how participants themselves would approach the family. Two items were included to check the approach position- and distance manipulation. Here participants were provided with statements such as *"the robot generally approached from the same direction"* and *"the robot generally approached from different directions"*. Participants were forced to choose which of the statements was true. A final item was included in which we asked participants if they could indicate where they thought the family they had seen in the situations originated from.

The second block of the questionnaire consisted of a series of validated scales measuring four dependent variables. An indication of whether participants were members of a high-contact or low-contact culture was assessed by measuring *closeness* as people from a high-contact culture have been found to sit significantly closer to each other compared with members from a low-contact culture [19]. Five items from the IPROX (iconic proximity) questionnaire were used [7]. Participants' general attitude towards robots was measured by the *Negative Attitude Towards Robots* scale, a 14-item 7-

point Likert scale. Hofstede [6] identified five dimensions of culture, one of these being Individualism-Collectivism. One way to explain cultural differences is by measuring *individual* and *group self-representations*. Individual self-representations refer to whether the self is represented as "a separate, unique individual" [1] whereas group-self representation refers to one who is "an interchangeable part of a larger social entity" [1]. This was operationalized using 7 items, by Brewer & Chen [1].

The final construct in this block was personality as we figured this could influence people's preference for a robot position (e.g., more extrovert people preferring the robot to come closer or to approach at their side of the group). We measured the Big Five personality traits using the 20-item Mini-IPIP scale [2].

The final block of questions included demographic questions like gender, age, nationality, and level of education. Social-demographic questions like nationality of ancestors, marital status and number of children were also included.

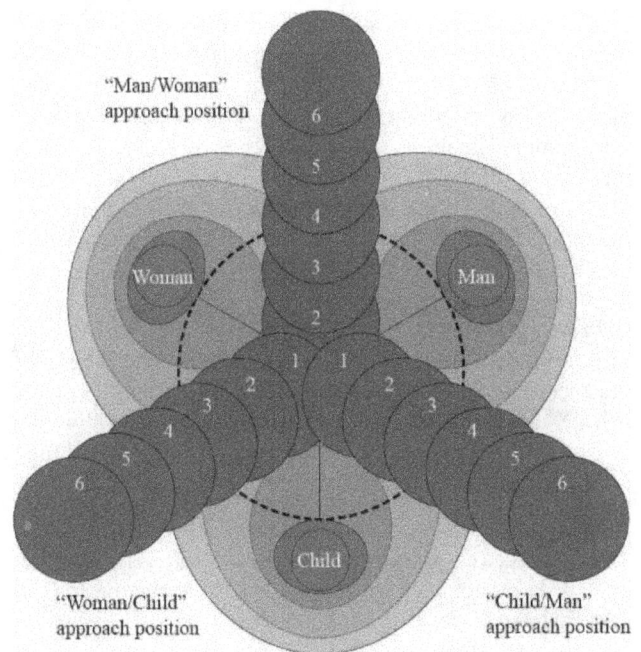

Figure 5: Participants standing in a circular F-Formation with a diameter of 122 cm. Dark grey indicates possible location of the robot. Grey: intimate zone, light grey: personal space zone.

	N	Mean age (sd)	Male / Female
U.S.	86	43.27 (12.25)	26 / 60
China	29	30.48 (8.93)	19 / 10
Argentina	66	33.06 (10.90)	48 / 18
Total	181	37.50 (12.54)	93 / 88

Table 2 Number, nationality, mean age, and gender of the participants

Participants

Participants were recruited from three different countries: China, Argentina and the United States. People from these three countries are generally considered culturally different; not only because they are geographically on different continents, but also because various studies have shown cultural differences [3, 4, 17] in for instance societal values.

For each country, participants were recruited through the Crowdflower platform, which allows for specification of the target country. 244 participants completed the questionnaire; each being paid $1 for completion of the survey. Responses were limited to one per IP address. Participants who failed to correctly answer the two manipulation checks were excluded from the sample. A second control method was the analysis of the robot-scene questions, which were 18 situations rated twice by each participant on a 7-point Likert scale. Participants who rated four or more situations with a difference of 3 or more points were also excluded from the survey. In total 63 participants (26%) were excluded. After applying the exclusion criteria, the total sample contained 181 participants, as specified in Table 2.

Data analysis

The results presented in this paper focus on the ratings of the scenes and on the closeness scale (five items from the IPROX questionnaire, see Dependent variables). Internal reliability of all scales was assessed by calculating Chronbach's α, and deemed acceptable for all scales.

As stated in the previous section, the participants rated all scenes twice as form of control method. After having excluded participants these ratings were averaged per participant and scene.

Approach in between	Mean	SD
Man-Woman	4.11	0.095
Woman-Child	4.16	0.100
Man-Child	3.93	0.093

Table 3 Mean appropriateness scores and standard deviation grouped by approach direction

To determine whether the participants found an approach more appropriate if the robot stayed out of every group member's personal space zone (H1), we conducted a repeated-measures ANOVA with one within-subjects variable (being intimate- or personal space zone), and two between-subject factors (nationality and gender). For the purpose of analysis of this hypothesis, ratings for circles 1 and 2 (intimate space zone) were averaged as well as the ratings of circles 3, 4, 5 and 6 (outside intimate space zone).

To analyze whether an approach between the child and one of the parents was rated as being less appropriate (H2) and whether participants from higher contact cultures were more comfortable with a closer approach (H3), we conducted factorial repeated-measures ANOVAs with two factors as within-subjects variables; these being the average ratings of the position in the group (3) and distance from the group (6). Nationality and gender were used as between-subject factors.

RESULTS

In this section we present the results of the survey that we acquired from the analysis of the ratings of the scenes and the closeness scale

Participants prefer a robot that stays out of our intimate space zone

In H1 we hypothesized that participants would rate it as more appropriate if the robot was positioned out of every group member's intimate space zone. A repeated mixed-model ANOVA revealed that participants rated the robot positions in the intimate space zone as significantly less appropriate (M=3.14, sd=1.25) compared with those positions where the robot was positioned outside the intimate space zone (M=4.61, sd=.99), $F(1, 100.658) = 109.567$, $p<0.01$. We therefore **accept H1**: a robot which stays out of the intimate space zone of each of the group members is considered to be more appropriate. These ratings were neither affected by gender ($p=.87$) nor by nationality ($p=.60$).

Appropriateness of a robot's approach is not always affected by its position relative to the family members.

A factorial repeated-measures ANOVA with two independent variables (distance and position) and two between-subjects factors (gender and nationality) was conducted. Mauchly's test indicated that the assumption of sphericity had been violated for the main effects of distance, $\chi^2(14) = 613.9$, $p<0.001$, and angle, $\chi^2(2) = 76.37$, $p<0.001$. Sphericity had also been violated for the interaction effect (distance*direction), $\chi^2(54)=183.55$, $p<0.001$. The degrees of freedom were corrected using Greenhouse-Geisser estimates of sphericity ($\varepsilon=.42$ and $\varepsilon=.74$ for the main effects, and $\varepsilon=.81$ for the interaction effect).There was a significant main effect of the approach distance ($F(2.09,365.19)=54.37$, $p<0.001$), and a non-significant effect of approach angle on the appropriateness of the robot's position ($F(1.47, 258.25)=2.857$, $p=0.075$).

Post-hoc contrasts revealed a significant difference of appropriateness between the "Woman/Child" and "Man/Child" approaches: the appropriateness of the "Woman/Child" approach was significantly higher compared with the "Man/Child" approaches, $F(1, 175) = 11.71$, $p<0.001$ (See Table 3). The appropriateness of the "Man/Woman" approaches was equally appropriate as the "Woman/Child" approach, We therefore only **partially accept H2**, in which we hypothesized that participants would rate a robot approach as less appropriate if a robot approached in between a child and parent, as compared with approaching in between both parents. Instead, participants indeed found an approach between parent and child less appropriate but only for the position between father and child. The most appropriate approach position was generally thought to be in between the mother and the child (see Table 4).

Influence of cultural background on appropriateness

To check whether the countries that we chose actually differed in the low-high contact dimension, we analyzed the items from the closeness questionnaire. There was a significant difference between the ratings, $F(2) = 15.528$, $p<0.001$. As can be seen in Figure 6, participants from the United States gave significantly higher ratings on the closeness measure (M=4.96, sd=1.05), which indicates they put more distance between themselves and other people. This effect was vice-versa for Chinese people, as expected (M=3.88, sd=1.20). The Argentinian participants rated in between (M=4.11, sd=1.19).Therefore, we can assume that

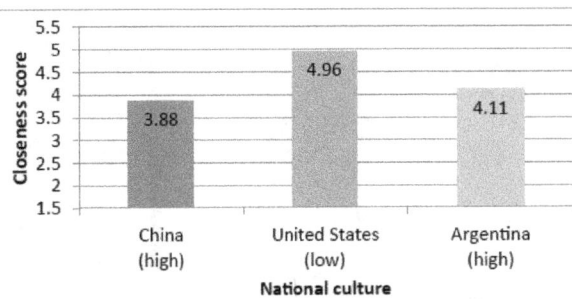

Figure 6 Participants from what are considered low-contact cultures scored indeed significantly higher on the "closeness" construct (scale: 1: high contact, 6: low contact. Mean scores provided in bars).

the national groups included in this sample can indeed be considered to have different cultural backgrounds concerning the low-high contact dimension.

Our third hypothesis was that participants from high-contact cultures (such as China and Argentina) would rate a close approach as more comfortable than participants from a low-contact culture (United States). There was a significant three-way interaction effect between the nationality of the participant, distance, and position of the robot on appropriateness of the scene, $F(16.20, 1417.24)=1.912$, $p<0.05$. This effect can be seen in Table 4 and Figure 7.

The Table and Figure show that the U.S. and Argentinian participants gave similar appropriateness ratings for the

dista nce	China			United States			Argentina		
20	3.052 (1.555)	3.862 (1.870)	3.741 (1.751)	2.721 (1.560)	3.023 (1.627)	2.721 (1.516)	2.697 (1.544)	2.909 (1.446)	2.530 (1.364)
40	3.345 (1.748)	4.017 (1.740)	3.310 (1.785)	3.552 (1.690)	3.843 (1.676)	3.407 (1.474)	3.477 (1.515)	3.614 (1.230)	3.038 (1.178)
60	3.862 (1.737)	4.155 (1.895)	3.759 (1.740)	4.308 (1.478)	4.552 (1.596)	4.128 (1.468)	4.083 (1.583)	4.439 (1.383)	3.689 (1.202)
80	4.259 (1.766)	4.466 (1.732)	4.414 (1.547)	5.047 (1.490)	4.988 (1.538)	4.709 (1.523)	4.795 (1.48)	5.000 (1.547)	4.220 (1.356)
100	4.517 (1.825)	3.672 (1.649)	4.414 (1.753)	5.337 (1.428)	4.977 (1.439)	4.994 (1.610)	5.136 (1.423)	5.220 (1.465)	4.644 (1.315)
120	3.724 (1.893)	3.103 (1.749)	3.603 (1.655)	4.913 (1.722)	4.692 (1.736)	4.837 (1.591)	4.917 (1.690)	4.841 (1.813)	4.689 (1.583)

Table 4 Mean appropriateness ratings for the Chinese, U.S. and Argentinian sample. Distance indicates distance between the center of the circle and the robot (in cm). Mean appropriateness ratings on a scale from 1 to 7, standard deviations between brackets.

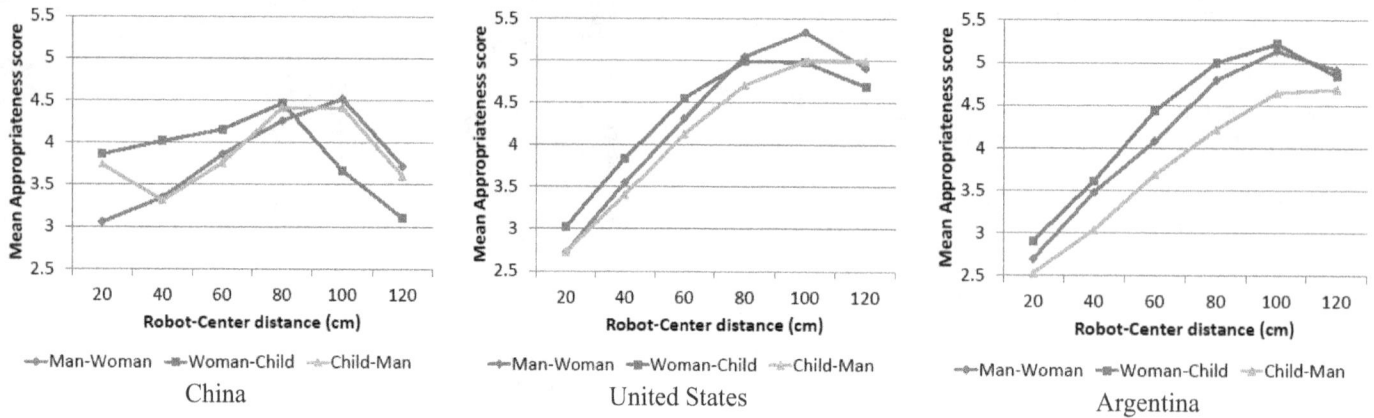

China   United States   Argentina

Figure 7 Mean appropriateness ratings for the Chinese, U.S. and Argentinian sample. Appropriateness on a scale from 1 to 7.

approach distances, but that one particular approach in between the "Man/Woman" was considered most appropriate by the U.S. participants, whereas the Argentinian believed the "Woman/Child" position was more appropriate.

The Chinese participants' ratings were generally lower and a notable difference was that the closer approaches (within the intimate zone) were actually considered to be quite appropriate. Like the U.S. and Argentinian participants, the Chinese also had a preference for a further stop distance (80-100 cm), though this difference was much less pronounced.

We therefore **partially accept H3**. We hypothesized that participants from high-contact cultures (such as China and Argentina) would rate a close approach as more comfortable than participants from low-contact cultures. Chinese participants saw a closer approach as more appropriate. However, we expected similar results for Argentinians, which we did not find. Interestingly enough the ratings the Argentinians provided were quite similar to those provided by the U.S. participants. We will reflect on this in the discussion.

DISCUSSION

In this paper we presented the methodology and first results of a survey investigating cross-cultural HRI proxemics preferences. This paper shows that there are indeed cultural differences in spatial behaviors in HRI. Thus, taking culture into account is an important next step for HRI if social robots are designed to operate all over the world in various cultural contexts or in environments where people from different cultures are around (such as airports, fairs and museums). We will now discuss both the methodology and the results to retrieve directions for future research.

We hypothesized that participants would find approaches in between the parents more appropriate compared with the approaches where a child is cut off from one of the parents. The reason for the unexpected finding that approaches between mother and child were found quite appropriate

could be a pragmatic one, which we had not considered. By approaching in between the mother and child the robot directly faced the father of the family. It could be that a robot's frontal approach to a male is seen as more appropriate. Even though previous work by Walters et al. [24] did not confirm this notion, this warrants further investigation into differences in gender preferences.

Figure 7 shows similarities in the appropriateness ratings of the U.S. and Argentinian samples respectively, despite the fact that Argentinian's closeness scores indicate a higher-contact culture. Therefore, we expected they would find it more appropriate if the robot approached closer. Thus, it could be that the high-low contact culture dimension is too simple and did not completely capture the subtleties of high-low contact cultural backgrounds and that there are more factors at play. One possible explanation can be found in Hofstede's work [6]. On the Individualism dimension, the U.S. scores are high (91 points), and Chines scores are relatively low (20). Argentinians scores are at 46 points. This is still closer to China than the U.S., however, if we look at other Latin American countries, such as Ecuador (8), Venezuela (12), Colombia (13) and Chili (23) it appears to be that Argentina is a rather individualistic country. This might partly explain why Argentinian participants showed a preference for a further positioning of the robot. However, this issue deserves further investigation.

Furthermore, we have not yet analyzed the relation between personality and the appropriateness of robot scenes. Previous work in HRI has shown that a high score on extraversion leads to more tolerance to uncomfortable robot approaches [20]. It could very well be that personality also influences ratings of appropriateness. In a similar way *attitude towards robots* and *individual* and *group self-representations* could influence the results in subtle ways, which we have not yet analyzed.

To analyze cross-cultural differences in proxemics, we used an online questionnaire as this allowed us to distribute the survey to geographically dispersed samples. The survey contained static images, and while the results do support most of our hypotheses, the ecological validity of our research is limited because groups are dynamic entities. The formation of the group changes when a new member joins the group, and our images might very well not have been able to capture these subtle dynamics. In future work, we will conduct a study where actual groups of people are approached by a robot– primarily to see if the results found with this survey are replicable when such an experiment is conducted in a lab or real world setting.

Furthermore, participants viewed the robot-group scenes from above. This may – unintentionally – have caused a limitation as participants were not able to take the height of the actors into account. In retrospect it is possible that participants would provide different ratings had they been provided with different camera angles next to the top-view.

Another limitation of the experimental design concerns the chosen *F*-formation. As we explained in the methodology section, we chose for a closed circular formation with congruent angles (Figure 2). It could very well be that another formation, for instance with incongruent angles, yields different results; either because of the position (and status) of the members within the group, or simply because there is more room for a robot to approach when the angles are not congruent. This issue will also be addressed in future research.

Finally, the context of our stimuli could be debatable. The reason for not providing a specific context in which this group and the robot would interact (for instance a domestic environment, airport or shopping mall) was that we did not want our participants to have a predisposed opinion on for instance the feasibility or acceptability of a robot in a certain context. However, how different real-world contexts influence the ratings is a highly interesting question as future robots will be operating in such contexts.

As stated in the introduction, this is a first study. In order to improve ecological validity and generalizability of our results more research has to be conducted. Our future work will focus on replicating a similar experimental setup in either a physical lab or field setting in order to account for some of the limitations that arose in this experiment, as also pointed out in literature (f.e. [10]).

CONCLUSION
In this paper we have presented the first results of a survey that we distributed to three countries (China, the U.S. and Argentina). We were interested in finding out whether or not people from different nationalities have different proxemics expectations from a robot which approaches a small family.

The most appropriate approach distance appears to be somewhere near 80 cm from the center of the circle. Our results also show that while participants found a robot more appropriate when it stayed out of the intimate space zone,

there are cultural differences which surface when comparing China with the other two countries:

- Argentinian and U.S. participants rated approaches in Hall's intimate space zone as clearly inappropriate whereas the Chinese participants rated approaches farther away (100-120 cm) as more inappropriate.

- Argentinian and U.S. participants rated an approach in between the child and man as less appropriate, Chinese participants did not have a clear preference.

Unexpectedly, the Argentinian ratings were closer to the U.S. ratings even though both Argentina and China were considered to be high-contact cultures, and both scored as such on our closeness measure. Hence, there seem to be many factors that contribute to the cultural identity of people that we will look into in the future, among others the interplay between personality and culture, as well as to the limitations caused by the methodological choices.

Overall, the influence of culture on HRI has turned out to be a promising research direction with respect to proxemics. Our first research shows that researchers need to take culture into account when building robots that operate in intercultural environments.

ACKNOWLEDGEMENTS
This work has partly been supported by the European Commission under contract number FP7-ICT-600877 (SPENCER).

REFERENCES
1. Brewer, M.B. and Chen, Y.-R. 2007. Where (who) are collectives in collectivism? Toward conceptual clarification of individualism and collectivism. *Psychological review.* 114, 1 (Jan. 2007), 133–51.

2. Donnellan, M.B., Oswald, F.L., Baird, B.M. and Lucas, R.E. 2006. The mini-IPIP scales: tiny-yet-effective measures of the Big Five factors of personality. *Psychological assessment.* 18, 2 (Jun. 2006), 192–203.

3. Gupta, V., Hanges, P. and Dorfman, P. 2002. Cultural clusters: Methodology and findings. *Journal of World Business.* 37, (2002), 11–15.

4. Hall, E.T. 1963. A system for the notation of proxemic behavior. *American anthropologist.* 65, 5 (1963), 1003–1026.

5. Hall, E.T. 1966. *The Hidden Dimension.* Anchor Books.

6. Hofstede, G. 2001. *Culture's Consequences: Comparing Values, Behaviors, Institutions and Organizations across Nations.* Sage Publications, Inc.

7. Høgh-Olesen, H. 2008. Human Spatial Behaviour: The Spacing of People, Objects and Animals in Six Cross-Cultural Samples. *Journal of Cognition and Culture.* 8, 3 (Aug. 2008), 245–280.

8. Hüttenrauch, H. and Eklundh, K. 2006. Investigating spatial relationships in human-robot interaction.

Proceedings of the 2006 IEEE Conference on Intelligent Robots and Systems. (2006), 5052-5059.

9. Kendon, A. 1973. The role of visible behaviour in the organization of face-to-face interaction. In M. von Cranach and I. Vine, eds., *Social Communication and Movement Studies of Interaction and Expression in Man ad Chimpanzee*. New York: Academic Press, p. 29-74.

10. Kendon, A. 1990. *Conducting interaction: Patterns of behavior in focused encounters*. Cambridge University Press.

11. Kuzuoka, H., Suzuki, Y., Yamashita, J. and Yamazaki, K. 2010. Reconfiguration Spatial Formation Arrangement by Robot Body Orientation. *Proceedings of the 5th ACM/IEEE international conference on Human-robot interaction*, 285-292

12. Little, K.B. 1968. Cultural variations in social schemata. *Journal of Personality and Social Psychology*. 10, 1 (Sep. 1968), 1–7.

13. Nomura, T., Kanda, T., Suzuki, T. and Kato, K. 2008. Prediction of Human Behavior in Human--Robot Interaction Using Psychological Scales for Anxiety and Negative Attitudes Toward Robots. *IEEE Transactions on Robotics*. 24, 2 (Apr. 2008), 442–451

14. Patterson, M.L., Mullens, S., and Romano, J. 1971. Compensatory Reactions to Spatial Intrusion. *Sociometry*. 34, 1 (1971), 114-121

15. Reeves, B. and Nass, C. 1996. *The Media Equation: How People Treat Computers, Television and New Media Like Real People and Places*. Cambridge University Press.

16. Rehm, M., André, E. and Nischt, M. 2005. Let ' s Come Together — Social Navigation Behaviors of Virtual and Real Humans. *INTETAIN 2005* (2005), 124–133.

17. Remland, M.S., Jones, T.S. and Brinkman, H. 1995. Interpersonal distance, body orientation, and touch: Effects of culture, gender, and age. *The Journal of Economic Perspectives*. 135, 3 (1995), 281–297.

18. Sardar, A.H., Joosse, M.P., Weiss, A. and Evers, V. 2012. Don't stand so close to me: users' attitudinal and behavioral responses to personal space invasion by robots. *Proceedings of the 2012 ACM/IEEE Conference on Human-Robot Interaction*, 229-230.

19. Sussman, N.M. and Rosenfeld, H.M. 1982. Influence of culture, language, and sex on conversational distance. *Journal of Personality and Social Psychology*. 42, 1 (1982), 66–74.

20. Syrdal, D.S., Dautenhahn, K., Woods, S.N., Walters, M.L. & Koay, K.L. 2006. 'Doing the right thing wrong'- Personality and tolerance to uncomfortable robot approaches. *Proc. of the 15th IEEE Symposium on Robot and Human Interactive Communication*, 183-188

21. Takayama, L. and Pantofaru, C. 2009. Influences on proxemic behaviors in human-robot interaction. *Proceedings of the IEEE/RSJ International Conference on Robots and Systems (IROS2009)* (2009), 5495–5502.

22. Walters, M.L. 2008. *The design space for robot appearance and behaviour for social robot companions*. University of Hertfordshire.

23. Walters, M.L. and Dautenhahn, K. 2005. Close encounters: Spatial distances between people and a robot of mechanistic appearance. *Proceedings of the 2005 IEEE-RAS Conference on Humanoid Robots* (2005), 450-455.

24. Walters, M.L., Dautenhahn, K., Woods, S.N. and Koay, K.L. 2007. Robotic Etiquette: Results from User Studies Involving a Fetch and Carry Task. *Proceedings of the 2007 ACM/IEEE Conference on Human-Robot Interaction*, 317-324.

25. Yamaoka, F., Kanda, T., Ishiguro, H. and Hagita, N. 2008. How close?: model of control for information-presenting robots. *Proceedings of the 3rd ACM/IEEE international conference on Human-robot interaction*, 137-144.

Marius, the Giraffe: A Comparative Informatics Case Study of Linguistic Features of the Social Media Discourse

Chris Zimmerman[1], Yuran Chen[1], Daniel Hardt[1], and Ravi Vatrapu[1,2]
[1]Computational Social Science Laboratory (CSSL)
Department of IT Management, Copenhagen Business School, Denmark
[2]Norwegian School of Information Technology (NITH), Norway
cz.itm@cbs.dk, yc2779@columbia.edu, dh.itm@cbs.dk, vatrapu@cbs.dk

ABSTRACT

On February 9, 2014, a giraffe named Marius was put to death by the Copenhagen Zoo in Denmark, sparking a storm of public discussion nationally and internationally. This paper presents a comparative informatics case study of the event. We employ the method of grounded comparison in the examination of the text of postings and articles in social media as well as mainstream media in Danish and English languages. At the macro-structural level, the social media discourse is characterized by arguments grounded in scientific and bureaucratic rationality, cultural and linguistic relativity, and animal ethics. At the micro-genetic level of language use, our findings show that international discourse was much more intense and emotional than the discourse in Danish media as evidenced by the differences in volume, sentiment and topics in English vs. Danish data. While these differences undoubtedly reflect a broad range of cultural, linguistic, organizational and societal factors, we suggest that to some extent the differences might result from specific features of the media landscape in Denmark.

Author Keywords

Comparative informatics, grounded comparison, computational linguistics, social data analytics, social graph, social text, sentiment analysis,

ACM Classification Keywords

H.5.3 Group and Organization Interfaces: *Theory and models, Asynchronous interaction Collaborative computing, Evaluation/methodology.*

INTRODUCTION

On February 9, 2014, a giraffe named Marius was put to death by the Copenhagen Zoo, sparking a storm of reaction in Denmark and throughout the world. Local and global reactions to the killing of the giraffe ranged from rational justifications and emotional condemnations to nationalistic stereotyping and reported death threats to the Zoo

employees. In this paper, we present a comparative informatics case study of that reaction based on data from social media as well as mainstream media (online newspapers, magazines, TV channels, and other news story websites). Such intense international controversies are nothing new, of course (a recent example is the Danish cartoon crisis [1] which has international diplomatic implications and foreign policy consequences [2]).

One of the most striking features of this Danish Giraffe Affair is the difference between Danish and international reaction. In general, international reaction was much more intense and emotional than reaction in Denmark: our analysis shows clear differences in volume, sentiment and topic of texts in Danish and English data. In this paper we will focus on these differences, addressing two main questions.

1. *What specific differences are there in the Danish vs. international interactions?*

2. *Can these differences be traced to features of the media landscape in Denmark?*

Both questions concern a comparison between Danish and international reactions: the first question, concerns **what** the reactions were, while the second question attempts to approach the issue of **why** the differences were found. In addressing the **what** question, we deploy a sophisticated arsenal of tools and analytical techniques; as we describe below, this analysis uncovers a fine-grained picture of the detailed differences in the Danish and English data. Addressing the **why** question must be approached with more caution, and the answers we arrive at are necessarily limited and rather speculative. Still, we argue that there is reason to believe that features of the media landscape in Denmark might well contribute to precisely the sort of general differences that we have found.

The remainder of the paper is organized as follows. We begin with a description of conceptual, methodological and analytical foundations and related work followed by a description of our data and methodology, outlining our use of data collection and visualization tools as well as the techniques for sentiment analysis, volume comparison, and topic analysis. Next we present our analysis, which includes the sub-sections volume, sentiment, topic and influencers.

Following this is a discussion and conclusions section. Here we return to our main research questions: we sketch what we believe are the main observations concerning **what** the data shows about differences between Danish and international reactions. We then discuss at length some suggestions about **why** those differences may have in part arisen from differences in the social media landscape in Denmark: in particular, we point to the following factors: 1) a high proportion of mainstream media 2) a low proportion of Twitter use. We suggest that these factors might partially explain the fact that there is far less emotional and subjective language use observed in the Danish data, which in turn, we argue, is a key factor in the difference between Danish and international reaction.

FOUNDATIONS AND RELATED WORK

Conceptually, our research is informed by the notions of public sphere as originally formulated by Habermas [3, 4] and its subsequent development into online public spheres[5, 6]. A public sphere is *"a domain of our social life in which such a thing as public opinion can be formed"* [7]. In this paper, we focus on describing and explaining the interactional dynamics of the public opinion formation in the Danish Giraffe affair. As such, we are not concerned with the consequences of the public opinion formation (as in Danish Cartoon Crisis [2]). That said, we speculate the public opinion formation in this case could have partially influenced the decision to spare the life of that another giraffe (also named Marius) at another Danish Zoo[1] (Jyllands Park Zoo).

Methodologically, in order to answer the research questions, we employ the grounded comparison method of the Comparative informatics (CI). CI *"is the application of the comparative method to the study of information and communication technologies (ICTs) across diverse contexts"* [8]. The analytical aim of CI *"is not laws or generalization, but heightened awareness of the uneven surface of ICT practices locally and globally"*. The CI method of "grounded comparison" [9] involves careful micro-genetic analysis of nuances in actual usage to complement the macro-structural observations similarities and differences across local and global cultures, languages, and technologies.

Analytically, we situate our work in the emerging fields of data science [10] and computational social science [11] in general and social data analytics [12] in particular. Extant literature in the emerging field of social data analytics can be broadly classified into two main categories:

(a) *description and explanation* of *interactional aspects* such as social influence [13], passivity [14], virality [15], persistence [16], sentiment analysis[17-19], opinion mining [17], and political deliberation [20-22].

(b) *Correlation to and/or prediction of real-world outcomes* such as movie revenues [23], stock prices of the companies based on the analysis of content from the online media such as news items, web blogs, and Twitter feeds [24-29], product sales [30], and quarterly revenues [12, 31].

Our study focuses on descriptive and explanatory aspects of the Danish and International reactions on social media channels. In our case, the prevalence of social media certainly provides new ways of looking at micro-genetic nuances in terms of the interactional dynamics. Specifically, the social media reactions of ordinary people can be stored and analyzed in detail using newly developed techniques of social data analytics to complement online discourse analysis methods based in ethnography [32, 33]. In this paper we exploit these social data analytics techniques to present a detailed, fine-grained analysis of the linguistic features of this international controversy, analyzing 315 thousand posts from 40 online channels with 2449 and 150947 unique actors in the Danish and English datasets respectively.

DATA AND METHOD

Data Collection

A full month of data was collected (January 17th – February 16th, 2014) one week after the event took place so as to capture the entire long tail of activity as well as to contrast with a calm period of three weeks prior to the media storm, which received less than 500 posts in total. Radian6[2] (a Salesforce enterprise tool) was utilized to fetch and download 315,000 posts from 40 online channels. The resulting dataset was then visualized using Tableau Desktop[3] (an enterprise software tool for visual analysis) to examine the unfolding of the incident online. Figure 2 below illustrates that social media channels like Facebook and in particular Twitter, dominated the overall volume and the distribution illustrates that they held uninterrupted activity of posts throughout the timeline of events. Conversations on blogs, video/photo-sharing sites, and mainstream media articles as well as their comments were all captured as well. These channels, such as 'mainstream media', are pre-defined by Radian6.[4]

The search strings for data collection were aimed at capturing all English instances of "Marius + Giraffe" and "Copenhagen Zoo" in several variations (Figure1). Meanwhile an additional fetch was initiated to capture the

---

[1] http://edition.cnn.com/2014/02/15/world/europe/denmark-zoo-giraffe/

---

[2]http://www.salesforcemarketingcloud.com/products/social-media-listening/

[3] http://www.tableausoftware.com/products/desktop

[4]'Mainstream Media' includes newspapers, television, or any written news stories that exist openly online (not behind a paywall) from tens of thousands of mainstream news websites.

Danish language conversation utilizing the alternate spellings of "Marius + Giraf" as well as variances of "København Zoo"

```
"copenhagen" AND "zoo"
OR "copenhagenzoo"
OR "københavn" AND "zoo"
OR "københavnzoo"
OR "marius" AND "giraf"
OR "marius" AND "giraffe"
```

Figure 1: Data fetching queries

The raw data was first examined to identify the very first online post mentioning the scheduled event, a Danish mainstream news article. A line-by-line examination of posts also allowed us to identify the first Facebook post, tweet, forum thread, and key catalyst events on social channels. These were collected in a separate archive to form a timeline and were eventually transposed with volume and sentiment escalations in our analysis.

Automatic Sentiment: Pre-defined and Detected

When the full conversation data was extracted, the raw dataset was pre-coded by Radian6 with automatic sentiment detection at the post level for English-language content. It could be expected that the overall conversation surrounding something inherently negative as the event relating to death would unavoidably be negative in nature to a certain degree. However, it quickly became apparent that the tool was labelling a significant portion of negative and even outraged language as neutral (79% of English-language posts coded as neutral). Re-tweeted messages were consistently given the same sentiment coded for the initially

broadcast, since they were considered to be echoing the sentiment of the original author. For sentiment analysis, retweeted contents from Twitter have been removed. The way of detecting retweets is to identify RT string at the beginning of each content. This process is done by R.

Manual Sentiment: Facebook Annotations

In order to improve the accuracy of results an eventual sentiment analysis, we enlisted the help of a group of 50 corporate communications students from the Copenhagen Business School, Denmark. The students manually annotated all 442 Danish-language Facebook posts and comments that mentioned the giraffe incident, in addition to a random sample of English-language Facebook posts of corresponding size and equal time distribution throughout the event. All but three students were fluent in both Danish and English. However, other nuances to sentiment detecting had to be explained and fully elaborated. For the most consistent human interpretation, the students annotated each post individually being either positive, negative or neutral, as if they were unaware of the surrounding controversy simply by evaluating the text itself, and not following any links leading to additional content besides the post-level text. Permalinks were accessible to see each Facebook post on the platform should there be a need to read the post in context with a dialogue of comments. They carefully disassociated key actors from the controversy (avoiding negative connotations say for any one actor such as the well-being of the giraffe or image of the zoo itself) and were asked to subjectively interpret the intended sentiment broadcast by the message sender. These human interpretations were integral for interpreting irony, flagging irrelevant content and filtering non-Danish noise within the

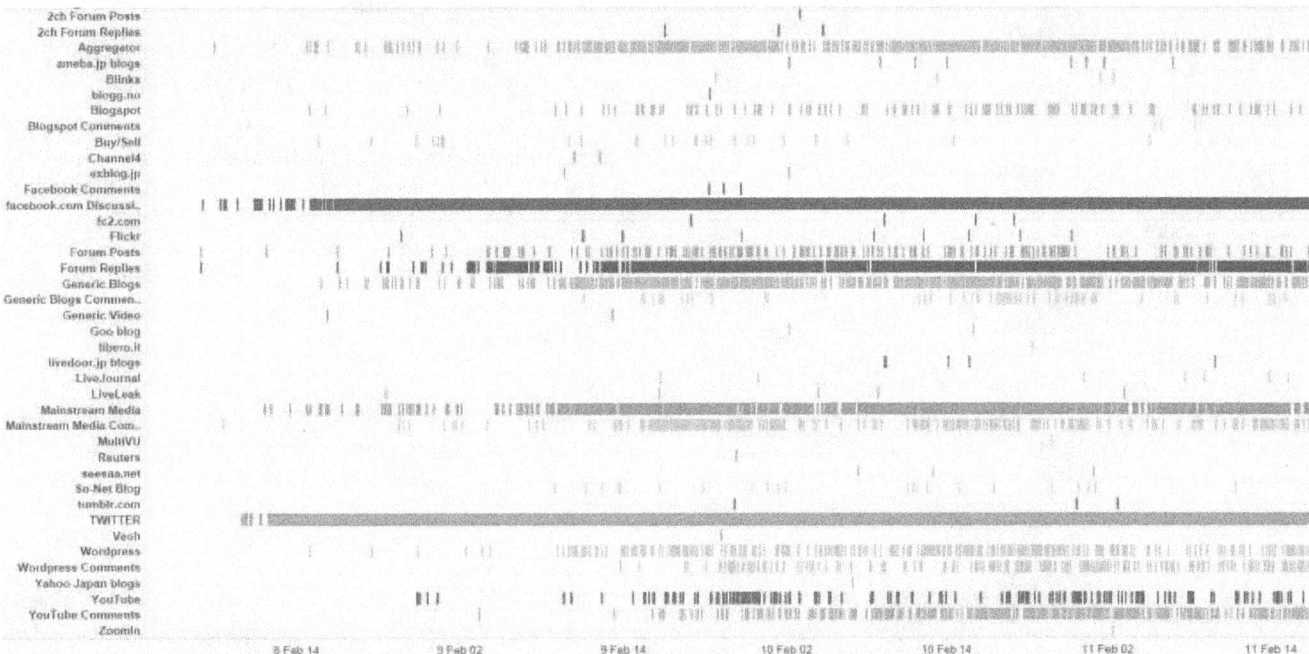

Figure 2: Whole data collection across channels and over time – A strip plot distribution of activities shows which channels were more consistently present during real world events at the Copenhagen Zoo, revealing differing activity footprints

data, mostly emanating from Dutch similarities in spelling of the search string. An automatic sentiment system was also run on these Danish Facebook posts, using a classifier that we trained ourselves with Danish online reviews from Trustpilot.dk.

Text Mining: Word Frequency Comparison
The Danish and English raw data is initially fetched by distinguishing the way of spelling Giraffe (ENG)/Giraf (DNK) and Copenhagen (ENG)/København(DNK), which inherently brings some noise. In order to effectively compare the difference between languages, a language identification tool (LangID)[5] was used to keep only Danish and English word frequencies which were then stored as two different datasets. These two datasets were then tokenized in the form of unigrams (single words), bigrams (two words) and trigrams (three words). Frequency of each form is calculated at the same time (see appendix).

Facebook: Complete Data Archive of Copenhagen Zoo
Social Data Analytics Tool (SODATO) [34] was used to fetch the complete data record of the Facebook page of the Copenhagen Zoo from Jan 1st 2009 to Mar 11th 2014. The data corpus consists of 11,652 posts in total, giving a full historical context to the size and scale of activity that occurred during February 2014.

Netnography of Online Media
Netnographic observations were conducted by one of the authors on different English mainstream and social media channels, the Facebook page of the Copenhagen Zoo, and the Twitter streams for #Marius and #CopenhagenZoo and its Danish variants. Notes from the observations and interpretations informed the macro-structural analysis of the discourse in terms of key argument types deployed in the discussions.

ANALYSIS

Netnographic Observations: Argumentation Types
During the crisis, the zoo was overwhelmed with the volume of the online reactions as well as the accusations of animal rights violations on social media channels. The zoo's Facebook page was inundated with user-generated content containing accusations and outrage. It took days for the staff to respond, and when they did, the zoo posted responses to the most frequently asked questions from the public throughout the week of giraffe controversy. Such postings received more engagement levels than the zoo had ever experienced in the lifespan of its Facebook page. In addition to receiving high levels of (often negative) comments below the post, the original explanation from the zoo also received unprecedented levels of likes, offering both negative and positive reactions at the same time. Since their page administrator had simultaneously posted these broadcasts in Danish and English, the performance of these parallel messages could thus be contrasted in terms of

the reaction from different language audiences. To isolate the reaction to Copenhagen Zoo's own posts on Facebook from the total discussion, we used the free version of the Quintly[6] online social media tool and SODATO to extract post-level performance figures. Our netnographic analysis reveals that the stakeholder groups involved in the public debate employed one or more of the following argument types:

- *Rationality(Scientific and Bureaucratic):* These arguments had their warrants [35] in the sciences of genetics and conservation (that the Copenhagen Zoo was a scientific institution and the giraffe had to be killed because of its redundant gene type) and organizational rules (Copenhagen Zoo as member of European Association of Zoos and Aquaria, EAZA is rule-bound not to transfer the giraffe to a non-EAZA zoo or to a circus)
- *Relativity (Cultural and Linguistic):* Cultural relativism arguments were employed by some Danish commentators to justify the public dissection of the dead giraffe as well as the carcass feeding to the lions at the zoo. Note that these acts were rationalized by the zoo as part of their public education service mission. Linguistic relativism was seen in action with dual-language posting policies of the organizational stakeholder, the zoo as well as the Danish commentators supporting or opposing the incident.
- *Animal Ethics:* These arguments discussed animal rights with accusations of animal cruelty and professional misconduct on the part of the scientific staff of the zoo as well as *ad homenium* attacks of hypocrisy on meat-eating commentators that opposed the killing of the giraffe.

We now focus our attention on the micro-genetic analysis of the linguistic features of the public discourse on Danish and International mainstream and social media.

Micro-Genetic Analysis of Media and Language Use
This analysis gives insight into the evolution of volume and sentiment that progressed throughout a week of intense social media reaction to breaking news, detailing how it broke, where and when the conversation escalated, who initiated it, where negativity existed, and what words were used the most.

Timeline
The initial unfolding of the outcry to the planned event was rather slow during the four days preceding the killing, as reflected by online reaction globally. It is possible that perhaps early word-of-mouth (WOM) reaction could have been intense in Denmark or Scandinavia. However, given that most of the reaction volume took place internationally and in English, this traction was sparked by several key events the day before the scheduled euthanasia. On

---

[5] https://pypi.python.org/pypi/langid

[6] https://www.quintly.com/

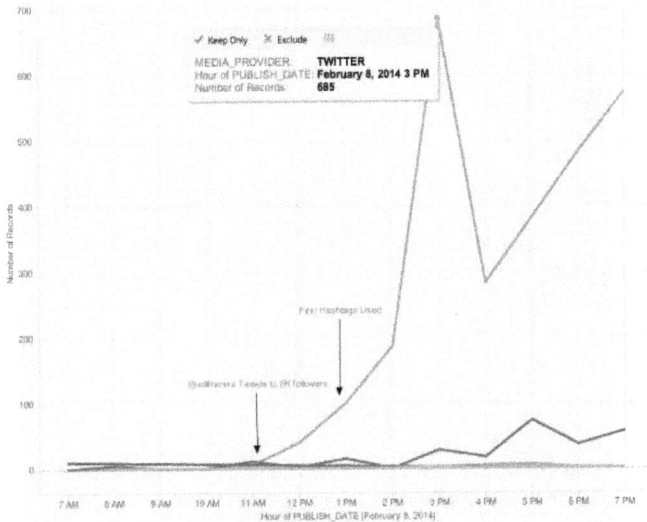

Figure 3: Activity escalates the day before the killing of Marius - the international news story breaks as a story from the Independent newspaper at 3pm

February 5th 2014, the news story first broke from a newspaper article that day in the Danish tabloid paper Ekstra Bladet that the zoo was planning a public autopsy event in four days' time. The first Facebook post (in Danish) and then a tweet (in English) surfaced that very day. However very little traction took place on social channels in the subsequent two days while Swedish and Norwegian newspapers also published their stories on the 6th and 7th respectively. But for the most part there was minimal activity in forums, article comments and on social channels.

Several Twitter posts continued to surface two days later including a direct-address tweet from one animal rights advocate (@rearwindow1) to another (@longleat). This tweet in particular would eventually serve as a catalyst for the onset of an avalanche of tweets that would ensue the next day. Before the first international press caught wind the following day, this tweet was responded to at 11am by Will Travers, founder of the Born Free foundation for animal welfare and wildlife conservation and a contributor to the Huffington Post. Travers was the first actor to have significant followers (8,200 followers) and his message directly addressing @CopenhagenZoo therefore was the first to have a wide potential reach on Twitter, sparking an upward trend in volume (Figure 3).

Within two hours the first hashtag was utilized, forming a way for participants in the global conversation (irrespective of language) to include their message in the stream of #Marius discussions. One minute later, another hashtag #SaveMarius was also coined as tweet volumes about the incident broke the 100/hour rate. This secondary hashtag was an appeal to speak out and protest against the zoo in hopes of saving the animal from its ill fate the next morning (Figure 3). However the original #Marius hashtag would

carry on traction for many days to come. Finally, the global news story broke via an English-language, non-Scandinavian article from the Independent on Feb 8th, 2014 at 15:39:00 began to spark world-wide attention, as Twitter volume jumped to 685 tweets that hour. See appendix for examples of postings on Facebook and Twitter.

Volume

The Copenhagen Zoo received fewer than 500 posts in the three weeks before the news surrounding their decision to euthanize a giraffe. The zoo and their giraffe were subsequently mentioned 232,323 times during the week of February 5th to the 12th, and a further 82,052 times when a second giraffe named Marius emerged briefly in the online debate (5:30 12-Feb - 2:00pm 16-Feb).

1	27.8%	TWITTER-original	1	37.3%	TWITTER-original
2	24.8%	facebook.com Discussions	2	37.2%	TWITTER-Retweets
3	14.0%	Mainstream Media	3	20.8%	facebook.com Discussions
4	10.4%	Mainstream Media Comments	4	1.3%	Forum Replies
5	9.7%	TWITTER-Retweets	5	1.2%	Mainstream Media
6	5.3%	Forum Replies	6	0.4%	Aggregator
7	2.8%	Generic Blogs	7	0.4%	Generic Blogs
8	1.3%	Aggregator	8	0.3%	YouTube Comments
9	1.1%	Wordpress	9	0.3%	Mainstream Media Comments

Table 1(left): Channel distribution of Danish data
Table 2(right): Channel distribution of English data

In terms of channel amplitude, Twitter posts totaling 232,285 represented 75% of the total online conversation about Marius the giraffe. Facebook followed with 20.8% of the discussion, with far less commentary existing on other social channels, news media, and forums or in the blogosphere. This abundance of tweets was largely in the English language where Twitter is a relatively-highly adopted social channel in the United Kingdom and United States. Yet Twitter volume provided the most accurate pulse as volume spikes appeared most dramatically on Twitter at the time of the public giraffe killing and especially upon news of plans for a second potential giraffe euthanasia.

The online reaction to the media storm in Denmark was not only smaller than the international reaction, but also different in nature. Distribution was still consistently strongest over time on unique contributions on Twitter (27.8%) and Facebook (24.8%). Twitter is not as widely adopted in Denmark as in Anglophone countries. Denmark currently has a very high adoption rate of Facebook users when compared to the rest of the world, which explains the greater percentage of Facebook commentary than the English conversation. Without the predominance of Twitter, other online channels were less broad in diversity but more richly represented, implying that mainstream media play a greater role for expression (with 24.4% news articles and commentary).

This is in contrast to countries where social media may now occupy much larger proportions of the media distribution, as displayed in the English dataset. Finally, we note that the Twitter proportion of retweets-to-tweets was less in Denmark perhaps suggesting a different use of the medium. This may imply that Danes use social media more to

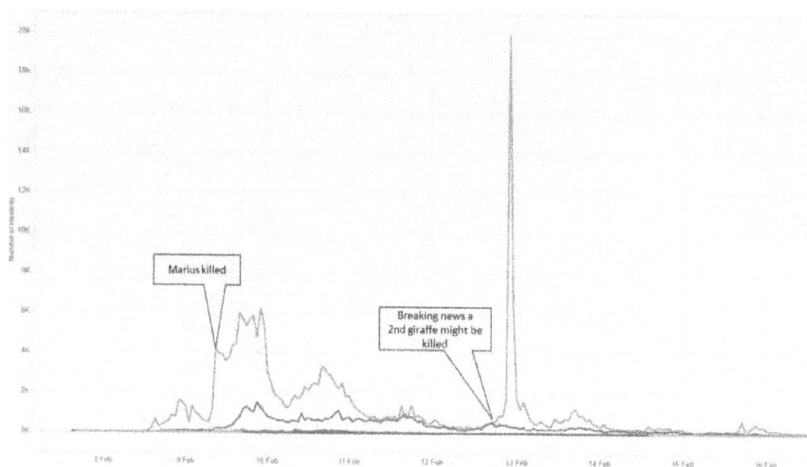

Figure 4: Twitter Volume Distribution - The killing event at the zoo had many peaks of activity throughout the weekend (left hand side of the graph) while a subsequent news story later that week overshadowed the main event unexpectedly with one intense, resurgence of activity.

express themselves rather than to share information about the incident. Tables 1 and 2 show the volume distributions across channels.

Twitter Volume over Time

The bulk of volume thus occurred during the day before (Feb 8), day of (Feb 9) and day after (Feb 10) the events unfolded at Copenhagen Zoo. Twitter served as the most intense outlet of reaction, and the most accurate pulse of real world events. As shown in Figure 4, during these three days the steepest upturn on Twitter began during the actual hour of euthanasia to that of the autopsy, with hourly tweets climbing from 1152 to 413, a 359% rise. Activity continued to climb late into the evening, as mainstream media reported the events that had taken place at the zoo that day, peaking in volume at 5pm. Reaction on Facebook also escalated that day, and while not nearly as much as Twitter with a substantial percentage of retweets, Facebook discussions maintained their elevated levels of activity for several days.

Nevertheless the unexpected pinnacle of the online media storm came with the surprising news later that week when the news that a second potential giraffe euthanasia may take place, at another Danish zoo, and also with the same name of Marius. This unexpected and coincidental final chapter of the news story tapped into an already sensitive and controversial global conversation about how animals are treated by humans. Thus the second news story generated an intense peak of 19,936 posts in one hour -- over three times the peak achieved on Twitter from the actual death the weekend before. An activity rate of 332 Posts / Minute occurred almost entirely on Twitter and only during a sudden spike from 9PM growing 1206% in the next 60 minutes before falling again after 10pm. This final and most dramatic spike occurred in Denmark on Twitter, as well as a smaller spike in Facebook activity that did not occur externally.

Online Community Characteristics

The community at large could be generally described as social media natives, with 95% of the global conversation emanating from Twitter and Facebook. Given that a large portion of population originated from public Twitter accounts, some investigations could be made to better understand the community of engaged actors. The frequency of words within the Twitter bios of actors who utilized the #Marius hashtag revealed a few patterns about this population. The highest frequency terms suggested several common traits including *Liberal* (6%), *Progressivism* (5%), *Vegan* (4%), *Activist* (2%) and *Animal Rights* (1%). One could note that the total Twitter conversation from these publishers of content had a potential reach of 681 million total impressions. Certain actors however injected more influence than others, either with influential messages (as mentioned earlier) or a substantial Twitter following. Specifically the Danish blogger @FieLaursen posted her appeal five hours before the giraffe was euthanized to 21.7 thousand twitter followers. Secondly the @BBCBreaking news service posted its live report of the killing to 8.9M million followers of the broadcasting service's breaking news handle on Twitter. Finally the post that generated the most amplification came from actor and producer Ricky Gervais, expressing his disappointment while gaining 5,003 retweets of his opinion.

Sentiment

As previously mentioned, automatic sentiment from the Radian6 data was remarkably neutral-biased. In examining this pre-coding of sentiment over time, one could still notice however an increased relative amount of negativity during the timeframe of the zoo killing, autopsy, and disposal of the carcass to feed other animals. Initial sentiment detection also revealed that English-language Facebook content may offer a greater portion of original, polarized debate language due to the infrastructure and mechanisms of the friends-based social network (Radian6 does not detect Danish sentiment). Nonetheless, with only

16.2% of posts in a global controversy being marked as negative by the tool, a more thorough annotation of sentiment was needed for English in addition to a full examination of the Danish language reaction. We used the following formulas from Asur and Huberman [23] for calculating subjectivity and polarity. Table 3 presents the subjectivity and polarity results.

$$Subjectivity = \frac{Positive\ Posts + Negative\ Posts}{Neutral\ Posts}$$

$$NP\ ratio = \frac{Negative\ Posts}{Positive\ Posts}$$

	Neutral		Positive		Negative		Total	Subjectivity	NP ratio
facebook.com Discussions	43254	66.8%	5930	9.2%	15606	24.1%	64790	0.50	2.63
Forum Replies	3459	85.5%	145	3.6%	441	10.9%	4045	0.17	3.04
Twitter	191378	82.4%	6842	2.9%	34065	14.7%	232285	0.21	4.98
Mainstream Media	2733	74.4%	323	8.8%	618	16.8%	3674	0.34	1.91
Others	5570	82.1%	5570	82.1%	886	13.1%	6787	1.16	0.16
Total	246394	79.1%	13571	4.4%	51616	16.6%	311581	0.26	3.80

Table 3: Subjectivity and Polarity of Online Media

English Sentiment on different channels

An early assessment of Radian6 pre-coded sentiment showed an overall level of subjectivity at 0.26 (total polarized posts vs total neutral posts). This level is obviously low due to an overwhelming amount of neutrally coded posts however one can still examine the relative differences in subjectivity per channel, as well as the relative rate of negative polarity across channels ignoring the neutral majority. It was expected that mainstream media would be the more objective and contain less negative polarity. Indeed the popular news stories did contain the lowest level of negativity (1.91), and low levels of subjectivity. Subjectivity was however shown to be highest on Facebook (0.50), almost double the number for all the posts on other channels (0.25). This would indicate that the English-language Facebook conversation could serve as the most effective channel to measure sentiment reactions from the most emotional discussions. In terms of polarity, the global English conversation revealed a total negative polarity of 3.80 for all postings on all channels. The largest portion of negative polarity came instead from Twitter with a negative polarity of 4.98, based on a statistically significant number of 34,065 negative tweets versus 12,211 positive tweets. The most intense negative polarity was detected from the comments portion of English mainstream media (negativity factor of 10), however this was based on a very small number of posts (50 negative, 5 positive) with an overwhelming amount of neutrality in the online English press.

Echoing Sentiment

Finally we examined the division of Twitter data between the 116,233 tweets and compared them with the 116,052 re-tweets. While these volumes were virtually the same, re-tweet sentiment showed both higher degrees of subjectivity and negative polarity. Twitter already had the highest degree of negativity for any channel, but an even higher negative polarity of 5.56 for re-tweets suggests that people who read original tweets, then echoed negative sentiment at a higher rate than those who authored the original post (Table 4).

	Neutral		Positive		Negative		Total	Subjectivity	NP ratio
Twitter(original)	97279	83.7%	3498	3.0%	15456	13.3%	116233	0.19	4.42
Twitter(retweets)	94099	81.1%	3344	2.9%	18609	16.0%	116052	0.23	5.56
Total	191378	82.4%	6842	2.9%	34065	14.7%	232285	0.21	4.98

Table 4: Twitter's Sentiment Distribution

Comparison of Sentiment: Danish vs English

Due to the aforementioned indications of higher degrees of Facebook subjectivity, this medium was further investigated with manual interpretations of all Danish Facebook posts over time, as well as an opportunity to contrast with a corresponding sample of English posts on Facebook. The data was then first examined for its evolution over time. A heat map of manually coded Danish Facebook posts shows almost exclusively positive activity before the event began to unfold in the popular press on the 5th of February, then showing negative and neutral activity taking over the conversation (see appendix). The manual sentiment coding further indicated that an overwhelming amount of negativity existed in the English Facebook posts (63.0% negative) when compared to half as much neutral posts (31.6%) and very few positive English posts (5.3%). Meanwhile for Danish text, a stark contrast existed in Facebook sentiment. Manual annotations indicated only 39% negative sentiment in all Facebook posts, overshadowed by 44% neutral postings from Danes, including even a substantial portion of positive postings (17%). We also measured the ratio of negative to positive tweets finding that negative polarity has a much stronger ratio of 11.81 in English than 2.32 in Danish. We again calculated the overall subjectivity by the combined number of positive and negative tweets divided by the number of neutral tweets. The resulting subjectivity was also much higher in English (2.16) than in Danish (1.29) Facebook discussions. These finding show a stark contrast between the local Danish reaction and that of the global English-speaking community.

Topics/Aboutness

We compared the frequency of unigrams (single words), bigrams (two words) and trigrams (three words) in the Danish and English data. We find that the traces of punctuation marks (/ :) are the most frequently used characters, remains from both languages use of links. This illustrates how much both speakers engaged in pointing activity, referring to a link to elaborate their understanding of the story and often support their particular point of view or sentiment. Following these two top occurrences, both languages also have zoo (#3) and Marius, Giraffe and Copenhagen all appearing in the next five most frequent positions, unsurprisingly. The exclamation point and question mark punctuations also appear similarly in both, prominently expressing emotion or inquiry within the top 20 terms.

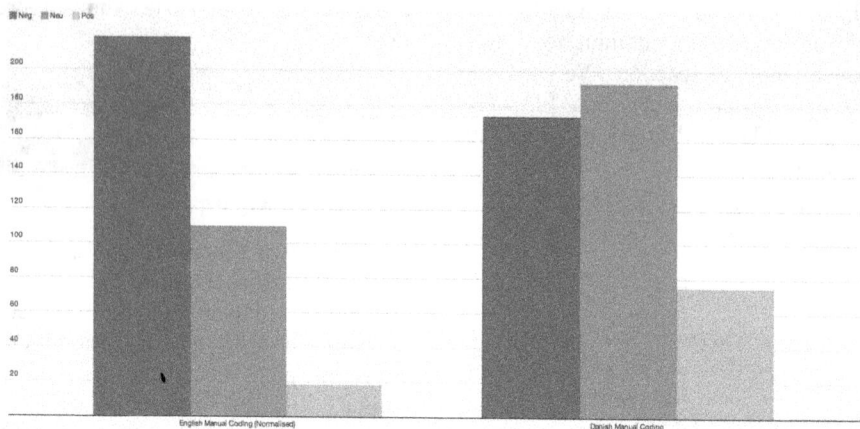

Figure 5: English vs. Danish POS / NEU / NEG Sentiments on Facebook

Another structural nuance of the data is apparent in the English frequency list which shows the abundance of tweets with 125,054 uses of "RT" as the 12th most used term, the # character the 11th, and the @ sign as the 4th most occurring morsel of modern day language in English.

English Unigrams

English terms describing the nature of the giraffe had high degrees of frequency such as healthy (#15), young (#22), baby (#39), and beautiful (#96). These words do not appear in the top of the list for Danish language. The words death and its Danish equivalent, død, both appear with similar frequency (29 and 37 respectively). This can be expected as it describes the outcome of the event. But overall there are several other "killing words" appearing prominently in English. Killed (16), killing (20), kill (31) and kills (45) all appear with very high frequency. These all precede the clinical term, "euthanize". By contrast, the Danish frequency list shows the inverse in death-related words. Variants of "euthanize" (aflivede) occur at 33, 41, and 60, much higher than variants of "killing" in Danish (dræb at 349, 552, 769 and 778).

Furthermore, in English there are intensely negative death words such as "destroying" (91), "murdered" (108), "slaughtered" (112), "butchered" (136), "slaughter" (138) and "execution" (14). Some of the corresponding words also appear in Danish, however with less frequency, such as butcher (slagte - 271) or murderers (mordere - 298).

Danish Unigrams

Among the most frequent Danish are objective fact or descriptive words around what happened at the zoo. Referring to the time of public autopsy, the number 10 and "kl" (o'clock) appear at 34 and 35th. And the word "shot" (skud-38), "boltgun" (boltpistol-42) and "dissect" (parteres-53) all appear higher in Danish than in English.

There is one highly frequent discourse in the Danish list: "fordi" (because). This term does not appear among the high-frequency English words, where the only highly frequent discourse particle is "despite".

Advocacy Similarities

In terms of advocacy words, the hashtag #holsttzooshame appeared with similar agency in both languages (23/26). The combination refers to the scientific director, Bengt Holst, who as a figurehead took much of the blame/credit for how the zoo handled the event. His first and last names appears extremely high in Danish at 16 and 17. Additionally the words "petition" (38) and "sign" (53) are prominent examples of activism activity. This suggests that perhaps more people in English decided to sign a petition or simply retweet their opinion. It is possible in Denmark people encouraged others to write directly to the zoo.

Medium / Transparency Differences

One explanation for why this zoo incident received such immense public outcry on social media perhaps relates to the openness of the event itself. The use of graphic photos could reinforce the emotional weight that user posts carry on social channels. The use of such photos may have had greater effect and reaction in international activity than in Danish. In the list of unigrams, for example, the word "photo" appears much higher in English than in Danish (42 /141). The fact that the giraffe was a visually appealing animal only added to the visual and emotional viral potential of messages propagating across social networks. Finally another small pattern emerges in the words that are associated with how the zoo chose to deal with the giraffe so openly. A point of public outrage was the fact that in the photos people saw online, children were allowed and encouraged to witness the scientific autopsy of the animal. For this reason the words "children" (40) appears higher in the English data than in Danish (børn-73).

An Animal with a Name

The hashtag #Marius helped to categorize and launch the conversation worldwide, as was shown in the analysis of an outbreak in volume. In addition to visual qualities, the fact that the giraffe had a name, Marius, increased the attachment ability when compared to other controversial human incidents with animals. For example, the animals we eat, use in lab research, or even die in other tragic occurrences such as the beached whales that Danes walked on top of the following week. The images of curious humans walking all over these nameless wales (one dead and one still alive) made television newscasts but were not spread as virally on digital media. The unigram frequency reiterates this point with high frequency in both languages such as "named" at 33 in English and "navn" at 89 in Danish. When examining trigrams, indeed the phrase "giraffe named Marius" is one of the very most frequent (11) with 15,225 occurrences in English.

DISCUSSION

Under these circumstances the prevalence of Social Media provides new ways of expanding and provoking the global conversation for actors and potential actors involved. An inflamed, controversial incident of this nature has likewise provided a unique opportunity to capture the global and local reactions via social media, as this investigation has shown. It first offered a stark contrast between reactions locally in Denmark and internationally among the English speaking community. Both subjectivity and negativity were shown to be higher on Facebook in the English language than in the Danish language. Generally speaking, Facebook and Twitter serve differently in sharing signals. Given that 10% or less of Twitter users have a private social network, the intended audience is mostly public in nature, making the intended signal different to that of the friend-directed social network of Facebook. Twitter is therefore seen as a proxy for semi-public voice and Facebook as a proxy for semi-private voice. In our examination of a highly controversial global issue, the discussion in the form of a directed debate is higher on Facebook, which showed higher levels of English subjectivity. However English negativity existed to the highest degree of polarity on Twitter. Roughly half of all global tweets (116,052) were detected as retweets, echoing the sentiment of the original authors. This amplification reflected over a third of total posts that surrounded the story. The English usage of Twitter showed much higher level of amplification than the Danish dataset, with no less than 50% of activity stemming from re-tweets. Furthermore the negative polarity of retweets exhibited even higher levels than those of original tweets, suggesting that this mechanism strongly served as a means for echoing sentiment. Because people used the re-tweet mechanism to echo sentiment more intensely for negative posts, this offered a clear distinction with the tone of Facebook conversation (highly subjective, but not so negatively polarized). Herein lies a virality nuance in the Twitter medium and its 1-click rebroadcasting mechanisms with a feed of conversation. With Twitter re-tweets showing the highest degrees of both volume and negativity overall, the entire data set of this event may reflect Twitter's role within a media storm supporting 'slacktivism' to a larger extent than the directed discourse on Facebook. In general, our analysis reveals that the international reaction in this case was much more intense than the Danish reaction; not only in the volume of postings, but more importantly in the subjectivity, sentiment, and also the frequency of more emotional and inflammatory words. Our analysis also points to some intriguing possibilities for why this might be so: we found that mainstream media constitutes a much higher proportion of the Danish media landscape than observed internationally. Furthermore, Twitter is used much less in the Danish context than internationally. Given that mainstream media tends to be less subjective and extreme than social media, and that Twitter is conversely more echoed and extreme than other media, we hypothesize that the Danish media landscape is structured to inhibit the kind of extreme media storms observed internationally. Prior work [36] in CABS (formerly ICIC) has proposed a research program on micro-genetic analysis [37-41] in order to " investigate how *cultural code, ecological data* and *interactional structure* intertwine to account for social interaction". Our paper is a study of human actors from different cultures and countries interacted with each other using different technologies and languages in terms of the linguistic aspects of the interactions at the micro-genetic level and argument types at the macro structural level.

REFERENCES

[1] Modood, T., Hansen, R., Bleich, E., O'Leary, B. and Carens, J. H. The Danish cartoon affair: free speech, racism, Islamism, and integration. *International Migration*, 44, 5 2006), 3-62.

[2] Larsen, H. The cartoon crisis in Danish foreign policy: A new balance between the EU and the US. *Danish Foreign Policy Yearbook* 2007), 51-85.

[3] Habermas, J. *The Structural Transformation of the Public Sphere: An Inquiry into a Category of Bourgeois Society*. MIT Press, Cambridge, MA, 1991.

[4] Calhoun, C. *Habermas and the public sphere*. MIT press, 1993.

[5] Dahlberg, L. Computer-mediated communication and the public sphere: A critical analysis. *Journal of Computer-Mediated Communication*, 7, 1 2001), 27.

[6] Robertson, S. and Vatrapu, R. *Digital Government*. City, 2010.

[7] Habermas, J. *The Public Sphere*. University of California Press, City, 1991.

[8] Vatrapu, R. *Comparative informatics: investigating cultural and linguistic influences in computer supported collaborative learning*. International Society of the Learning Sciences, City, 2010.

[9] Nardi, B., Vatrapu, R. and Clemmensen, T. Comparative informatics. *interactions*, 18, 2 2011), 28-33.

[10] Loukides, M. What is data science? the future belongs to the companies and people that turn data into products. *An OReilly Radar Report (June 2010)*2010).

[11] Conte, R., Gilbert, N., Bonelli, G., Cioffi-Revilla, C., Deffuant, G., Kertesz, J., Loreto, V., Moat, S., Nadal, J. P., Sanchez, A., Nowak, A., Flache, A., San Miguel, M. and Helbing, D. Manifesto of computational social science. *Eur Phys J-Spec Top*, 214, 1 (Nov 2012), 325-346.

[12] Mukkamala, R., Hussain, A. and Vatrapu, R. Towards a Formal Model of Social Data. *IT University Technical Report Series*, TR-2013-1692013), https://pure.itu.dk/ws/files/54477234/ITU_TR_544720 13_54477169.pdf.

[13] Cha, M., Haddadi, H., Benevenuto, F. and Gummadi, K. P. Measuring user influence in twitter: The million follower fallacy. *ICWSM, 10*2010), 10-17.

[14] Romero, D., Galuba, W., Asur, S. and Huberman, B. Influence and passivity in social media. *Machine Learning and Knowledge Discovery in Databases*2011), 18-33.

[15] Leskovec, J., Adamic, L. and Huberman, B. The dynamics of viral marketing. *ACM Transactions on the Web (TWEB)*, 1, 1 2007), 5.

[16] Asur, S., Huberman, B., Szabo, G. and Wang, C. *Trends in social media: Persistence and decay*. City, 2011.

[17] Yang, M., Kiang, M., Ku, Y. C., Chiu, C. C. and Li, Y. J. Social Media Analytics for Radical Opinion Mining in Hate Group Web Forums. *Journal of Homeland Security and Emergency Management*, 8, 1 2011).

[18] Hardt, D. and Wulff, J. What is the Meaning of 5*'s? An Investigation of the Expression and Rating of Sentiment. *Empirical Methods on Natural Language Processing : Proceedings of the Conference on Natural Language Processing 2012*2012), 319-326.

[19] Pang, B. and Lee, L. *Opinion mining and sentiment analysis*. Now Pub, 2008.

[20] Robertson, S., Vatrapu, R. and Medina, R. Off the wall political discourse: Facebook use in the 2008 U.S. presidential election. *Information Polity*, 15, 1,2 2010), 11-31.

[21] Robertson, S. P., Vatrapu, R. K. and Medina, R. Online video "friends" social networking: Overlapping online public spheres in the 2008 US presidential election. *Journal of Information Technology & Politics*, 7, 2-3 2010), 182-201.

[22] Vatrapu, R., Robertson, S. and Dissanayake, W. Are Political Weblogs Public Spheres or Partisan Spheres? *International Reports on Socio-Informatics*, 5, 1 2008), 7-26.

[23] Asur, S. and Huberman, B. A. *Predicting the future with social media*. IEEE, City, 2010.

[24] Bakshy, E., Simmons, M. P., Huffaker, D., Teng, C. and Adamic, L. The social dynamics of economic activity in a virtual world. *ICWSM2010*. *http://misc.si.umich.edu/publications/18*2010).

[25] Bollen, J. and Mao, H. Twitter mood as a stock market predictor. *Computer*2011), 91-94.

[26] Dorr, D. H. and Denton, A. M. Establishing relationships among patterns in stock market data. *Data & Knowledge Engineering*, 68, 3 2009), 318-337.

[27] Gavrilov, M., Anguelov, D., Indyk, P. and Motwani, R. *Mining the stock market (extended abstract): which measure is best?* ACM, City, 2000.

[28] Kharratzadeh, M. and Coates, M. *Weblog Analysis for Predicting Correlations in Stock Price Evolutions*. City, 2012.

[29] Mittermayer, M.-A. *Forecasting intraday stock price trends with text mining techniques*. IEEE, City, 2004.

[30] vd Reijden, P. and Koppius, O. R. *The Value of Online Product Buzz in Sales Forecasting*. City, 2010.

[31] Lassen, N., Madsen, R. and Vatrapu, R. Predicting iPhone Sales from iPhone Tweets. *Proceedings of IEEE EDOC 2014, Ulm, Germany*in press/2014).

[32] Kozinets, R. V. *Netnography: Doing ethnographic research online*. Sage Publications, 2010.

[33] Hine, C. *Virtual ethnography*. Sage, 2000.

[34] Hussain, A. and Vatrapu, R. Social Data Analytics Tool. *DESRIST 2014, Lecture Notes in Computer Science (LNCS)*, 8463, Springer 2014), 368–372.

[35] Toulmin, S. E. *The uses of argument*. Cambridge University Press, 2003.

[36] Vatrapu, R. Explaining culture: an outline of a theory of socio-technical interactions. *Proceedings of the 3rd ACM International Conference on Intercultural Collaboration (ICIC 2010)*2010), 111-120.

[37] Sanderson, P. and Fisher, C. Exploratory sequential data analysis: Foundations. *Human-Computer Interaction*, 9, 3 1994), 251-317.

[38] Fisher, C. and Sanderson, P. Exploratory sequential data analysis: exploring continuous observational data. *interactions*, 3, 2 1996), 25-34.

[39] Jordan, B. and Henderson, A. Interaction Analysis: Foundations and Practice. *The Journal of the Learning Sciences*, 4, 1 1995), 39-103.

[40] Goodwin, C. Seeing in Depth. *Social Studies of Science*, 25, 2 1995), 237-274.

[41] Goodwin, C. Action and embodiment within situated human interaction. *Journal of Pragmatics*, 32, 10 2000), 1489-1522.

Evolution of Human Mind and Culture Viewed from the Study of Chimpanzees

Tetsuro Matsuzawa

Professor, Section of Language and Intelligence, Primate
Research Institute, Kyoto University,
President of the International Primatological Society
matsuzaw@pri.kyoto-u.ac.jp

ABSTRACT

I have studied chimpanzees both in the wild and in the laboratory. My talk illustrates the evolutionary origins of human mind and culture. The human mother–infant relationship is characterized by physical separation, and the stable supine posture of infants; enabling face-to-face communication via facial expressions, vocal exchange, and manual gestures, and also demonstration of object manipulation. I have used the novel 'participant observation' method in the laboratory and through "field experiments" in their natural habitat. There are several critical differences between the two species: chimpanzees lack the social referencing ability observed in human children and chimpanzees seldom engage in active teaching. Moreover, although young chimpanzees showed unique working memory capacity, often superior to that of human adults, they are less able to learning symbols. In sum, mind and culture in humans is fundamentally influenced by the manner of raising young children; characterized by collaboration among multiple adults. This aspect of human rearing may be linked to the development of empathy, altruistic behavior, reciprocity, understanding others' minds, and so on. Taken together, my talk presents evolutionary and ontogenetic explanations for the uniquely human cognition and culture. For further information, please visit the following web site: http://langint.pri.kyoto-u.ac.jp/ai/

Author Keywords

Culture; evolution; chimpanzees and human comparison

ACM Classification Keywords

J.4 Computer Applications, SOCIAL AND BEHAVIORAL SCIENCES: Psychology

BIO

Tetsuro Matsuzawa is a Professor at the Primate Research Institute, Kyoto University, Japan. Matsuzawa studies chimpanzee cognition both in the laboratory and in the wild. The Ai project began in 1978 with research on language-like skills and number concepts in a female chimpanzee named Ai. The focus is now on the cultural transmission of knowledge, skills, and values, across generations, in a group of chimpanzees living in a semi-natural setting. Recent studies from this research project have demonstrated that young chimpanzees have an extraordinary working memory; often better than that of humans. Matsuzawa has achieved parallel progress in both laboratory work and fieldwork. Research on the behavior of wild chimpanzees in their natural habitat has been carried out in Bossou-Nimba, Guinea, West Africa, since 1986. Researchers at the site have documented the use of a pair of mobile stones as hammer and anvil to crack open oil-palm nuts, and have examined hand preference, critical periods in development, education by master-apprenticeship, and cultural variation across adjacent communities. Matsuzawa's many publications include: "Primate origins of human cognition and behavior" (2001), "Cognitive development in chimpanzees" (2006), "The mind of the chimpanzee" (2010), "Chimpanzees of Bossou and Nimba" (2011). He received the Jane Goodall Award in 2001, the Purple Ribbon Medal of Honor, and the Person of Cultural Merit in 2013 (awarded by the Government of Japan for exceptional academic contribution). He is the current President of the International Primatological Society.

CABS '14, August 21-22, 2014, Kyoto, Japan.
ACM 978-1-4503-2557-8/14/08.
http://dx.doi.org/10.1145/2631488.2637432

Author Index

www.ingramcontent.com/pod-product-compliance
Lightning Source LLC
Chambersburg PA
CBHW080557220326
41599CB00032B/6507